新东方
XDF.CN

新东方雅思(IELTS)考试指定辅导教材·强化培训

IELTS Speaking
雅思口语特训

孙 涛 编著

浙江教育出版社

图书在版编目(CIP)数据

雅思口语特训 / 孙涛编著. —杭州：浙江教育出版社，2015.8
ISBN 978-7-5536-2477-8

Ⅰ.①雅… Ⅱ.①孙… Ⅲ.①IELTS—口语—自学参考资料 Ⅳ.①H319.9

中国版本图书馆CIP数据核字（2015）第003833号

雅思口语特训

出版发行	浙江教育出版社 （杭州市天目山路40号　　邮编：310013）
编　　著	孙　涛
责任编辑	孔令宇
责任校对	赵露丹
责任印务	温劲风
封面设计	大愚设计
印　　刷	北京慧美印刷有限公司
开　　本	787mm × 1092mm　1/16
印　　张	18
字　　数	260 000
版　　次	2015年8月第1版
印　　次	2015年8月第1次印刷
标准书号	ISBN 978-7-5536-2477-8
定　　价	45.00元
联系电话	0571 - 85170300 - 80928
电子邮箱	bj62605588@163.com
网　　址	www.zjeph.com

前 言

2013年，雅思官网公布了2012年全球雅思考生分数分析。在全球41个主要雅思考生国中，中国考生排第34名，大陆考生总分平均分为5.6，听力、阅读、写作、口语分别为5.8、5.9、5.2、5.3，其中口语考试成绩又一次垫了底。这成绩是对中国传统语言教学最大的挑战和喝问：我们花费了那么多的时间、金钱和精力，却为何总是得不到相称的回报，哪怕是像世界上其他普通英语学习者那样用这门并不是那么复杂的语言去表达自己？

作为北京新东方学校的雅思口语教师，我有幸接触到了全国甚至是全世界最庞大的学员群体。多年的教学实践过后，面对逐年递增的学员和始终停步不前的雅思口语成绩，最初的成就感转化成一种更强大的责任感和紧迫感——我要把这多年的教学经验和我教授的数万名学员的感受转换成一本雅思口语学习的好书，算是对曾经奋斗过的"烤鸭"们和那些曾经那么信赖和支持我和我的同事的学员们一个交代。为了编好这本书，我把身边能用上的所有资源都用上了——网络，同事，甚至是目前在北京新东方学校担任雅思模考考官的外教几乎全都被我"逼"着贡献了一些精彩的答案和素材。希望所有人的努力没有白费，我也相信这本口语书会成为广大考生的良师益友。

这本书有几个特点是其他同类参考书所不具备但却对雅思考生提供最大的帮助的：

1. 所有话题答案均由外教编写、考官审订，使本书不仅成为最权威的口语教材，更为学员提供了最地道的口语素材。
2. 增加话题背景阅读，不单单提供可供模仿的口语材料，更能帮助学员突破语汇、思维瓶颈。
3. 所有答案均配有外教录音，既可用于口语训练，又可以用于练习听力和改善语音语调。
4. 话题进行分类分级，易于安排复习计划。

本书的最终完成，绝不是我一个人的努力。新东方教育科技集团高级副总裁、新东方前途出国咨询有限公司总经理周成刚老师对此书高度重视，给予了热情的鼓励和莫大的支持；北京新东方学校英联邦考试部总监何钢老师对此书提出了专业的见解；北京新东方学校的外教Joe和Laurie及雅思前任考官Chris Green都为本书做出了重要贡献。最后还要感谢北京新东方大愚文化传播有限公司的编辑们，没有他们的认真工作，估计这本书还会晚半年跟考生见面。

诚然，一本书解决不了雅思口语的所有问题，但它起码能让考生去感受英语学习的步骤，去理解阅读、听力以及网络这些看上去跟口语毫不相干的事物和活动对口语的巨大帮助。在此，祝所有的雅思考生考试顺利，心想事成。

孙 涛

目 录

第一章 雅思口语考试介绍 …… 1

Ⅰ. 概述 …… 3
Ⅱ. 口语水平提高策略 …… 4
Ⅲ. 口语考场应试技能 …… 6
Ⅳ. 如何使用此书 …… 8

第二章 雅思口语最新话题选材 …… 9

1. Education and Learning 教育和学习 …… 11
2. Working Life 工作 …… 14
3. Towns and Cities 城镇家乡 …… 17
4. Daily Routine and Leisure Time 日常生活和休闲 …… 20
5. Holidays and Traveling 节日和旅游 …… 24
6. Housing and Accommodation 家居 …… 27
7. Sports and Exercise 体育锻炼 …… 30
8. Interests and Hobbies 兴趣和爱好 …… 33
9. Mass Media（TV, Radio, Newspapers）大众传媒 …… 41
10. Nature（Flowers, Birds, Weather, Seasons）自然界 …… 44
11. Social Issues（Transport, Noise）社会问题 …… 49
12. Food and Restaurants 饮食 …… 54
13. Relationships（Family, Friends）关系 …… 57
14. Science and Technology（Mobile Phone, Email）科技 …… 61

第三章 雅思口语话题卡 …… 63

人物类核心级（Topics 1~3） …… 66
Topic 1 Senior Citizens 老人 …… 66
Topic 2 Children 孩子 …… 71
Topic 3 Celebrities 名人 …… 76

人物类进阶级（Topics 4~6） …… 81
Topic 4 Adventurous People 有探险精神的人 …… 81
Topic 5 Leaders 领袖人物 …… 86
Topic 6 Neighbours 邻居 …… 91

地点类核心级（Topics 7~8） …… 96
Topic 7 A Building in Your Hometown 家乡建筑物 …… 96
Topic 8 Your Childhood Room 童年房间 …… 102

地点类进阶级（Topics 9~11） …… 107
Topic 9 A Leisure Centre 休闲健身中心 …… 107
Topic 10 A Hotel 旅馆 …… 112

Topic 11 A Library 图书馆 …… 117
喜好类核心级（Topics 12~14） …… 122
Topic 12 A Film 电影 …… 122
Topic 13 An Outdoor Activity 户外活动 …… 127
Topic 14 Favorite Time of the Year 喜欢的季节或月份 …… 132
喜好类进阶级（Topics 15~17） …… 137
Topic 15 A Walk 经常走的一段路 …… 137
Topic 16 Sporting Events 体育赛事 …… 142
Topic 17 Foreign Cultures 外国文化 …… 148
物品类核心级（Topics 18~20） …… 153
Topic 18 Clothing and Fashion 服饰和时尚 …… 153
Topic 19 Wild Animals 野生动物 …… 158
Topic 20 Electrical Appliances 电器 …… 163
物品类进阶级（Topics 21~26） …… 168
Topic 21 An Important Letter 重要的信件 …… 168
Topic 22 Books 读物 …… 173
Topic 23 Furniture 家具 …… 178
Topic 24 Advertisements 广告 …… 183
Topic 25 A Childhood Present 童年礼物 …… 188
Topic 26 News Reports 新闻报道 …… 193
经历类核心级（Topics 27~28） …… 198
Topic 27 Public Events 公众活动 …… 198
Topic 28 Life-changing Moments 改变人生的事件 …… 203
经历类进阶级（Topics 29~36） …… 208
Topic 29 English Class Activities 英语课堂活动 …… 208
Topic 30 Advice 建议 …… 213
Topic 31 An Unsatisfactory Purchase 不愉快的购物经历 …… 218
Topic 32 Exhibitions 展览 …… 223
Topic 33 Being Late 迟到的经历 …… 228
Topic 34 A Time When You Help Someone 帮助别人的经历 …… 233
Topic 35 Busy Days 忙碌的日子 …… 237
Topic 36 Practical Skills 实用技能 …… 242
假想类进阶级（Topics 37~40） …… 247
Topic 37 To Start A Small Business 创业 …… 247
Topic 38 A Large Sum of Money 大笔钱财 …… 252
Topic 39 A Goal You Want to Achieve 想做成的一件事 …… 257
Topic 40 A Meal 一顿饭 …… 262
练习题答案 …… 267
附录 雅思考试口语评分标准 …… 280

第一章 雅思口语考试介绍

Ⅰ. 概述

口语考试时间

口语考试可能安排在笔试前一周至笔试后一周的任意一天。考试具体时间可在笔试日期前十天登录雅思报名网站(http://ielts.etest.net.cn)查询。

口语考试特点

考试一对一进行(即一名考官考核一名考生)，双方隔着桌子面对面坐着。考官均为母语为英语的外籍人士。

口语考试形式与内容

时间	11-14 分钟
备考	考生应至少提前 30 分钟到达考场并签到，然后进入候考区待考。口试截止入场时间为口试时间前 15 分钟。迟到考生将无法进入考场。 考试开始后，考官会询问考生的全名并要求考生出示身份证件，整个考试过程会被录音，目的在于保证考官正确地执行了考试程序。
考试形式	考试分为三个部分。首先是一般交谈（introduction and interview)，接着是个人陈述(individual long turn)，最后是双向讨论(two-way discussion)。 **第一部分：一般交谈(4-5 分钟)** 进入考场后，考生与考官互致问候。在自我介绍并核对考生身份后，考官会问一些关于你的生活、背景、喜好等基本问题。 **第二部分：个人陈述(3-4 分钟)** 考官给考生一张话题卡。考生有 1 分钟准备时间，并可以做笔记。之后考生要围绕话题卡内容作 1-2 分钟的陈述。考官会在 2 分钟后打断考生，然后会就考生的阐述内容提一两个相关问题，由考生做简要回答。 **第三部分：双向讨论(4-5 分钟)** 考官与考生围绕由第二部分引申出来的一些比较抽象的话题进行讨论。第三部分的话题是对第二部分话题卡内容的深化和拓展。

口语考试评分标准

口语考试同样采用 9 分制，雅思出题方对口语各级别的鉴别方法做了细致的描述，从四个方面对考生的英语交流能力做全面的评估。这四个标准分别是(详细描述可参见附录)：

- 流利性和连贯性
- 词汇多样性
- 语法多样性与正确性
- 发音

四个标准份量相同，最后经过计算得出一个分数，这就是考生的口语最终得分。口语和写作自 2007 年 7 月 1 日起引入半分制。

口语考试到底有多难

四项当中口语部分肯定不是最轻松的，也不是中国考生最容易得高分的（那应该是阅读和听力），但也并非那么可怕。以一个目标是 6.5 分的考生为例，四项考试最经济的分布是：

听力 6　　阅读 7

写作 6　　口语 6

目前中国考生口语的平均分在 5.3 分左右。因此只要目标不是太高，有大学 4 级水平的考生一般经过 3 个月左右的努力学习，口语分数是可以提高到 6 分及以上的。

II. 口语水平提高策略

工具书的使用

拥有一定的词汇量无论是对提高雅思成绩而言还是对提高口语水平而言都是相当重要的。雅思口语 6 分对于词汇量的要求是“has a wide enough vocabulary to discuss topics at length”，即“有足够的词汇量维持长时间的讨论”。所谓“足够”，很多人都有误解，以为必须得到七八千词汇量才可以，其实不然。就口语交流而言有三四千的词汇足已。中国大学四级考试大纲中规定考生得掌握 4,500 个词汇，也就是说只要考过四级就掌握了日常口语交流所需的大部分词汇了。但问题在于在拥有了一定的词汇之后，如何实现“uses some less common and idiomatic vocabulary and shows some awareness of style and collocation”(7 分)甚至“convey precise meaning”(8 分)。无论是“风格”也好，“搭配”也好，还是“精准”也好，传统的背单词方式已经满足不了要求，熟练的使用一本英-英工具书才是实现词汇好分数最根本的办法。

举例说明，在口语中想表达“我昨天买了一本书”时，有些考生可能会想到“purchase”一词，虽然也是“购买”的意思，但用在这里却不恰当，因为它的风格属于“formal”，在词典里有清晰的标识。再比如说“sophisticated”一词，大部分中国学生在头脑中的反应可能是“世故的”、“城府深的”，但实际上在英文中它的含义没有那样含有贬义，相反，它表示“having a lot of experience of life, and good judgment about socially important things such as art, fashion, etc.”，指的是“高雅的”、“有涵养的”。类似的例子举不胜举，看来要想了解英文单词真正的含义和使用方法，最好的办法还是要看看英语国家出版的词典，这样才能看清词汇的本来面目。

目前市面上存在着各式各样的工具书，其中有两本很适合雅思考试的，一本是Longman Dictionary of Contemporary English，一本是新东方与柯林斯出版集团合作编写的IELTS Examination Dictionary(《新东方 - 柯林斯雅思备考词典》)，两者都备受雅思考生青睐，使用很方便。

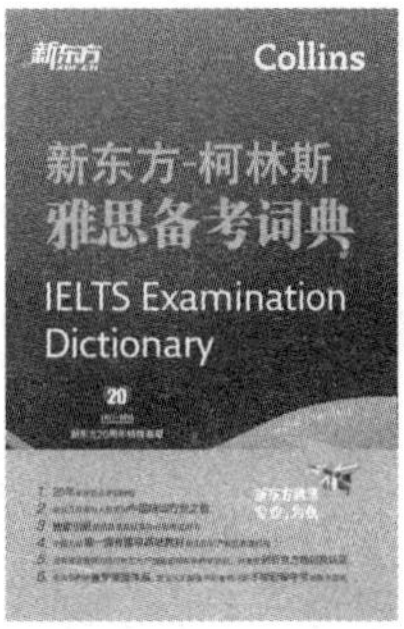

增加背景阅读

练习口语时很多人会感觉无话可说，面对话题无从谈起，有人会把这个问题归结于词汇量不够。其实词汇只是问题的一部分，缺少以句子、段落为形式的资源才是根源。如果光有大量的词汇，却不能用连贯的语句把这些词汇呈现出来，同样无法实现“谈笑风生”。而要提高词汇量、增加句子和段落储备，最好的办法莫过于针对特定话题搜集背景材料，然后进行阅读和分析。本书中每个话题单元都提供了背景文章，供考生研读之用。

此外，网络上丰富的英语资讯加上强大的搜索引擎，使得互联网成为了巨大的英语资料库。读者在备考雅思或学习英语的过程中如果遇到词汇匮乏、思路狭窄等问题，不妨试一下网上淘宝，相信会有惊喜收获。下面给大家介绍几个最常用的网站：

	百度网站	Answers 百科全书	Yahoo 帖吧
	Baidu百度	Answers.com™	YAHOO! ANSWERS
网址	www.baidu.com	www.answers.com	answers.yahoo.com
概述	强大搜索引擎	网上英文百科全书	英文帖吧，话题无所不包
应用举例	雅思口语和写作中的任何话题，均可以直接或提取关键单词输入搜索框。 如：输入“research using animals”或“benefits of walking”，便可找到大量相关文章。	关于人类文明的概括，对雅思考试最有用的莫过于对中国文化和现象的介绍，考生只要知道想查询的中国文化的英文名称，基本都可以找到英文的解释。 如：输入“CCTV New Year’s Gala”(春节晚会)或“Yang Ge”(秧歌)，或者“Super Girl”(超级女生)，都能查到英文介绍。	网上问答网站，基本囊括了所有的日常话题，最适合搜寻口语素材。读者可直接将口语问题输入搜索框查询相关帖子。 如：输入“Do you like dancing?”或“What is your favorite piece of music?”。
使用注意事项	搜索结果过多，使用需耐心；文字风格多为书面，比较适合在雅思写作中借鉴，用于口语时应略加修改。	文字风格书面，不适合直接应用到口语中。	语言多为日常口语，偶尔夹杂俚语和不良信息；美国英语为主。

反复演练

口语学习的过程中，反复练习占据着很重要的地位。如果说在整个口语备考过程中搜集资料、整理答案要花费 40%的时间的话，那么反复练习就应该占到剩下的 60%的时间。练习的方法有很多，粗略地讲有两种，一是自练自说，二是实战练习。

所谓自练自说，就是自己把准备过的材料或答案反复练习，直至纯熟而且自然。在使用此方法时，可考虑对着镜子，并适当加上肢体语言。这种方法听上去比较好笑，但口语学习的确是需要一点点激情和疯狂的。此方法适合各类层次的考生，特别是基础较薄弱、缺乏自信的同学，可以通过这样 1-2 个月的练习培养语感、增加流利性，从而树立自信。

所谓实战练习，即找个练习口语的伙伴，约定话题后集中练习。伙伴可以是外国朋友，也可以是中国同学。但使用这种方法最需要注意的一点是要尽量避免两个人毫无目的的“free talk”，最好是在实战练习前先规定话题，然后对要讨论的话题进行大量的准备后再进行练习。不做准备就直接开练的做法不可取，因为那样做的效率太低，效果最差，而且有时候会产生挫败感。

III. 口语考场应试技能

雅思口语准备情况如何，最终都要到口语考场上接受检验。考场上紧张的气氛和快节奏为口语最终得分带来很大变数。就像所有的竞技比赛一样，有了扎实的基础之后，还要力争将自己的竞技状态在比赛现场调整到最佳。下面所列出的“考场发挥 5 原则”是帮助考生在考试现场发挥出最好水平的重要技巧。

主动交流

口语考试旨在考查考生能否“communicate effectively in English”，因此交流技能是考官重点考查的能力之一，而交流的主动性是最显而易见、也是最容易被考官注意到的交流能力。考生应该在考试中表现出“willing to speak”，即表现出一种“我虽然英语不好，但我特别想交流，而且尽量去交流”的态度来，这对于基础较薄弱的考生来说尤为重要，它可以帮助考生保住基本的 5 分或 6 分。表现交流主动性最简单的办法就是在问答时尽量避免只用一个单词或者“Yes”、“No”，或者简单的一句话来做答。在回答出考官的问题后，后面可以再加个“1”——即一条额外的信息，比如说对前面的回答做更细致描述，或者加以解释等，如下面的例子：

—(考官在第一部分问到)**Where do you live now?**

—(考生回答)I live in Beijing now. *I am happy to be here because the city is really on the move and there is a lot of excitement here.*

—(考官在第一部分问到)**What kinds of films do you like best?**

—(考生回答)My favorite kinds of films are comedies. *I like movies that can make me laugh.*

在上面两个例子中，考生在给出问题的答案后（即下划线部分），又主动给出了附加的解释说明(斜体部分)，非常好地体现出交流的主动性以及语言能力。这样的答案肯定要比单单给出下划线部分或者光给出"Beijing"和"comedies"两个单词要好得多。在本书后面真题演练部分，书中给出的答案都反映出了这一交流策略。

微笑＋眼神交流

微笑是交流的润滑剂，也是给自己加油鼓劲的心理暗示。此外，在考试过程中，跟考官的"eye contact"也是必不可少的，微笑的眼神流露出自信和交流的意愿。

自然

雅思口语固然需要准备，但考试时尽量不要一字不漏地背诵已经准备好的答案。考官可以看出来你准备了，那样的话，即使你说得再好也不会得到理想的分数了。有时可以用一些表示犹豫的词语如 er, erm, uh, and, yes, right, yeah, oh right 等增添一分自然的味道，但是不能过度频繁地使用这些词语。

得体着装

口语考试毕竟是个较为正式的场合，考生固然不需要穿得太正式，但得体的服装能体现出对对方的尊重。

礼貌

进入考场后大大方方地问候，口试结束后向考官表示谢意并告辞。切忌在离开考场时向考官询问自己的成绩或表现情况，这在考官看来是不成熟的表现。

Ⅳ. 如何使用此书

使用《雅思口语特训》四步骤

1. 研读样板、消化吸收

先熟悉真题本身以及样板答案，用精读的方式研究文本，并反复听配套 MP3。

2. 拓展词汇、背景阅读

阅读话题补充素材，或者按照“Ⅱ. 口语水平提高策略”中介绍的方法去网上搜集更新的材料，尽量扩大阅读量。

3. 组织答案、融入个性

到此考生已经对话题非常熟悉，而且掌握了足够的语言资源，现在可以开始准备自己的答案，最好在准备的初期阶段把答案整理成文字，随着复习的推进再考虑用笔记的形式准备答案。

4. 反复练习、实战演练

自己准备的答案要反复练习，一开始可以自说自练，尽量做到看到一个话题稍加准备就可以比较流利地进行作答。而后，可以利用光盘中的“实战演练”进行模拟练习。

雅思口语话题更新速度快，在备考过程中遇到新题也可以按照本书所介绍的方法去准备，甚至可以直接到本书中去寻找需要的素材，比如说 2007 年出现的新题 “Describe a modern interesting building”，考生也可以直接去“地点题”部分参考“重要建筑物”话题卡，其实旧题中提供了足够的用来描述新题所需要的语言资源。

第二章
雅思口语最新话题选材

Introductory questions:

口语考试开始前考官要对考生进行身份确认，下面几个问题是最常见的开场白，考生应对其熟练掌握，以便在考试之初就给考官留下自信、友好的第一印象。

1）Good morning/afternoon.

2）Can you tell me your full name, please?

3）What shall I call you?

4）Can you tell me where you're from?

5）Can I see your identification, please?

1. Education and Learning 教育和学习

1）Do you work or are you a student?

Presently I am a student. I have been studying at Beijing University for three years. I will graduate in one year.

2）What subject are you studying?

I am studying Accounting. Along with Accounting, I am also majoring in Business Finance.

3）Why did you choose to study that?

My father has a business and I want to work with him. I plan to take over company finances.

更多资源

It's practical and useful in getting a job because many companies are interested in hiring students with a background in international business.

I've always liked reading, especially novels, history, literature. That's why I chose Humanities.

I didn't choose my major, I just went with the flow. I was taking maths courses left and right and I found myself majoring in Applied Maths with a Computer Science option.

It was the easiest decision ever. I chose it because I have passion for it.

4）Do you like your university?

It's OK. I am not thrilled with it but I am getting the education that I wanted.

更多资源

大学 I'm in university and it's awesome! I've never had so much fun or learned so much about a topic, or most importantly, learned so much about myself. I've met so many great and diverse people and been in situations that I never thought I'd ever be in. I wouldn't trade my years at university in for anything.

I went to Northeastern in Boston: not a good choice for me—big commuter school, not a big "campus" atmosphere. I transferred and ended up at Ithaca College in Ithaca, NY. It was great, mainly because of my program in the communications school and because there were things going on around campus.

中小学 It's the best school we have in... This school's history goes back many months, but everything is nice and kept in good condition in addition to some new things. Plus the teachers are cool and so is the current principal. Everything is cool there.

5）Is there anything you don't like about your studies?

Basically studying, just joking. Some of my studies I just have to take for the credits and that gets a little tedious sometimes.

6）Which subject do you like the most?

I like Math. For some reason math comes easy to me. It could be because my father was a math teacher.

更多资源

Right now my favorite subject is Physics. I have an absolutely amazing professor and I love the class. I am learning so much!

7）Which subject do you think will be the most useful to you after you leave university?

I suppose my English class will be the most useful since I am planning on studying further in Australia. Probably 90% of what I've learned I will never use though.

8）Do you often get together with your classmates after classes?

I get together with my classmates as much as I can after class. Getting together with them really helps to relieve the pressure for me.

9）What was your favorite subject in high school?

Well, I think my favorite subject in high school was art. One reason was I sat next to the prettiest girl in the class.

更多资源

History was always enjoyable for me. Math was highly dependent on the teacher, but I typically enjoyed physics and chemistry. Really, it was teachers more than the subject that made a subject unpleasant.

I like science because I think it is very interesting to learn about new things that we hadn't even thought of before.

Science (e.g. Biology). It tells about how life works and it's useful, too. I like biology because that is the study of living organisms, which really fascinates me.

10) Which school subject do you think is the most useful for people in adult life?

Any subject having to do with communication would be the most useful when you graduate from school. Geography is also a subject that is nice to know, if you are going to travel. You would want to know what country you are in and which country is north and which is south.

教育话题必备词汇

1. learning atmosphere 学习氛围
2. academic standards 学术水平
3. faculty *n.* 系
4. lecturer *n.* 讲师
5. supportive *adj.* 支持的
6. academic subject 学术课程
7. skip classes 逃课
8. sit an exam 参加考试
9. do badly in an exam 考的不好
10. transcript *n.* 成绩单
11. drop-out *n.*辍学
12. social skills 社交技能
13. life skills 生活技能
14. transferable skills 受用终身的技能
15. internship *n.* 实习
16. association *n.* 联盟，社团
17. extracurricular activities 课外活动
18. social and cultural life 业余生活
19. develop talents and interests 发挥聪明才智
20. tuition fees 学费
21. grant *n.* 助学金
22. dormitory *n.* 宿舍
23. reach one's full potential 实现全部潜能

2. Working Life 工作

1) Could you tell me what you do for a living?

I work in the foreign trade department, I am in sales. It is my job to bring foreign investors to the city to open up a business here.

> 更多资源
>
> I work for a large European car maker. I work on car design. In fact, I run the design department and I manage a team of designers: 20 people work under me. One of my main responsibilities is to make sure that new model designs are finished on time. I'm also in charge of design budgets.

2) What are your responsibilities at work?

I have to develop a strategy for bringing foreign investment to Beijing. I work together with other departments to basically sell and promote Beijing as a good place to start a business.

3) What is the most interesting part of your work?

The most interesting part of my work is meeting people from other countries. To me people are very interesting and I am keen on learning the customs and cultures of other countries.

> 更多资源
>
> I do like my job, been here for 6 years! It's a small office; the work environment is great; everyone is chill, laid back. I don't have to dress up. I can wear jeans everyday if I wanted.
>
> I definitely love my job... it is something that I enjoy doing. I meet so many cool people daily and I have opportunities to learn more about myself and others.
>
> I like dealing with people from different cultures and traveling. I also like the 30 days paid holiday.

4) Is there anything you don't like about your job?

The pay is one thing that I don't like about my job. My boss is another thing that I don't like about my job. The distance to the office is the last thing that I don't like about my job.

> 更多资源
>
> I work as a system developer. I'm stuck with the same client, the same users, the same programs for the last 3 and a half years, so it's now boring, and not exciting as it was before. Besides, I haven't acquired any new knowledge, or have any new challenges.

5）Is your job very important to you?

My job is very important to me. If I didn't have my job, I wouldn't be sitting here in front of you, applying for a chance to go overseas.

6）Would you like to change your job?

I don't want to get stuck at this job that I am working at now. I am still young, so I want to learn as much as I can and then I plan on starting my own business.

7）Do you often get together with your colleagues（workmates）after work?

I do get together with my colleagues after work as much as I can. When I get together with them, we can shoot the breeze and have a few beers. I really look forward to getting together with them and count on it to make my week.

补充资源

"描述你将来想从事的工作"是第二部分的话题卡之一，下面是国外网友对自己理想工作的描述，从里面可以找到很多用来评价工作的语汇。

What is your dream job?

My dream job is one that combines traveling, teaching and doing voluntary work. So in a sense, the ideal job is to teach kids in a foreign country and have the ability to travel to the different parts of the world/country. I hope it's achievable.

I am doing my dream job right now actually, I am a children's literacy tutor. I love to work with kids and helping them learn to read is the most rewarding experience. It is fun and every session is different and full of challenges. I wouldn't want to do anything else. I have had my share of dead-end, low-wage jobs and now this is the ultimate dream job for me!

My dream job would be:

1. A job with flexibility of time.
2. A job where I can learn and grow as a professional.
3. A job with a nice environment.
4. A job that pays well.
5. A job not so far from home.
6. A job where I could feel security, and not feel that if the project finishes I have the risk of loosing it.
7. A job where I could have better benefits than I have now.

工作话题必备词汇

1. working hours 工作时间
2. make a living 谋生
3. daily routine 日常事务
4. in charge of 负责

5. paperwork *n.*文书工作
6. work nine to five 朝九晚五
7. flexi-time 灵活工作时间
8. work overtime 加班
9. work experience 工作经验
10. administration *n.* 行政管理
11. colleague *n.* 同事
12. business associates 商业伙伴
13. client *n.* 客户
14. retire *v.* 退休
15. workaholic *n.* 工作狂
16. trainee *n.* 实习生
17. promote *v.* 升迁
18. training course 培训课程
19. freelance *n.* 自由职业者
20. in-job training 在职培训
21. job satisfaction 工作满意度
22. opportunity to learn 学习机会
23. fringe benefit 额外福利
24. well-paid *adj.* 高薪的
25. pay rise 涨工资
26. paid holiday 带薪假期
27. sick pay 病假工资
28. medical insurance 医疗保险
29. working environment 工作环境
30. commuting time 上下班时间
31. dream job 理想工作
32. challenging *adj.* 有挑战性的
33. prospects *n.* 前景
34. rewarding *adj.* 有益的，值得的
35. engaging *adj.* 让人投入的
36. pension scheme 养老计划
37. sense of accomplishment 成就感

3. Towns and Cities 城镇家乡

1）Whereabouts did you grow up?

I grew up in Tianjin, a city that is southeast of Beijing. It is closer to the sea than Beijing, and is also a municipal city like Beijing.

2）Do you still live there?

No, I haven't lived there for many years. I went to school here in Beijing and have simply settled here and made it my hometown. I still go back to Tianjin every once in a while.

3）What's the most famous place in your hometown?

Well, there isn't much in Tianjin that is famous, not like Beijing, where there are so many famous places, but the TV tower is where most people want to go when they come to Tianjin.

4）How has your hometown changed in recent years?

I hardly even recognize it, it has changed so much. Just like most of China, Tianjin is changing rapidly at an alarming rate.

更多资源

It's quite amazing, from 1990 to 2006, my state has grown from 660,000 residents to 783,000 people. There is nothing recognizable of my hometown except the historic area.

My hometown has changed dramatically over the past 20 or so years. Downtown does not look the same and real estate prices went through the roof. All the roads are under constructions and places that were considered the Ghetto when I moved to Miami in 1999 now have homes that are over $500,000.

While much of the place is the same and seems familiar, it does not feel like home. I can drive right by the house that I lived in through Junior High and High School and feel completely disconnected from the place. It isn't home anymore.... a rather bittersweet feeling if you ask me.

5）Where do you live now?

I live in Beijing now. I am happy to be here because the city is really on the move and there is a lot of excitement here because of the Olympics.

6）What part of the city do you like best?

I like the CBD the most because there are a lot of clubs there and also a lot of hustle and bustle and that is what I am into. I like to be where the crowds are, the same as most young people.

更多资源

The one thing I do like: people here are nice; there is a good sense of community. Also, there is not the traffic problem that you'd find in larger cities.

I love where I live because I have so many friends here, I've lived here all my life, I like the weather, and there are so many fun things to do.

7) Is there anything you don't likc about this city?

The springtime when the winds from the Gobi desert blow in and the sky turns a hazy orange is one thing I don't like about Beijing. Another one of my least favorite things is having to fight rush hour traffic on the subway.

8) Do you want to live in a big city or a small town?

I just couldn't go back to living in a small town. I have gotten accustomed to life in the big city and it would be hard to get me back to those "country roads."

更多资源

I like living in a small town within driving distance of a city. That way I can enjoy the craziness of the city for a time and then return to the simplicity of the small town life.

Big city. It's hard to get bored when you live in a city that never sleeps, like NYC, LA, Miami, Rome, Paris. There's much to do.

I really love to live in the small city, because there is less traffic and it's not so crowded. The small city looks so peaceful to me, but I love to visit the big city also, to go shopping, have fun with friends and stay for a couple of days, but not to live there.

I grew up in a small town, and could not wait to get out... now, as an adult, I'd love to go back.... I am tired of all the traffic... all the crime... all the rushing around like ants.

城镇家乡话题必备词汇

1. ancient *adj.* 远古的
2. cosmopolitan *adj.* 国际化的
3. cultural atmosphere 文化氛围
4. tourist attraction 游览胜地
5. situated *adj.*位于
6. suburb *n.* 郊区
7. scenery *n.* 景色
8. population *n.* 人口
9. inhabitant *n.* 居民
10. spectacular *adj.* 引人入胜的
11. historical site 历史遗迹
12. public library 公共图书馆
13. well-preserved *adj.* 保存完善的
14. specialty *n.* 特产
15. pace of life 生活节奏
16. lifestyle *n.* 生活方式
17. living standard 生活水平
18. cost of living 生活消费

19. sense of community 相互关爱和谐的感觉
20. downtown *n.* 市区
21. job opportunity 就业机会
22. air quality 空气质量
23. architecture *n.* 建筑
24. infrastructure *n.* 基础设施
25. city service 市政服务
26. sightseeing *n.* 观光
27. night-life 夜生活
28. bustling *adj.* 熙熙攘攘的
29. lively *adj.* 活跃的
30. vibrant *adj.* 充满生机的
31. dynamic *adj.* 生机勃勃的
32. well worth a visit 值得一游
33. holiday resort 度假地
34. seaside resort 海滨胜地
35. art gallery 艺廊
36. concert hall 音乐厅
37. exhibition center 展览中心
38. opera house 歌剧院

4. Daily Routine and Leisure Time 日常生活和休闲

Daily routine 日常生活

1）What part of your day do you like best?

My favorite part of the day is late afternoon, because the day's work is coming to an end, I can go home, and I have the evening to look forward to, and the weather is generally pleasant and cool.

更多资源

Late night, when I can mess around here for a bit, play a computer game or two, then snuggle down and read a book or watch TV until I fall asleep. No worries, nothing to do, just relax and sleep. I love it.

I like the evening after I get off of work. I can then cook a good meal, work on my hobbies, and read as late as I want. I am not on a schedule then.

When I get up. No one else in the house is awake yet. That's my quiet time when I can do what I want. For most people it would be in the evening when everyone else goes to bed, but for me I'm exhausted by then.

2）What is the busiest part of the day for you?

From about 10 o'clock to noon. That is when I have to take care of my work and things are a bit hectic.

3）When do you have free time?

I have free time during the evenings and on the weekends. I guess you could say that I have it pretty good, because a lot of people here in China don't have so much free time.

4）What's your favorite way to relax?

I take a long hot shower and then I jump in bed with a good book and something to snack on. It is a little hard on my figure but then it just means that I have to do a few more exercises the next morning.

更多资源

I sit in a hot tub with bubble bath. Candles light the room and there is good music playing in the background. Perfect way to end the day.

I usually listen to music or just play around on the Internet. I pretty much do anything that makes me forget about my school work.

Sometimes I like to drink alone and listen to music. They say you shouldn't drink alone, but it is probably okay once in a while, and it is a very relaxing experience.

I love to go for a long walk...listen to jazz in my little radio, or some kind of nice music...and then go home, put on pyjamas, turn on the heat and have a little something that tastes really good and curl up and watch the Movie Channel, with all the old movies...

The best way I relax after work is to clean up my house! Even just tidying makes me feel so much more relaxed. I sort myself out by doing this and for me it works.

5) Do you do things in your leisure time with friends or family?

Mostly with my friends. I often go out to eat or go shopping with my friends, and sometimes we stay in and watch a movie or play games. Sometimes we just talk together.

6) Do you have any hobbies or interests?

I love to read novels, go go-carting, hiking, watch movies and write. I have lots of different interests.

更多资源

I go to the gym a few days a week. It is a great way to let off stress. It also has a jacuzzi and a steam room so if I have extra time on the weekends, it is a great place to relax.

I like to knit and do other forms of needlework. I find it relaxing and creative.

I love taking my pictures and putting them into albums to catalog my family's "stories". It's the way I express myself creatively, and it serves the purpose of capturing and enjoying our memories, and preserves them for future generations!

I have tons of hobbies, I knit, crochet, cross-stitch, latch-hook, draw, paint, write, play the violin, piano and video games, and the list keeps growing as I find other things to try. What I love about my hobbies is that they keep me sane, they're great stress relievers too (it's been proven, trust me), and it gives me a sense of accomplishment and a feeling of self-worth. We all need those little pick-me-ups at some point in our lives no matter how fortunate we are.

Weekends 周末

7) How do you (usually) spend the weekend?

I sleep late, and watch movies, I go out with my friends, or I work on different projects I haven't had time for during the week. Sometimes if I am really tired or stressed from the week I will just stay in bed all weekend.

更多资源

It depends what time of year it is. But most Saturdays I go grocery shopping in the morning and sometimes I go shopping after that for things I might need around the house. If not, then I work in the house and clean. On Sundays, it is wash day. I wash all the dirty clothes from the week.

I usually hang out with my sisters or just go shopping or study.

Saturday is mostly shopping and cleaning the house. Sunday I relax, play computer games and go to the movies.

8) Which do you prefer, Saturday or Sunday?

Saturday, because I can go out in the evening and stay out late and I don't have to worry about waking up early for work the next morning.

9) Are weekends important to you?

Very, it's some of the only time I can use for my hobbies or spend with my family. On the weekends I feel free to do exactly what I want.

10) Should people be paid overtime for working at the weekend?

Definitely, working overtime is extra, and it takes away the relaxation time so many people need, so people should be compensated for it.

Shopping 购物

11) Do you like shopping?

No, I actually don't like shopping; I hate making decisions, and it irritates me to spend all that time looking for what I want. It irritates me even more if it's too expensive on top of that!

更多资源

I hate shopping. I don't see how women can find it enjoyable. I buy stuff I need from eBay, no people, no waiting in line to pay, no shop staff, no parking.

I absolutely love shopping! It's like my drug. It makes me feel good. I love fashion so it's cool to see what everyone is wearing, showing and buying.

12) Are there many shops near where you live?

Yes, but only small shops, which sell all kinds of curious things, no big shopping malls. I think there is going to be a shopping center opening up soon near where I live and that should be nice.

13) Who usually does the shopping in your home?

My mum does the shopping, and sometimes I go along too. Sometimes I have to go out and do the shopping and I enjoy haggling with the vendors. I look forward to it.

14) Do you have a regular time to go shopping?

For some things, yes — for example, my mum goes food shopping twice a week, but I only go shopping for clothes when I feel like it.

15) What things do you usually buy when you go shopping?

I buy way too much jewelry, and peculiar hats that I will never wear, and lots of scarves. It's hard for me to make decisions on what to buy when it's anything real big or costly.

16) Do you prefer shopping in small shops or big supermarkets and department stores?

I prefer shopping in small shops because you can find more unusual things and they come cheaper, too. I like to get to know the owners and sometimes they will cater to me a bit.

日常生活和休闲话题必备词汇

1. be crazy about 痴迷于
2. be keen on 热衷于
3. entertainment *n.* 娱乐
4. spare time 业余时间
5. mahjong *n.* 麻将
6. Karaoke bar 卡拉 OK 歌厅
7. massage *n.* 按摩
8. sauna *n.* 桑拿
9. Tai Chi 太极
10. gardening *n.* 园艺
11. Peking opera 京剧
12. pastime *n.* 消遣

5. Holidays and Traveling 节日和旅游

1）What do you do in your holidays?

For most holidays, I just stay home and rest and enjoy myself, but if it's a particularly long holiday I like to travel. If I stay home I can read and play computer games and do what I like to do. I can spend time with my friends, although often my relatives want me to visit them as well. So there is a lot to do.

2）Do you think holidays are becoming more and more important?

Not necessarily; holidays have always been important to people. But of course the harder your work, the more important your holiday becomes to you, because you need that relaxation more.

更多资源

To be honest, I'm not big on holidays. I don't really like all of the pressure and attention that go with them. The honest truth is I do often use holidays as an excuse to get people together (otherwise some won't). I enjoy having fun and spending time with the people I love, and there are some people I only get to see on holidays.

Yes, because it gives you time to be with your family and friends. Many young people live away from their parents, so it's a perfect time for them to get together and have fun.

3）Do you like to travel in your holidays or free time?

If it's a long holiday, I love to travel, especially to places I have never been to before; it's an adventure and you see so many great and beautiful and strange things. I really enjoy traveling because when you have a change of scenery and a change of environment for a while, it helps you to relax and is good for your health.

更多资源

I love traveling! There are so many places I want to see and so many things I want to do, but lack of funds has been a big obstacle! One day though I will travel to the four corners of the world and beyond, with nothing but a knapsack on my back....

I love traveling. I've been to Taiwan, Hong Kong and Singapore. I hope to visit Europe with my husband in the near future.

4）What kind of places do you like to travel to?

I like to travel to exotic places, different countries, and places with beautiful natural scenery.

However I don't often have the opportunity to go to places like that. So instead I like to go to places where I can enjoy myself with my friends and where there are fun things to do together.

> 更多资源
> I like the mountains myself. Nothing makes me happier than to be exploring a new backwoods trail.
> I love to go around the world and explore. But if I were to choose a region, it would be Europe. Every part of Europe interests me. Specifically, I like to go to Rome, Paris and Vatican city.
> I love to travel—going to new places and seeing things I've never seen before. My favorite places to travel to are beaches.

5）Have you ever been to the seaside?

Yes, I've had several vacations on the seaside. There is a beach not too far from where my family lives, so every time I go to visit my family, we spend a lot of time on the beach.

6）Why do some people take their holidays at the seaside?

I guess they like to swim, lie on the sand, tan, and go sailing on the sea. Plus there are usually a lot of nice restaurants near the seaside and it is a good opportunity to enjoy fresh seafood.

7）Do you want to live near the sea?

No, I don't like the sea. It's so salty and deep and there are all kinds of fish and other creatures swimming about in it. On the other hand, the air is often quite clean near the sea and the weather very pleasant compared to farther inland. So if I was concerned about my health I would probably choose to live near the sea.

节日和旅游话题必备词汇

旅游

1. check-in desk 登记前台
2. backpack *v.* 背包旅游
3. sunbathing *n.* 日光浴
4. get a suntan 晒太阳
5. get away from it all 摆脱所有烦恼
6. destination *n.* 目的地
7. route *n.* 路线
8. travel agency 旅行社
9. tour guide 导游
10. package holiday 旅游套餐
11. self-catering holiday 自助游
12. go sightseeing 观光
13. board（boat / plane）登上
14. hitchhike *v.* 远足
15. set off 出发
16. campsite *n.* 露营地

旅游住宿

17. tranquil *adj.* 安静、祥和
18. awesome *adj.* 极好（口语）
19. stunning *adj.* 惊人的好
20. courteous *adj.* 有礼貌的
21. lobby *n.* 大厅
22. adjacent *adj.* 临近的

23. frequent *v.* 经常光顾
24. be located 位于
25. basic utilities 基本设施
26. homey（homely）*adj.* 像家一样的
27. all year round 常年
28. hang out 打发时光
29. disco *n.* 迪厅
30. spa *n.* 矿泉，矿泉疗养地
31. cafeteria *n.* 餐厅
32. maid *n.* 女服务员
33. guesthouse *n.* 客栈

6. Housing and Accommodation 家居

1）What kind of housing/accommodation do you live in?

I live in an apartment building. My family owns two apartments right next to each other and I live in the smaller apartment with my sister. My mother and father and my father's parents live in the other.

2）How do you like it?

Oh, I like it very much; I live quite high up and I have a wonderful view of the city. And it is very convenient to live near my parents, as my mom often cooks for us when we are very busy.

3）What kind of decorations does it（do the rooms）have?

The apartment is very nicely furnished, though simple. We have a brand new living room set, a couch and two chairs, which my parents picked out. My sister and I picked out the curtains and lamps and knicknacks, so that it has kind of a Middle Eastern style. We decorated our own rooms with all the things we saved from growing up.

4）What kind of house or apartment do you want to live in?

I want to live in a little house in the country, with two floors and a big attic and basement, and wide gardens and orchards around it. I would probably have to live in an apartment in town most of the time and I would like my apartment to also have two floors.

更多资源

I would love to own a nice brickfront townhouse close to work. Something with a deck above a patio, a big kitchen, and plenty of room to entertain. That would be so wonderful...

5）Which is your favorite room in your home?

My favorite room is my room, because it has my bed and things in it and a little window seat where you can sit in the sunshine and look outside. When I want to get away from everything for a while, I can escape to my room surrounded by the things I love that remind me of happy memories and if I want to chill I can play computer games whenever I want.

更多资源

I like the living room because there I can relax on the couch.

Of course, my bedroom, because I can do whatever I want in it. No noise, but my own.

I would have to say that it would be my room. It's clean, well kept but comfortable and relaxing.

It's my territory. I could do what ever I want and it wouldn't matter because it's my room.

The kitchen. It is the hub of the house. More activities there than anywhere else. And I like to cook.

6）Which room does your family spend most of the time in?

My family spends most of their time in the living room. We often watch DVDs together or we just talk about our day. And if we have friends or relatives over, we will all go into the living room to sit and talk and eat some snacks.

7）What would you say is the best thing about your home?

My favorite thing about my home is the big terrace we have; it's a very pleasant place to sit in the warm weather. There is a "secret" door inside a closet that leads out onto the terrace and we have a picnic table and chairs out there, so you can just go out there under the sky and read a book or look up into the clear blue sky.

更多资源

Probably my comforter set. I didn't like it much when I first bought it—I originally wanted another design—but it's grown on me in the past few months.

It depends. If you're talking about my apartment or my parent's house, their house, I like the family room—awesome couches and big-screen TV. In my apartment, my bedroom—comfy king-size bed.

8）Would you like to move to another place?

Not now, but eventually yes, because I think I would be bored to live in the same place for too long. I would miss my parents so it would be hard to move away from home, but at the same time I am anxious to have a life of my own. Plus I think that living in a big city is very impersonal and I would like to live in a different place.

家居话题必备词汇

1. neighborhood *n.* 小区
2. housing *n.* 住房
3. two-bedroom flat 两居室
4. studio flat 小户型一居
5. guesthouse *n.* 招待所
6. bungalow *n.* 平房
7. ground floor 一层
8. study *n.* 书房
9. courtyard *n.* 院子
10. balcony *n.* 阳台
11. attic *n.* 阁楼
12. ceiling *n.* 天花板
13. lounge *n.* 客厅
14. basement *n.* 地下室
15. mortgage *n.* 房贷
16. décor *n.* 装饰风格

17. interior design 内部装饰
18. rent *n.* 房租
19. cramped *adj.* 狭促的
20. spacious *adj.* 宽敞的
21. airy *adj.* 通风的
22. cozy *adj.* 舒适的
23. symmetry *n.* 对称
24. furnished *adj.* 装修过的
25. in good condition 保养的不错
26. clean and tidy 干净整洁
27. storey *n.* 层
28. plant *n.* 绿植

7. Sports and Exercise 体育锻炼

1）What is your favorite sport?

My favorite sport is definitely soccer. I love the feeling of being out there on the field and just running with the wind.

更多资源

Soccer! It's one of the most highly athletic, demanding, and competitive sports!

My favorite sport is basketball. I like watching it. I'm not really good at any sport, because I'm not athletic.

Volleyball! I like serving in V-ball. It is all I can do well. When I was in high school, I was not popular, but I was ALWAYS called on to serve in V-ball. It was the only time I was popular!

2）Why do you like it so much?

In soccer the rules are not too complicated, but it's very competitive and takes a lot of skill and talent to play well. I always have fun when I'm playing or watching it on TV.

更多资源

These sports make you move a lot, thus giving you more adrenalin and exercise!

It's just awesome, the thrill, the rush and then there are the dunks which can be so cool!

Because those are really the only sports I excel at. In track I am the best girl long-distance runner and in softball I am one of the better pitchers. They are also very fun and get you in shape!

I grew up in Huntington Beach California, so it was as natural to me as breathing.

3）What is the most popular sport in your country?

I think it's basketball. Football also has always been the most popular sport in China. Badminton and *ping pong* are close behind.

4）Do you like to exercise daily?

No, I don't. I'm awfully lazy. I know that I need to change this habit or I'm afraid it is going to come back and bite me in the butt.

更多资源

No. I like to walk but that's it.

I do enjoy exercising but finding the time is the hard thing.

Walking is very good and cheap. Sit-ups and push-ups are great too. I do them when I wake up and before I go to sleep. The push-ups and 25 crunches. It's not a lot, but it's better than nothing.

5）How much time do you spend exercising?

Probably five or six hours a week. I know that I will not make the Olympics at that rate, but then again sports is not my field.

6）What are the advantages of regular exercise?

There's the obvious advantage that if you regularly exercise you will stay stronger, more fit, and healthier, but you also get better sleep and it helps calm your busy mind.

7）Where do people in China usually exercise?

Young people go to the gym or go to a playground and play basketball. Older people will just go outside their apartments and do Tai Chi.

8）What forms of exercise are most popular in China?

Badminton or *ping pong* are very popular here in China. Basketball and football are also very popular.

9）Do you think primary school children should have sports classes at school?

I certainly think so, because primary school children have a lot of energy and if they must remain cooped up at a desk all day, they will not be able to concentrate because they will want to go out and play.

体育锻炼话题必备词汇

1. work out 锻炼
2. gym *n.* 体育馆
3. leisure centre 健身娱乐中心
4. membership scheme 会员制
5. exercise machines 锻炼器材
6. fitness instructors 健身教练
7. treadmill *n.* 跑步机
8. championship *n.* 冠军赛
9. tournament *n.* 锦标赛
10. trek *v.* 长途跋涉
11. badminton *n.* 羽毛球
12. racket *n.* 球拍
13. break record 打破记录
14. stadium *n.* 大型体育馆
15. atmosphere 气氛
16. cheerleader *n.* 啦啦队长
17. spectator sport 观赏性运动
18. extreme sport 极限运动
19. draw *n.* 平局
20. quarterfinal *n.* 四分之一决赛
21. knockout *n.* 淘汰赛
22. extra time 加时赛
23. stimulant *n.* 兴奋剂
24. golf course 高尔夫球场
25. court *n.* 场地
26. time out 暂停

27. athlete *n.* 运动员
28. amateur 业余爱好者
29. gold medal 金牌
30. jersey *n.* 球衣
31. sports gear 运动装备
32. referee *n.* 裁判
33. score（a point / a goal）*v.* 得分
34. bowling alley 保龄球场
35. health benefits 保健作用
36. lower blood pressure 降低血压
37. lower stress 减压
38. character building 塑造性格

8. Interests and Hobbies 兴趣和爱好

Film 电影

1）Do you like films?

Yes, I enjoy watching films. When I want to relax, or have some fun, I like to watch movie.

2）What kinds of films do you like best?

My favorite kinds of films are comedies. I like movies that can make me laugh.

更多资源

My favorite kinds of films are action films, with exciting stories and lots of special effects.

Mostly romantic comedies, but I like some of the ones that keep you thinking all the way through too, like *A Beautiful Mind*, *The Fifth Element* and *The Sixth Sense*.

Romance, comedy, drama, some action but not much though, mystery, horror and suspense. I guess everything but westerns and most action, oh and some classic old movies are OK too.

3）How often do you watch films?

If there is an interesting movie playing at the cinema, I'll go to see it. It's nice to go out to see a movie with my friends sometimes, and get to see it on a big screen.

4）Do you like to watch films alone or with your friends?

I'd rather watch films with my friends. We always have a good time together, and afterwards we talk about the movie, whether we enjoyed it or not.

5）Do you prefer to watch films in the cinema or at home?

I prefer to watch movies at the cinema, because then you get to see the movie on a big screen, with a better sound system. I think it makes the movie more impressive, you know.

更多资源

I prefer to watch movies at home, because then I can choose any movie I want to watch, and I can pause it if I need to go get something.

I prefer watching movies at home because you can watch at your leisure and it is so convenient to pause or go back a few scenes and just stop and continue watching hours or days later. Whereas in the cinema, you do have a bigger screen but you do not have any control whatsoever.

Depends. If it's a big action film with lots of explosions, I would see it at the cinema, but others I like to watch on DVD. There's nothing better than kicking back on your comfy old couch in front of the box.

电影话题必备词汇

1. blockbuster *n.* 大片
2. action films *n.* 动作片
3. kung fu film 功夫片
4. musical *n.* 音乐剧
5. science fiction 科幻电影
6. animated films 动画片
7. release *v.* 发行
8. hero *n.* 男主角
9. heroine *n.* 女主角
10. cast *n.* 全体演员
11. subtitle *n.*字幕
12. dubbed *adj.* 无字幕而有本国人配音的
13. genre *n.* 风格
14. classification *n.* 分级
15. plot *n.* 情节
16. gripping *adj.* 引人入胜的
17. feature *v.* 由…主演
18. box-office 票房
19. censorship *n.*审查制度
20. freedom of speech 言论自由
21. uproar *n.* 一片哗然
22. celebrity *n.* 名人
23. video clips 视频片段
24. review *n.* 评论

Dance 舞蹈

1）Do you like to dance?

Yes, I like to dance, 'cause I really enjoy moving to the music.

更多资源

No, I don't like to dance, I don't know how to dance very well, and I feel uncomfortable.

I love to dance, in fact I take belly dance classes and I've performed a couple of times...it's actually quite addictive once you get used to it!

I love to dance! I've been taking dance class since I was 5 years old. Jazz, tap, ballet and modern. I find dancing very exiting and sensual. It most definitely keeps you in shape. You don't realize how many calories you are burning and the positive effects it has on the heart while you are just enjoying yourself.

2）What kind of dancing do Chinese people like?

Chinese people like to do ballroom dancing, but outside on the street. Young people like to go to discos and dance techno and hip hop.

3）Does China have any traditional dances?

China has a lot of traditional dances. There are as many traditional dances in China as there are ethnic minorities.

更多资源

Yang Ge（秧歌）is a style of celebration dance very popular in the countryside of Dongbei, China. Dancers typically use a red silk ribbon around the waist and swing the body to music. In different areas Yang Ge are done in different styles but all express happiness.

Er Ren Zhuan（二人转）is a local folk dance from Northeast China. It usually consists of two people, a boy and a girl. They sing as well as dance, using folded fans during the dancing portion.

4）Is traditional dance still popular today in China?

Yes, I think so. Many Chinese young people go to school in order to learn it; it's part of our culture.

No, I don't think so. Nowadays, more people prefer modern music and dancing styles.

5）What kinds of dancing are popular with young people in China?

Young people are interested in many forms of dancing here in China. We like to go to clubs and dance to hip-hop and techno music.

舞蹈话题必备词汇

1. performing arts 表演艺术
2. sense of rhythm 节奏感
3. folk dance 民间舞蹈
4. modern dance 现代舞
5. ballet *n.* 芭蕾
6. hip-hop 街舞
7. gymnastics *n.* 体操
8. ethnic minorities 少数民族
9. lion dance 舞狮子
10. bring luck and happiness 带来运气和幸福
11. coordination *n.* 协调
12. flexibility *n.* 灵活性
13. stamina *n.* 耐力
14. build confidence 树立信心
15. positive self-esteem 自尊
16. well-being 健康快乐
17. dance studio 跳舞房

Music 音乐

1）Do you like to listen to music?

Yes, I do. I'll often listen to music on my MP4 when I'm traveling from place to place, or when I'm at home, relaxing.

2）What kinds of music do you like?

I like to listen to love songs/ pop music/ rock music/ traditional Chinese music/ jazz/ hip hop / Latin music.

更多资源

I have an open mind when it comes to music. If it's great music, it's great music. I would have to say my favorite genre is Heavy Metal and my favorite bands are Metallica and Pantera!

I don't have a favorite type. I like a little of everything, but I do have a favorite band, Bon Jovi.

I love all kinds of music. I think it's important to be open enough to enjoy all types. I like R&B, hip hop, jazz, rock, oldies, classical and alternative.

I like rock because of the guitars. I like loud music. I like the energy it has and gives off. A lot of rock I listen to is about experiences and relationships gone bad. I like the heavy guitars behind the lyrics it really adds more meaning to the songs.

3）What kinds of music are popular in China?

Everybody has different tastes, but I think love songs and pop music are the most popular kinds of music in China. Older classics from America and Europe are pretty popular here too. Rap is also getting to be very popular as well.

4）Have you ever learned to play a musical instrument?

Yes, when I was in school, I learned to play the violin, but I don't play it anymore, and I think I've forgotten how.

5）Is music an important subject at school in China?

Unfortunately music is not such a popular subject at school in China. Math and Science are much more important in China although maybe not so popular.

6）What benefits do children gain by studying music or learning to play a musical instrument?

By learning how to play a music instrument, children can learn many things. They can learn self-discipline, determination, and how to appreciate music better.

更多资源

There are benefits indeed. Playing an instrument makes you smarter, it teaches you discipline, it helps to relieve stress, it can give you a sense of achievement and most of all, it's fun. And it's proven that people playing an instrument since children become smarter, more articulate and have a higher chance of having a successful life.

音乐话题必备词汇

1. classical music 古典音乐
2. pop music 流行音乐
3. folk music 民乐
4. rap 说唱音乐
5. soothing *adj.* 起镇定作用的
6. melody *n.* 旋律
7. spontaneous *adj.* 内在的，自发的
8. beat *n.* 拍子
9. rhyme *n.* 压韵
10. musical instruments 乐器
11. lyrics *n.* 歌词
12. music education 音乐教育

13. band *n.* 乐队
14. orchestra *n.* 管弦乐队
15. symphony *n.* 交响乐
16. temperament *n.* 气质
17. creative-thinking 创造性思维
18. enrich *v.* 丰富
19. enlighten *v.* 启蒙
20. music therapy 音乐疗法

补充资源

中国古典音乐是中国文化的瑰宝。下面所列的是中英文对照的乐曲名称，看翻译的怎样？

The ten greatest Chinese classical music

1. White Snow in Early Spring（Pipa）阳春白雪（琵琶）
2. Ambush on All Sides（Pipa）十面埋伏（琵琶）
3. Flute and Drum At Sunset（Pipa）夕阳箫鼓（琵琶）
4. High Mountain and Flowing Water（Gu zheng）高山流水（古筝）
5. The Autumn Moon over the Han Palace（Erhu）汉宫秋月（二胡）
6. Guang Ling Verse（Gu qin）广陵散（古琴）
7. Three Variations of the Plum Blossom（Dizi）梅花三弄（笛子）
8. Wild Geese Descending on the Sandbank（Song qin）平沙落雁（宋琴）
9. Dialogue between Fisher and Woodcutter（Qin, Xiao）渔樵问答（琴、箫）
10. Eighteen Tragic Parts of Barbarian Pipes（Gu qin）胡茄十八拍（古琴）

Drawing and Painting 绘画

1）Have you ever learned to draw?

To tell you the truth, I never really had the time to learn to draw. I also really don't have the talent to spend my time drawing.

2）Do you draw now?

Yes, I sometimes like to draw. Not only is it a good form of relaxation, but I enjoy creating beautiful things and using my imagination. Even if I can't draw very well, I still enjoy it.

3）What do you think are some of the benefits of drawing, for both children and adults?

Both children and adults need to use their creativity. Drawing teaches people to look at the world differently, more carefully and thoroughly, it helps people relax and have fun, and it gives you a chance to use your imagination.

更多资源

Kids get many benefits from drawing and painting. Artistic expression can offer urban children an appreciation of the beauty in the ordinary, like fruit, and expand their visual horizons beyond cityscapes to the wider world.

Drawing is fun and exciting. The benefits of drawing to every other facet of learning and communication are enormous. By learning to draw what we see, we also learn to make connections and we learn to be able to describe what we otherwise would not be able to express. We learn to solve problems and to think about areas of knowledge and ideas that would not otherwise have occurred to us.

绘画话题必备词汇

1. art skills 艺术技能
2. nurture *v.* 培养
3. Chinese painting 国画
4. wash painting 水墨画
5. ink stone 砚台
6. oil painting 油画
7. calligraphy *adj.* 书法
8. watercolors *n.* 水彩
9. portrait *n.* 肖像
10. landscape *n.* 风景画
11. still life 静物
12. graffiti *n.* 涂鸦
13. realistic *adj.* 现实主义的
14. concentration *n.* 专心
15. focus *n.* 专注
16. brush *n.* 画笔
17. technique *n.* 技巧
18. observation *n.* 观察
19. canvas *n.* 画布
20. Renaissance 文艺复兴

Photography 摄影

1）Do you like to take photographs?

Yes, I like to take photographs. It's great fun, and then afterwards you can always have the photos, and remember the good times you've had.

更多资源

I like photography. As they say, a picture is worth a thousand words. Through photography, you can find beauty in the most unlikely of places. Photographs are a means of showing and sharing experiences with those close by, or with the world. You put a little of your own self in every picture.

Yes I like photography. I just started and am doing good. It's so much fun!

2）When (= On what occasions) do you take photos?

Well, usually I take photos when I go out somewhere, to a park or to the beach or to a party. When it's somebody's birthday, Spring Festival, at graduations, or any other important occasion, I take photos.

3）What kind of photos do you like to take?

Mostly, I like to take pictures of nature or of beautiful scenery. Also I like to take silly pictures with my friends. We always laugh a lot and have a good time.

更多资源

Animals and nature. I hate taking pictures of people because they are always posing and looking unreal, but animals and nature, are so natural and beautiful.

I am in no way a professional photographer, but I like to carry my camera around just in case I see something of interest, something beautiful that I'd like to capture. I also like to take photos of the people around me. Years later, I look at these photos and they help me to remember some great times in my life.

4）Is photography a popular hobby in China?

I think so. When Chinese people go out together, they often take photos of each other, or of the places they visit.

5）Do Chinese people like to visit photographic exhibitions?

You know that I don't really visit photographic exhibitions because they are a little hard to find here in China. There are some, but the content is really not so interesting.

摄影话题必备词汇

1. photography *n.* 摄影
2. digital camera 数码相机
3. develop films 冲洗底片
4. know-how 诀窍
5. close-up shots 特写
6. optical *adj.* 光学的
7. pixel *n.* 像素
8. patience *n.* 耐心
9. imagination *n.* 想像力
10. artistic *n.* 有美感的

Collecting 收藏

1）Do you collect anything?

Sure. I have a collection of postcards from different countries.

更多资源

I have a collection of interesting bags. I have many different sizes, some are clear, some are green or pink or black, many colors and some have cool designs on them like dollar signs, aliens, sports teams and 4-leaf clovers. I think it's pretty unique.

I'm addicted to gum, so I've started collecting gum wrappers. I have about 600 Trident wrappers and 900 Orbit. I also collect anything having to do with penguins, because they are my favorite animal.

I have always been attracted to coffee mugs with great prints or logos on them. Not the ones available in regular shops; I mean the ones in the souvenir shops in museums, national parks, monuments and such kind of places. They have such neat looking ones and I always get a couple of them wherever I go.

2）Why do you collect ....（that/those things）?

I collect those things because they are interesting and rare. I like to go over my collection and see all the cool things I've got stored away.

3）Is collecting a popular pastime in China?

It used to be but not anymore. Actually it is a little hard to find things to collect, except for maybe pictures of Chairman Mao on flags or coffee mugs.

4）Do a lot of people in China collect things and what do they collect?

People in China really don't collect too many things. They are pretty busy with the daily run of things and don't have the time or the resources to collect things.

5）What are the benefits of collecting?（= Why do people like collecting?）

Well people like to collect things mostly as a hobby and hobbies are good to have, because they help people to relax and get their minds off their jobs or problems they may have.

更多资源

Stamp collecting is a hobby that has been enjoyed by many people. It is a popular pastime that provides many educational benefits. It's a great way to learn history and past events.

Well, there is a good potential to learn a lot about our and other countries; that is, history. This is one benefit that I hear a lot about all the time. And this may be one of the best benefits for young collectors (but you are never too old to learn!). Coins can be a good way for children to learn about the history of their own country and to have something that will fit into a pocket for "show-and-tell".

There are all of the other coin collectors that you can meet and get to know. And they all have their own stories to tell.

收藏话题必备词汇

1. collector *n.* 收藏者
2. antique *n.* 古董
3. take up 开始从事
4. coin collecting 收藏硬币
5. stamp collecting 集邮
6. historical value 历史价值
7. educational benefits 教育意义
8. organizational skills 组织能力
9. rock collecting 收藏矿石
10. outdoor exercise 户外锻炼
11. identify *v.* 识别
12. worthwhile *v.* 值得
13. museum *n.* 博物馆
14. exhibit *n.* 展品
15. item *n.* 物品
16. curator *n.* 馆长
17. asset *n.* 资产

9. Mass Media（TV, Radio, Newspapers）大众传媒

1）What kind of entertainment do you prefer, TV or radio?

I definitely prefer to watch TV because then you not only get to hear, but to see, and you remember the story better when there's a picture to go with it.

更多资源

Sometimes I'll listen to the radio if there is something good on it.

Neither, I go to the website. I don't have time for TV or radio and I can watch clips on CNN.com.

2）What programs do you like to watch/listen to?

I like to watch different soap operas, and if it's a series, I never miss one.

更多资源

I like to listen to educational programs; there are so many things you can learn about nature, language, different countries, and different cultures. They're so interesting.

I like documentaries. Anything factual where I can learn something new and interesting. You discover a lot of new things, and get a scientific explanation to everything.

I like to watch animal shows because I find animals and their behaviors are very intriguing. It's surprising at times how much some animals seem to mimic behavior you would only expect from a human being.

3）How do you think TV/radio broadcasts in China could be improved? ?

It would be nice to have more variety in both TV and radio here in China. It is getting a lot better now and looks to get even better.

4）Do you prefer TV news or news on the radio?

I prefer news on the radio because then I am not distracted by the announcer and his or her presence. I like news on the radio also because of the fact that you can get it more often, on TV it is limited to certain hours of the day.

更多资源

I don't like TV news because it isn't really news. It is entertainment, and it is biased but doesn't acknowledge the fact. On radio you can get more information, and the bias is usually acknowledged. The internet is the best. You can go to multiple sources to find out what you want, and get different points of view.

5）Do you read newspapers?

Yes, I like to read them very much. They are a source of information for me and I can keep up with my favorite sports team through them.

更多资源

I rarely read newspapers or magazines. I prefer getting my news online or via local news.

Yes, I still read the newspaper. I mainly rely on it for local events that are coming up, or that have just happened recently. There is also a lot of other useful information in the paper that may not be on the web.

6）Which section of the newspaper do you like to read? Why?

My favorite sections of the newspaper are the sports section and the entertainment section. I like to keep up with personalities and what they are doing.

更多资源

I read the local news. There is always something exciting going on. It's good to stay informed, especially about things happening in your neighborhood.

I just like political news/world news. After that I go check out the cartoons.

The local news, the comics, and the sports. In that order. I also enjoy doing the puzzles.

7）Do you think the Internet will replace newspapers one day?

Yes, I definitely think so. I think that as more people have access to the Internet and computers, paper will eventually become a thing of the past. It's quicker and easier to update webpages on the Internet than to print a whole newspaper.

大众传媒话题必备词汇

1. mass media 大众传媒
2. ratings *n.* 收视率
3. episode *n.* 集
4. audience *n.* 观众
5. host *n.* 主持人
6. announcer *n.* 播音员
7. live broadcast 现场直播
8. sitcom *n.* 情景喜剧
9. current affairs 时事
10. soap operas 肥皂剧
11. documentary 记录片
12. variety show 综艺节目
13. talk show 谈话类节目
14. quiz show 知识问答节目
15. TV adaptation 电视改编
16. commercials 商业广告

17. public service advertisement 公益广告
18. sports news 体育新闻
19. weather forecast 天气预报
20. satellite dish 卫星电视接受器
21. couch potato 电视迷
22. regular media 常规媒体
23. daily *n.* 日报
24. quarterly *n.* 季刊
25. quality newspaper 严肃报纸
26. tabloid *n.* 小报
27. broadsheet *n.* 大报
28. circulation *n.* 发行量
29. headline *n.* 标题
30. editorial *n.* 社论
31. book review 书评
32. column *n.* 栏目
33. classified ads 分类广告
34. periodical *n.* 期刊
35. in-depth coverage 深度报道
36. domestic news 国内新闻
37. international news 国际新闻
38. comic strip 连环漫画
39. feature article 专题文章
40. agony aunt 回复读者情感问题的专栏作者
41. scandal *n.* 丑闻
42. human interest story 富有人情味的故事
43. timeliness *n.* 及时性
44. highlight *n.* 重要部分
45. opinion poll 民意调查
46. objectivity *n.* 客观性
47. watchdog *n.* 监督者
48. bias *n.* 偏见
49. hearsay *n.* 谣言
50. publicity *n.* 宣传
51. reliable *adj.* 可靠的

10. Nature（Flowers, Birds, Weather, Seasons）自然界

Flowers 花儿

1）Do you like flowers?

Yes, I like flowers. They're so beautiful and varied, and some have a wonderful scent, too. The world would be a little more boring without their cute faces and lovely scents.

> 更多资源
>
> Yes. They are pretty and smell nice. They cheer me up and make the place look nice and cheerful.
>
> I don't really like flowers. They die if you don't take care of them and I'm forgetful. They are pretty though and smell nice.

2）What is your favorite flower?

My favorite flowers change with the kind of mood that I am in. If I am happy I like carnations; if I feel romantic I like roses.

> 更多资源
>
> I love lilacs. I'm addicted to their fragrance.
>
> I'm partial to daisies. They're so cheerful and happy and not too expensive. They last a long time—sometimes two weeks.

3）What are the occasions when people send or receive flowers?

Usually people send flowers when it's a special occasion, such as when a friend has a birthday, or graduates from school, or has a new baby, or opens a new business, or gets promoted or married.

4）What flowers have special meaning in China?

You know if you asked my mom, she could answer that question, she is a florist. I never really was that interested in which flower goes on which day. I think roses go to someone who is in love. Peony is kind of the national flower and it represents prosperity and fortune.

花儿话题必备词汇

1. chrysanthemum *n.* 菊花
2. peony *n.* 牡丹
3. national flower 国花
4. symbol of prosperity 富贵的象征
5. jasmine *n.* 茉莉
6. daisy *n.* 雏菊

7. carnation *n.* 康乃馨
8. China rose 月季
9. orchid *n.* 兰花
10. symbolic meanings 象征意义
11. represent *v.* 代表
12. integrity *n.* 正直
13. virtue *n.* 美德
14. bloom *v.* 开花
15. fragrance *n.* 香味

Birds 鸟儿

1) Are there many birds near your home?

Yes, there are, but you usually can only hear them sing in the early morning. There are also a lot of sparrows flying around and pigeons on the roof on my apartment building.

2) How do you feel about birds?

I think some birds can be beautiful, and I enjoy listening to their singing. They're so small and sweet. They really help me to leave this world a while as I look at them flying about so gracefully.

更多资源

Yeah, they can be good companions, but my main problem with them is that they tend to poo all over when you let them out to fly around. They can also be loud for no reason at all. They are good pets because they are easy to maintain.

No, actually I hate birds... small cute birds are okay, as long as they are outside, but I hate birds. I think I have a bird phobia. My heart starts pounding every time I walk by the parrots in the pet store (they are not caged or chained or anything. they just sit on their little tree freely). Birds freak me out.

3) How do Chinese people feel about birds?

Just go to a park and you will see that Chinese people really like birds. They love to keep them as pets and fill their houses with them.

4) Do any birds have any particular significance in China?

The phoenix, which although is mythological, is a bird that has particular significance in China. It is a sign of good fortune and blessing.

5) Do you think birds should be protected?

Well, I think birds, like any other animal, need to be protected if they become an endangered species. They really have a hard time protecting themselves and if they were gone, something special would be missing from life.

6) How can they be protected?

We can protect birds by raising awareness about their situation, and by not buying endangered species, or destroying their habitats. We also need to keep an eye on the environment, which is their habitat.

7）Do Chinese people like raising (keeping) pet birds?

Yes, many people like to keep birds as pets. They like listening to the birds sing, and some birds can even be taught how to talk. Birds are great pets. They are so cute and sweet.

8）Is bird-watching popular in China?

If people have the time and the money and can get to a location that has a lot of birds, then people will do it, but unfortunately that is not the case here in China.

鸟儿话题必备词汇

1. magpie *n.* 喜鹊
2. sparrow *n.* 麻雀
3. crow *n.* 乌鸦
4. mandarin duck 鸳鸯
5. parrot *n.* 鹦鹉
6. phoenix *n.* 凤凰
7. peacock *n.* 孔雀
8. crane *n.* 鹤
9. longevity *n.* 长寿
10. elegance *n.* 幽雅
11. eat insects 吃昆虫
12. control pests 控制害虫
13. poo *v.* 排便
14. bird watching 观鸟
15. cage *n.* 鸟笼
16. eco-system *n.* 生态系统
17. variety *n.* 多样性
18. feather *n.* 羽毛

Weather 天气

1）What is the climate like in your hometown?

I live in Chongqing and the weather there is very wet in winter and extremely hot in summer.

The climate in my hometown is generally hot and sunny/ hot and rainy, especially during the noon/ very dry and dusty/ cold and cloudy.

2）Does it rain much here in Beijing?

No, it doesn't and that is getting to be a problem here with the threat of drought conditions appearing on the horizon. We really need the rain and sometimes I spend days just hoping the sky will pour down what we so desperately need.

3）Do you like rainy days or sunny days?

I like sunny days better than rainy days. Rainy days make me feel sad, and make me feel like not going outside.

更多资源

Well I suppose that it depends. If I have to work or have a lot to do that day, then I'd prefer it be sunny outside. If I don't have anything to do and I'm off work, which is rare, then I don't mind the rain. When it rains and I don't have anything to do and I can just curl up on the couch, watch movies, read a book, or nap then. Rainy days don't bother me. So, I suppose it depends on my mood and how busy I am that particular day.

I like sunny days. Rainy days are boring and sometimes they can make you sad.

4）When（in what month/season）does it rain most in your hometown?

My hometown is Chongqing and it rains mostly in summer, buckets of rain at a time. It is really refreshing when it comes down, and the sound of the rain is magical.

5）Do you think rain is good?

Of course, rain is good. Crops couldn't grow without it, and then we would all starve to death.

6）Does rain ever affect transportation in your hometown?

If it rains very heavily, then there are often traffic jams, because nobody wants to walk or ride bicycles. They all take taxis or cars, and this causes traffic jams.

天气话题必备词汇

1. agreeable weather 宜人的天气
2. humid *adj.* 湿润的
3. stifling *adj.* 气闷的
4. breezy *adj.* 微风轻拂的
5. scorching *adj.* 炎热的
6. freezing *adj.* 冰冻的
7. chilly *adj.* 寒冷的
8. depressing *adj.* 让人感到压抑的
9. drizzle *v.* 细雨
10. shower *n.* 阵雨
11. typhoon *n.* 台风
12. sunny days 大晴天
13. dust storm 浮尘、扬沙
14. temperature *n.* 气温

Seasons 季节

1）Which season do you like best? Why?

My favorite season is spring, because flowers begin to bloom and the weather starts to warm up.

更多资源

My favorite season is summer, because I like hot weather and lots of sunshine.

My favorite season is fall, because I like cooler weather, and then the leaves on the trees start to change color. It's really beautiful.

My favorite season is winter, because I like cold weather, and I always hope it will snow.

I like spring because it is starting to get warm and isn't too cold or too hot. I don't like the others because winter is too cold, summer is too hot and autumn is starting to get cold.

2）What do people do in this season?

In spring, because people have holidays, they often like to visit their hometowns or other beautiful places.

更多资源

In summer, because the weather is so warm, some people like to go to the beach, or go outside. Other people would rather stay indoors with their air-con on.

In autumn, because the weather starts to get cooler, people usually like to travel.

In winter, if you live somewhere where the weather gets very cold, people like to ice skate, or ski. If you don't like cold weather, you stay inside and keep warm.

3）Do you think the seasons have changed in recent years, compared to the past?

Nowadays, there are many changes in the seasons. Sometimes the summers are unusually hot, or the winters unusually warm, or the rains come too early or too late.

季节话题必备词汇

1. crisp *adj.* 干冷
2. warm *adj.* 温暖的
3. sunny *adj.* 晴朗的
4. wrap up warm 穿的暖暖和和的
5. still and quiet 静止的

11. Social Issues（Transport, Noise）社会问题

Bicycle 自行车

1）Are bicycles popular in your city?

Bicycles are generally popular in China, probably because they are cheap transportation and you can get good exercise from riding them.

2）Do you often ride a bicycle?

Yes, I often ride a bicycle, if I'm not going too far, or if I just want the exercise.

> 更多资源
>
> No, I don't ride a bicycle. The traffic is too dangerous and I'm scared of getting hit by a car.
>
> Wow! I do not think I have been on a bicycle for 10 years, I wonder if I can still ride one.
>
> I used to ride my bicycle when I was 18 almost everyday, but now I keep it in my garage because I now only drive my car, even if not going very far.

3）What do you think are the advantages and disadvantages of bicycles compared to cars or public transport?

Well, for one thing, traveling in cars and public transport is much quicker, and can be more convenient. But when you ride bicycles, you don't get stuck in traffic and you can get some good exercise.

> 更多资源
>
> Benefits of Bike Commuting
>
> **Fitness**
>
> Biking lets you incorporate low stress aerobic exercise into your daily commute.
>
> **Time**
>
> Bicycles are the fastest transportation on wheels in urban settings. Compared to driving a car, urban bicycle trips of three miles or less can actually decrease your travel time.
>
> **Parking**
>
> Forget about parking headaches. Riding a bicycle lets you park much closer to your destination than a car. Bike racks are free. A year-long bike locker can be rented for less than a month's worth of parking an auto in a garage.
>
> **Inexpensive!**

4）Do you think bicycles are suitable for present society?

Not always, because it takes too long to travel from place to place and this makes bicycles not so practical. On the other hand, bikes are very suitable for present society seeing we have reached the halfway mark in oil consumption. Maybe one day soon we will all be riding bikes.

自行车话题必备词汇

1. electric bike 电动车
2. folding bike 折叠车
3. mountain bike 山地车
4. pedal *n.* 脚踏板
5. tyre *n.* 车胎
6. bicycle lane 自行车道
7. environmentally-friendly 环保的
8. green *adj.* 绿色无污染的
9. less polluting 带来较少污染的

Transport 交通

1）What means of transport do you usually use?

I don't have a car, so I usually use public transport, like buses, or taxis, or the metro. It's quite convenient for me.

2）What's your favorite means of transport?

My favorite way to travel is by plane, because it's quick and convenient, even if it is expensive. I love to fly above it all and forget about traffic jams.

3）How do you like to travel for long trips?

By plane, because then it doesn't take me so long to get to my destination. I don't want to waste my valuable time just getting there. I have more important things to do.

4）What's the traffic like here in Beijing?

It's not so bad; because of the subway, it usually doesn't take long to get from place to place.

更多资源

The drivers are rude; they look at you and will just run you over.

It's one of the worst cities to live in because of the traffic it has. People generally give themselves at least an hour extra time to arrive on time.

The commuter traffic in the morning starts at 7a.m. and does not end until 10a.m. and then the afternoon traffic starts about 5p.m. and does not end until 8p.m.. And forget about it on Friday afternoons, especially in summer.

Beijing really does look like a giant car park, doesn't it?

5）How do you think the public transport could be improved?

Well, here in Beijing I think they just need to add a few more subway lines and add some more ring roads and have more buses available, in order to improve public transport.

更多资源

I think higher fuel prices are going to help. Having an on-line carpool database to get people from their homes to public transport nodes, or having secure cycle lockers at railway stations and bus stops might help too.

I have recently returned from a holiday in Switzerland. It is nice to go there occasionally to remind myself of how things should be done. In over a week I didn't see one traffic jam. Cities were all refreshingly free of cars. Yet the Swiss have a better standard of living than we do. The secret? Well there isn't one really—it's just that the government accepts that a comprehensive network of public transport is vital to the efficient running of the state. Therefore, all trains are electric; all run at regular times generally at least hourly 7 days a week. Bus stations are always located next to railway stations. Buses always connect with trains and with each other. Timetables are always available. Trams and trolley buses dominate transport in the cities. Everything runs with absolute precision (the lack of traffic jams helps facilitate this). Connections are guaranteed.... I could go on really, but I might start crying. All it takes is the political will to do something and it could be done—but as it is I suspect that politicians don't care so it isn't going to change. Learn to enjoy sitting in traffic jams—appreciate the freedom that a car brings you—and to the people sitting in the bus behind you.

Increased frequency of buses and trains, make transport more accessible to people with disabilities and those on low incomes.

交通话题必备词汇

1. bus fare 车票
2. light railway 轻轨
3. public transport 公共交通
4. bus lane 公交用道
5. priority *n.* 优先
6. cycle lane 自行车道
7. coach *n.* 大巴
8. congestion 交通拥堵
9. traffic jam 堵车
10. car pool 汽车合用
11. commute *v.* 上下班
12. traffic lights 交通指示灯
13. vehicle *n.* 交通工具
14. motor cycle 摩托车
15. speeding *n.* 超速
16. speed limit 时速限制
17. motorway *n.* 高速公路
18. pavement *n.* 人行道
19. parking metre 停车收费器
20. taxi rank 出租车站
21. car park 停车场
22. packed *adj.* 熙熙攘攘的
23. rush hour 高峰时间

Noise 噪音

1）Do you mind noises?（Do any noises bother you?）

Yes, I can't stand certain noises, like construction work going on in my apartment.

> 更多资源
>
> Not really, somehow I don't seem to notice noise. I could sleep through an earthquake. When I fall asleep I am dead to the world.

2）What type of noise do you come across here in your daily life?

Where I live you can hear a lot of noise from the construction and the traffic. At night I can almost literally feel the hum of all of the TVs and people talking in the area. People say that I am very sensitive to noise.

3）How do you feel if you work in a noisy environment?

I feel irritable and I can't concentrate. I need to work in a quiet, orderly environment.

4）Are there any sounds that you like?

I like the sound of rain falling, and of music, and of birds singing. I also like the sound of my mother's voice calling me to dinner. This is one of my favorite sounds.

> 更多资源
>
> I love the sound of the waves. I also love to hear babies laughing, it's so cute.
>
> When you walk on the snow and it crunches under your feet.
>
> The sound of the ocean waves breaking on the shore. To me it's one of the world's most relaxing sounds—nature's lullaby.

5）Are there any sounds you don't like?

I hate the sound of snoring, or of babies crying, or of people talking very loudly. I also really dislike the sound of people complaining, this is one of my pet peeves.

> 更多资源
>
> scraping a fork against a glass/china plate
>
> the sound of people chewing their food up with their mouth wide open
>
> finger nails scratching a chalk board
>
> wet rubber shoes on a hardwood floor

6）Are cities becoming noisier?

I suppose they might be, since cities are getting larger. But I think that we are all becoming a little deaf from the noise in the city and we don't even know it.

7) What about noise pollution? How do Chinese people feel about this form of pollution? Is it a problem in your hometown?

Well, if you have 1.4 billion people crammed into only about a fourth of the country's space you're bound to have problems with noise. In big cities noise is just a fact of life that you have to live with. In my hometown, it didn't use to be a problem, but when more people started getting cars, and construction sites started popping up all over the place, the noise went from bad to worse. Maybe someday it'll get better, although I'll probably go deaf before that happens.

噪音话题必备词汇

1. decibel *n.* 分贝
2. construction sites 建筑工地
3. scratch *v.* 擦、刮
4. hearing *n.* 听力

12. Food and Restaurants 饮食

1）What kinds of food do you particularly like?

I really like spicy food. I am actually wild about Beijing duck, I could eat it every day.

2）Is there any food you don't likc?

I don't like sweet and sour food, because I don't like mixing the two.

3）What kinds of food are the most popular in China? Or, what kinds of food do Chinese people like to eat?

Of course rice is the most popular food in China, but that goes without saying. Noodles are very popular along with breads.

4）Do you like cooking?

I love to cook, but not for very many people, because then it's just too much work. I think it's very interesting to come up with my own recipes, and experiment with different dishes.

更多资源

Yes! I love cooking, it's so much fun. I'm not very good at it but I find it fascinating. It's like a hobby to me!

I have to say I dislike cooking. I find it a chore. My husband loves cooking though so he does most of it when he is not at work.

I like to cook because I like to eat. I hate the clean up afterwards though.

I love cooking and it's good to try out new recipes or just improve some of the ones that you already know and make.

5）Who usually does the cooking in your home?

I do most of the cooking, but there are others, like my mother, who take turns too. I learned most of my cooking from my mom. She is a great cook.

6）Do you prefer to eat at home or in restaurants?

I prefer to eat in a restaurant, because then there's no washing up. The atmosphere and setting are usually more relaxing and pleasant.

7）Do you often eat with your family?

I eat with my family almost every day. Eating together is a special time for us, especially in the evenings, because then we spend time together and can talk about our day.

更多资源

I eat dinner with my family almost every night. If I miss dinner one night, it's always for a good reason: studying late at the library, working out late at the gym, or having dinner with friends. But we have dinner together pretty much every night, and it has always been this way.

I live alone. So I always eat solo.

8) Do you think it's important for people to eat with their family?

I think it gives people time to spend with their family, when they can eat good food and enjoy each other's company. It is almost the only time when you have all of the family together, so it is a good thing to do.

9) Do you often go to restaurants to eat?

Not often, but every now and again. If I had more money, I would be eating out every night. It would save time on cooking and washing dishes and shopping.

10) What kind of restaurants do you like?

For me, the most important part about the restaurant is the food. I like variety, too, so you will find me in just about any restaurant.

更多资源

Food wise, I like all kinds of restaurants—Italian, Mexican, Chinese. I tend to prefer smaller, non-chain type restaurants over the nationwide, homogenized places that advertise all over the television. I think restaurants are more about entertainment than the food these days. They have to have a "gimmick" to get people in the door.

11) How do you think restaurants have changed over the past few years?

I think that there are more restaurants in the city. The food that they serve is more varied, and from more countries than before. The nice thing that hasn't changed is the price, it is still pretty cheap to go out and eat.

饮食话题必备词汇

1. cuisine *n.* 烹饪
2. recipe *n.* 食谱
3. flavour *n.* 味道
4. tasty *adj.* 好吃的
5. tender *adj.* 嫩的
6. season *v.* 调味
7. greasy *adj.* 油腻的
8. stodgy *adj.* 不易消化的
9. done to a turn 恰到好处
10. past its sell-by date 过了保质期
11. raw *adj.* 生的
12. ripe *adj.* 熟的
13. overcooked *adj.* 煮的过久的
14. grill *v.* 烤

15. roast *v.* 烘烤
16. steam *v.* 蒸
17. stew *v.* 炖
18. portion *n.* 份
19. slice *v.* 切片
20. spoonful *n.* 一匙
21. bitter *adj.* 苦的
22. crunchy *adj.* 嘎吱脆的
23. salty *adj.* 咸的
24. savory *adj.* 可口的
25. spicy *adj.* 辣的
26. barbecue *v.* 烧烤
27. buffet *n.* 自助餐
28. picnic *n.* 野餐
29. snack *n.*小吃
30. fattening *adj.* 吃了容易长胖的
31. ready meals 快餐
32. homemade food 自制食物
33. dumpling *n.* 饺子
34. combo *n.* 套餐
35. nutritious adj. 有营养的
36. GM food 转基因食物
37. chemical additive 化学添加剂

13. Relationships（Family, Friends）关系

Family Life 家庭

1）Could you tell me about your family?

My father is a manager at a bank and my mother is a nurse in a hospital. I am an only child, but I have many cousins that I've grown up with.

2）Do you still have your grandparents?

I only have one grandmother, for my father's parents died when he was young, and my mother's father passed away recently.

3）What influence do they have on their children or grandchildren?

They have a big influence on their children and grandchildren, especially grandchildren. They spend a lot of time with their grandchildren, because their parents are usually working during the day.

4）How are you getting on with your parents?

I get on with my parents wonderfully; they're easy to talk to, kind, and I trust them completely.

更多资源

If you asked me that when I was in junior high, it would be a totally different point of view. But now, I love them! There are times when I don't like my parents and times when they argue—it tears me apart—but they always work through their problems and they care for their children like all parents should.

My mom is like one of my best friends. She's really smart, and I talk to her about everything. She helps me out of situations and gives me her honest opinions on everything.

I don't. I am trying to become the person my mom wants me to be, she has a list of things that she thinks I need to become, and that I need to better myself and all. But no matter how hard I try she never seems satisfied.

I get along with my parents greatly... I haven't been the perfect daughter by any means.

5）Do you prefer to spend time with your family or with your friends?

In many ways, my family are my friends. But at the same time, I sometimes have more fun with my friends because they are closer to my age.

6）Is family very important to you?

My family is one of the most important things in the world to me. When everything goes wrong and nothing is going right, my family is always right there for me.

更多资源

Family is important to me because it's really all we have in the long run. Once you grow up and move out and away, you then realize how important your family is. You start to miss them and wish that you were around to go to b-day parties, births, and reunions. Friends can't complete you like family.

Yes absolutely. I have been going through some very painful times. I do not know what I would do without the love, support and strength I have received from them. I love them and will always be there if they need me. Family is not always perfect, but most of the time they are there for you.

7) If you were married, how many children would you choose to have?

If I were married, I guess I'd want about four or five children. I would love to have a big family, because then family members support and help each other, and my children won't be lonely growing up.

家庭话题必备词汇

1. relative *n.* 亲戚
2. cousin *n.* 表兄弟姐妹
3. family planning 计划生育
4. only-child 独生子女
5. generation gap 代沟
6. family tree 家谱
7. home life 家庭生活
8. family roots 家庭传统
9. nursing home 养老院
10. medical care 医疗
11. single-parent family 单亲家庭
12. paternal *adj.* 父亲的
13. maternal *adj.* 母亲的
14. in-laws 亲家
15. divorce rate 离婚率
16. childcare *n.* 育儿
17. adorable *adj.* 可爱的
18. understanding and caring 善解人意的

Friends 朋友

1) What kind of people do you like to have as friends?

People that enjoy being around me and appreciate doing things with me. People who I can trust and have fun with.

2) Do you like to spend time with friends?

Yes, I love to spend time with friends. It's one of my favorite things to do, because we have fun together and we can learn to understand each other's personalities.

更多资源

I like to be with my friends. But sometimes I need to spend time by myself. I think it really depends—if we need to do some thinking, we really SHOULD spend some time by ourselves, even if we enjoy the company of our friends a lot.

Honestly, I like spending time alone. I am the independent kind.

3）Do you have a best friend?

Not really, I have many good friends or close friends, but no best friends. My nature is to be a little off to myself, so I really don't have a best friend.

更多资源

I have two best friends, Teresa and Katie, and I have known them for as long as I can remember. I can't remember the first time we met, but we are great friends and enjoy sleepovers and talks, that sort of thing.

Yes, my mother is my best friend. We became close after she was diagnosed with breast cancer 7 years ago. I have other friends but I am not as close to them. I can tell my mum anything.

Yes, I do have a best friend that's just like a sister to me. I'd do anything for her. We live over an hour apart so it's tough seeing each other, but we do our best.

My best friend and I first met way back in preschool. I remember the first time we met was at my house. His mom, his older brother, and he came over and I gave him one of my toy dinosaurs. To this day he still has that dinosaur and we are still the best of friends. Just to let you know we are both 20 and that just shows how long we've been friends.

4）What do you and your friends do together?

Often we sit around and chat, or we play games, or watch movies together. Sometimes we just like to chill and do nothing. I think that is important for friends.

5）Is friendship important to you?

Friends are very important to me, because if something's going badly for me or if I have a problem then I have someone I can tell my feelings to. Also, then I'm not lonely or bored.

更多资源

I used to place a lot of importance on my friendships but have been hurt, let down and disappointed so many times by people who I thought were friends that now I do not think it is the be all and end all of life. I have a few friends who I have known all my life and have built up trust with them, they are important to me and I maintain those relationships but I don't really worry about making new friends.

I think it's important to have friends because they make life and just about everything else so much less lonely. Friends are important to have, because they will be there to offer you advice, information, personal experience, and yes, sometimes even a smart-aleck remark to help you see a different point of view.

6）What are the ways to meet potential friends?

I believe that if you are friendly to others, and talkative, and courteous, wherever you go you will find friends.

朋友话题必备词汇

1. acquaintance *n.* 相识
2. best friend 最好的朋友
3. soul mate 知己
4. affectionate *adj.* 温情的
5. fall out with 闹翻
6. cheer sb up 让某人开心
7. interpersonal *adj.* 人际的
8. relationship *n.* 关系
9. stick up for 为…辩护
10. make up 和解
11. personality *n.* 性格
12. count on 依赖
13. hang around 闲荡

14. Science and Technology（Mobile Phone, Email）科技

Mobile Phone 手机

1）Do you have a mobile phone?

Yes, I have a mobile phone. I carry it with me everywhere I go, well, not everywhere but close to everywhere.

2）What do you use it for?

Sometimes I use it for business reasons, but mostly for personal conversations or text messaging. With the phone that I have I can go online or even download books and then read them off my phone. It is so cool.

3）Who uses a mobile phone the most often in your family?

Why, it's me! I talk too much on the phone, and then my phone bill is huge. It's terrible!

4）Is a mobile phone important in your life?

I guess so, for it makes life a lot easier and more convenient, but it's not like I couldn't live without it if I had to. Once I went for a whole three days without using my phone, my boyfriend was so proud of me.

更多资源

My cell phone comes in awfully handy when my car breaks down in the middle of nowhere, or if I get lost, or if something happens in my family and I'm not near any other phone. I'm in my car a LOT, and the cell phone helps immensely in those situations.

Cell phones are good for emergencies, like your car breaking down. It is a great way to get hold of someone when they aren't at home. They are starting to replace home phones too.

I personally couldn't care less about owning a cell phone. In my opinion cell phones are dangerous to your health, but on the flip side having a cell phone is good if you're stranded in traffic and need to call your boss to tell him you're going to be late for work.

手机话题必备词汇

1. hi-tech *n.* 高科技
2. ring tone 铃声
3. bluetooth 蓝牙
4. text message 短信
5. picture message 彩信
6. impact *n.* 影响、冲击
7. breakthrough *n.* 突破
8. novelty *n.* 新鲜事物
9. innovation *n.* 创新
10. enjoyable *adj.* 愉悦的
11. user-friendly 便于使用的
12. portable *adj.* 便携的

13. face-to-face communication 面对面交流
14. human contact 人与人之间的接触
15. status symbol 社会地位的象征
16. controversial *adj.* 有争议的
17. double-edged sword 双刃剑

Email 电邮

1）Do you often write letters?

Yes, sometimes I think I enjoy writing letters more than I enjoy talking to people.

2）Who do you usually write to and what do you write about?

I write to my family, and to my friends; we tell each other about our lives and work, and also we talk about our opinions and feelings.

3）What do you think is the most difficult kind of letter to write?

I usually have a hard time writing business or formal letters, because then I just don't know what to say, it's hard to formulate proper sentences.

> 更多资源
>
> I find it very difficult to write a letter rejecting someone. It's hard to tell them you don't want to date (or marry or whatever) them and not hurt their feelings any more than you have to.
>
> You have to word things carefully and make sure they get the point but be subtle.

4）Do you prefer to write letters or emails?

I definitely prefer writing emails because I can type quite quickly; when I write letters my hand gets tired and besides, the letter takes much longer to reach the person.

> 更多资源
>
> I personally like emailing better, because it's easier, less effort, and faster getting there. That's what I prefer doing when it comes to me sending letters. But I would rather receive a letter than an email, because a letter takes more time and effort, and it's a little more personal.

5）What are the differences between handwritten letters and emails?

Most people feel that handwritten letters are more personal, and they feel as if the writer has taken more time and thought in writing it. Emails are sometimes rather informal.

电邮话题必备词汇

1. personal *adj.* 有人情味的
2. word *v.* 措辞
3. mailbox *n.* 邮箱
4. handwriting *n.* 字迹
5. internet connection 网络连接

第三章　雅思口语话题卡

雅思口语话题卡

人物类

核心级

1. Senior citizens 老人
2. Children 孩子
3. Celebrities 名人

进阶级

4. Adventurous people 有探险精神的人
5. Leaders 领袖人物
6. Neighbours 邻居

地点类

核心级

7. A building in your hometown 家乡建筑物
8. Your childhood room 童年房间

进阶级

9. A leisure centre 休闲健身中心
10. A hotel 旅馆
11. A library 图书馆

喜好类

核心级

12. A film 电影
13. An outdoor activity 户外活动
14. Favorite time of the year 喜欢的季节或月份

进阶级

15. A walk 经常走的一段路
16. Sports events 体育赛事
17. Foreign cultures 外国文化

物品类

核心级

18. Clothing and fashion 服饰和时尚
19. Wild animals 野生动物
20. Electrical aplliances 电器

进阶级

21. An important letter 重要的信件
22. Books 读物
23. Furniture 家具
24. Advertisements 广告
25. A childhood present 童年礼物
26. News reports 新闻报道

经历类

核心级

27. Public events 公众活动
28. Life-changing moments 改变人生的事件

进阶级

29. English class activities 英语课堂活动
30. Advice 建议
31. An unsatisfactory purchase 不愉快的购物经历
32. Exhibitions 展览
33. Being late 迟到的经历
34. A time when you help someone 帮助别人的经历
35. Busy days 忙碌的日子
36. Practical skills 实用技能

假想类

进阶级

37. To start a small business 创业
38. A large sum of money 大笔钱财
39. A goal you want to achieve
    想做成的一件事
40. A meal 一顿饭

人物类核心级(Topics 1~3)

Topic 1　Senior Citizens 老人

一、考试说明

老人是雅思中的经典话题。具体题目的措辞可能不尽相同，有时考生被要求描述一起生活的老人，有时被要求描述见过的年纪相对大的人，因此考生在拿到话题卡后要仔细审题。第三部分通常围绕老人和老龄化问题展开。在"真题演练"部分外教讲述的是自己的爷爷，很有代表性。在"话题相关材料"部分，考生可以看到 *China Daily* 上一篇有关老人问题的报道，读完后会对中国的老年人问题有更多的了解。

二、真题演练

CUE CARD

Describe the oldest person you know.

You should say:

who this person is

how you know this person

what kind of person he or she is

and explain what you think about this person.

点题	The oldest person that I know is my grandfather. He is actually very close to me. When I was young, my father was away a lot in the army and my grandfather took on the role of my father.
描述	He is a very kind gentleman. He is a simple man in that he likes to socialize and drink with his friends at home. He is a carpenter **by trade**, and one time I was able to work with him when my father asked him to put a floor in our house. Once when I was going on a train trip, he gave me a whole **carton** of a special kind of candy that I liked.
评价	I really love my grandfather and I believe that he loves me. He has taught me a lot about just being happy with the things that I have to do, and also to take time to enjoy life. I think that I get some of my athletic ability from him as he knows *kung fu*. I haven't seen my grandfather for a few years, but I know that he is doing well and I know that he will be happy to see me when I go to visit him. I believe that he grew up in a pretty rough time here in China. Things were a lot more difficult than they are now, but through it all he always **maintained a happy outlook on life**. I would like to grow up and be like him in some ways, I wouldn't say that he is perfect in any way, but then who is?

重点词句

by trade 就职业而言

carton 硬纸盒

maintain a happy outlook on life 保持开心的生活态度

Part 3

Senior citizens in China

1. What do people in China do in their retirement years?

   A lot of them, especially if they don't have money, don't do a whole lot and this is a problem here in China. Some of them take care of their grandchildren and this takes up their time. In the warmer weather you will see them outside, playing **mahjong** and **Chinese chess**.

   - mahjong 麻将
   - Chinese chess 象棋

2. How have the lives of senior citizens in China changed in recent years?

   Things are not as hard for the elderly people in China now. They have it easier because their children have pretty good jobs and so they're taken care of well. They can go to more places and can even drive around with their adult children, something they couldn't do in the past.

3. Would you like to live with the elderly?

   I would really love to live with the elderly. They have so much experience and so many stories to tell. You can really learn a lot from them. Of course you have to be careful around them too, so as not to upset them or cause problems for them.

4. What changes do you think will take place in the future regarding seniors' lives in China?

   If China continues to make the kind of progress that it is making, then the seniors' lives will change very much. When you are richer and have money you can do so many more things. You will see that old people will live longer and have better lives. Of course in the **rural regions** and **mountainous areas**, seniors' lives haven't changed that much and probably won't.

   - rural regions 农村地区
   - mountainous areas 山区

5. Who do you think should take responsibility for looking after the elderly? Should they live with their children or is it better for them to live in nursing homes?

   Of course, children should **assume responsibility** for their parents. But if the parents' health is pretty bad and their children don't have the time to look after them, then they would have to find someone to look after them. Here in China, the parents live for their children, so it is expected that the children will live for their parents.

   - assume responsibility 承担责任

6. How do you think modern technology has affected senior citizens in China today?

   Seniors are not so much affected by modern technology, **other than** maybe some forms of transportation. If you mean the Internet or computers, I think that most seniors are not that concerned about them. Older values and going at a slower pace are more important to them than **fancy gadgets**.

- other than 除了
- fancy gadgets 奇妙的小玩意儿

Old and Young

7. What are some of the differences in attitude towards life between young and old people in China?

Young people want to see and experience all that they can. Old people are more content to just enjoy the simpler things of life, like getting together with their folks or helping with the childcare. Young people want to travel abroad and make a lot of money and buy a lot of things, old people are just thinking about the day and what they will do that day, even if it is not so **glamorous**.

- glamorous 迷人的，有魅力的

8. What are some of the main problems facing the elderly in China today?

Well in the city the elderly are not facing the problems that the ones in the country are. Health care is a big issue with all of the sickness that is so **prevalent** in today's society. Retirement is difficult because the small **pensions** that the old people get here can hardly sustain them. People here in China have to retire early, so there is the feeling of worthlessness that they have to face. There are some big problems facing the elderly here in China.

- prevalent 普遍
- pension 退休金

9. Do the elderly in China have a lot of influence on their children's and grandchildren's lives?

Oh yes absolutely, the elderly have a lot of influence in their family's lives. You see, here in China, the family unit is very important and always has been. Our culture, as you know, goes back many years and parents and grandparents have played an important role in this unit. Respect for fathers and mothers, grandfathers and grandmothers, is **instilled** in each generation.

- instill 灌输

10. What role do the elderly play in the family?

Well, old people play the role of **babysitter** for their grandchildren. Another role that they play is moral supporter for the family. They have to cheer for the parents when they get a good job, cheer for the child when he does good in school, and cheer for the family when they make progress together. They also have to be the family **counselors**, to listen to and give advice to younger members of the family.

- babysitter 临时照顾小孩的人
- counselor 顾问

11. It seems that grandparents love their grandchildren more than their own sons and daughters. Why do you think that is?

I don't think grandparents love the grandchildren more. They just have more time to play with them, more patience in guiding them and they don't feel the responsibility for the total well-being of the child **24/7**. Plus seeing the children of their children brings back memories of their younger years. I think it's a great thing. Grandparents give children something special... special memories to cherish and grow up with. I think that grandparents love their grandchildren so much because of how much they also love their children.

24/7　24 hours a day, 7 days a week

三、话题相关材料

A　中国的老龄人口(aging population)越来越多，如何让老人安享晚年成了一个普遍关注的社会问题。《中国日报》上曾刊登过一个有过老年人的调查，结果的确不容乐观。

Senior citizens find it difficult to adapt

They are called senior citizens, but their authority in family and social affairs is becoming more and more "junior," a survey reveals.

Older people are finding themselves in a more passive position in today's rapidly developing society, the survey found.

"In history, China has been a country where authority grows along with your age when deciding family and social affairs," said Zhang Xuwu, standing member of the National Committee of the Chinese People's Political Consultative Conference (CPPCC).

However, about 60 per cent of interviewed people said that their children do not consult them over some decisions, Zhang said.

Zhang made the remarks at a press conference organized to release the survey on the lives of today's senior citizens, according to a report by the Horizon Research Group and the Joymain Group.

The survey involved a total of 2,225 people aged over 60 from Beijing, Shanghai, Guangzhou, Chengdu, Shenyang, Xi'an and Wuhan.

China's society started aging several years ago. By the end of last year there were 142 million people over 60 in the world's biggest developing country, Zhang said.

Nearly 80 per cent of the 2,225 interviewed said they are satisfied with their present lives.

The survey also revealed many problems, however.

One is that the rapid economic and social developments in China, which is opening wider to the outside world, are leaving older people further behind, said Yuan Yue, president of the Horizon Research Group.

Only about 40 per cent of these people say they have frequent talks with their children.

But elderly Chinese say they still show great understanding and support to their children. "Young people are quite busy and have serious pressures from their work and study," has become a popular comment from parents who want to explain why their children have less time to share.

People over 60 have largely failed to benefit from rapidly increasing incomes, so their ability to financially support themselves now is very limited, the survey shows.

For instance, about 60 per cent of senior citizens have to depend on other family members to survive.

The survey shows senior citizens care about social issues, including unemployment, the environment and economic development. However, they have few opportunities to participate in social activities, Yuan said. Their lives are quite dull, and they spend too much time indoors.

The survey found that the most important leisure activity for 85 per cent of senior citizens is watching TV. More than 60 per cent say their main work is housework.

At the same time, seniors know very little about computers, mobile phones and digital cameras.

About 40 per cent of those interviewed have a mobile phone, but many of them do not know how to use it properly.（注：选自 China Daily 17/10/2005 page3）

四、练习

A 请将下列句子翻译成英文。

1. 他教给我去开心地面对生活中的琐事，去享受生活。

____

2. 那时候比现在困难多了，但他一直保持着开心的生活态度。

____

3. 我想长大后在某些方面像他那样，当然我不是说他很完美，可话又说回来，谁又是完美的呢？

____

4. 老人在家人的生活中发挥着很大的影响。

____

5. 他们扮演的另一个角色是家里的啦啦队队长。

____

（☞ P267）

B 听 MP3 实战演练。

Topic 2　Children 孩子

一、考试说明

儿童话题选材虽然范围广泛，比如说可以谈自己的 cousin，niece 或者 nephew，但描述孩子所使用的语言资源对很多考生而言还是比较欠缺的。在“真题演练”部分考生描述了一个中国小孩，答案本身比较简单。“话题相关材料”部分为考生提供了更多的材料，其中有国外父母描述自己孩子的段落，也有对家喻户晓的荧屏儿童形象的描述，比如说樱桃小丸子、蜡笔小新和 *The Simpsons* 中的兄弟姐妹。

二、真题演练

CUE CARD
Describe a child you know.
You should say
how you know him or her
what he or she likes to do
what kind of person he/she is
and explain how you feel about this child.

点题	I would like to tell you about my niece, MaoMao, who is seven years old. I stay with her and her family every national holiday and she is always so delighted to see me.
交往过程	I helped to take care of her after she was born, so I feel very close to her and we have a good relationship. We like to ride bikes together through our small city and often fly kites. Before going to sleep at night she always asks me to tell her a story and sing her some songs.
感受	I love this child very much because she is always so happy and I can't help but feel happy too when I'm with her. Although she goes to school now and has to study very hard, she still doesn't worry about life and is very optimistic. Some people think that children are happy only because they are **naïve**. Spending time with MaoMao has helped me to see that I can have **a positive attitude** towards my life and be happy even though I am no longer a child and have many responsibilities. MaoMao trusts her parents to take care of her, so she doesn't have to worry. I should trust that things will work out right also. That way I can be like her, cheerful and happy all the time.

重点词句

naïve 天真的　　a positive attitude 积极的心态

Part 3
Children, education and play

1. How do you think children benefit from playing with toys?

   I think it's very important that children have toys to play with to help stimulate a good imagination. Of course, it's very important to give them the right toys. Toy weapons can have an **adverse affect** on children and might encourage them to be more violent when they grow older. Different toys can help their **coordination abilities, artistic skills**, and even inspire them musically. I believe that toys can be very beneficial for children, if presented in the correct way and supervised well.

   adverse affect 负面影响　　artistic skills 艺术能力

   coordination abilities 协调能力

2. What do you think about children playing electronic games?

   Electronic games have become a must-have for many of today's children. The games can be very exciting and are highly entertaining. Unfortunately, if children spend most of their time sitting in front of a computer or TV playing games, then they rarely develop good communication skills or learn how to interact with others in real life. I enjoyed playing computer games when I was young, but if there's not a good balance then it's not good. If I had a child I would allow him a specific amount of time to play computer games, and encourage him/her to spend more time outdoors playing sports with other people his age. That way he will have good health and also learn how to communicate and interact with his **peers**.

   peer 同龄人

3. What do you think are the differences between home schooling and studying in school?

   I think there is a very big difference. Home schooling is more **personalized and focused** on the individual student's needs, whereas personal attention is not available in public schools due to there being many other students. Studying at home gives the student freedom to go faster in those subjects that he enjoys and to learn more about topics that interest him. Also, studying at home provides the opportunity to get more practical knowledge and experience that you cannot get from school.

   personalized and focused 个性化和有针对性

4. Why do you think learning theoretical material is emphasized more than learning practical skills?

   Learning theoretical material can help you to develop practical skills. I personally feel that there needs to be a balance between theoretical material, or in other words, knowledge from textbooks, and having **hands-on experience** and developing more practical skills. Both are needed and both are important. Right now, the education system **is geared to** passing exams, so theoretical material is emphasized and taught in classes to help the students get high marks on their exams. Unfortunately, most of this information is not very useful in finding a good job.

hands-on experience 动手能力　　　　be geared to/toward 适合

5. Do you think the education system in China should be reformed?

Yes, I do think that changes need to happen. The focus of today's education system is on passing exams, but when students graduate from high school or university, they find that the knowledge they gained in school cannot help them get a good job. I suggest that the courses and subjects studied in school be practical as well as **informative**. Personally speaking, experience is the best teacher, and I think that if the students can get hands-on experience in addition to studying from textbooks, it will give them a more **well-rounded** education.

informative 信息量大的　　　　well-rounded 全面的

Children and families

6. Who usually disciplines children in Chinese families, the mother or the father?

It all depends on the family. Often it's the father figure who gives the most **discipline** to the child. However, fathers now are busier with their careers and are often not at home, so the mother is left with the job of disciplining their child. Every child needs good, healthy discipline in order to have a good character. Fathers have this job by nature, though I think it's important that the mother and father work together to have a united discipline standard for their child so that he/she can feel loved and protected.

discipline 管教

7. Do you think it's a good idea for children to aim to be a professional athlete?

No. I think it's a waste of a person's energy and talents. But so long as **athletics** is promoted by the media, children will want to be sports stars. It's not a bad job, compared to many, but most who try it will not succeed. It takes a special kind of person to succeed in athletics.

athletics 体育

三、话题相关材料

A 补充语汇

儿童性格	儿童喜好
sweet 甜美的	slide 滑梯
loving 充满爱的	swing set 秋千架
cuddly 令人想拥抱的	teddy bear 泰迪熊
copycat（调皮的）模仿别人	doll 洋娃娃
curious 好奇的	blocks 积木

innocent 天真的

playful 爱玩的

adorable 可爱的

spoiled 宠坏的

hopscotch 跳房子

roller skating 滑旱冰

video games 电子游戏

lollipops 棒棒糖

B 下面列举的几段都是国外父母对自己孩子的描述，有深情的，有幽默的。虽然大部分青少年考生不会(也不可能)选择自己的孩子作为描述对象，但即使是描述 cousin 或者 niece & nephew 时，也可以利用下面段落里的语言资源。

- My son is six and he is amazing. He makes me smile every day. He is always getting awards in school and tries so hard in his Tae Kwon Do classes. Last night he broke a board for the first time and it was awesome! He is ready to fight the world if someone （even jokingly）calls me out of my name. He tells me he loves me all the time and tells me I am beautiful. He is so precious!

- I have loved my daughter from the time she was born. It is the little things that attach them so close to our hearts, like when out of the blue they turn to you and say, “I love you, daddy.” Or when they are playing in the yard and pick some wild flowers or something and run up and say, “These are for you, mommy.” Or just when they simply do something new for the first time or smile at you in a special way.

- I have a seven-month-old girl and she is my world. She doesn't do a lot at this age. But when she smiles and sticks her tongue out, it makes me feel such immense love for her. I love her reaching for my face and when she's sleeping; I pick her up and she lays her head on my shoulders. When my daughter started kindergarten, she asked me to walk her in and not her mother. I teased my wife and said, “Oh, you'd just cry, anyway.” Well, I took her by the hand and lead her into the gym where she was to get in line with her class. She walked away from me without looking back. She looked so tiny. When she got in line, she was facing my general direction, but not looking at me. The expression on her face was what I imagine the rangers who landed on Normandy showed: fear, but determination.

C 日本和美国动漫中有很多我们都熟知的儿童形象，看下面的描述，能猜出他们是谁来吗？

Chibi Maruko-chan

Maruko is a nine-year-old third grade student. She is lazy, disorganized and usually late for school, in strong contrast with her neat and tidy older sister who must share her room with her. Maruko, like many kids, tries to avoid homework and chores, takes advantage of her doting grandfather and squabbles with her sister. Nevertheless, she is a well-meaning child who tries to do good.

Crayon Shin-chan

Kindergarten-aged boy whose antics are the basis for the anime series. It is always stated that he is five years old, and loves chocolate biscuits（called 'Chocobee'）and an animated superhero named

'Action Kamen'. He is strangely attracted to older girls and women, despite his young age. He shares this trait with his father and paternal grandfather, but this will often result in his mother's brutal punishment. Some of his strange activities include dressing up as animals or plants (with appropriate costumes) and taking his pants off anywhere he feels the urge to.

The Simpsons

Bart Simpson is a ten-year-old troublemaker who thinks of himself as a rebel. Lisa Simpson is an extremely intelligent eight-year-old middle child who is often involved in left-wing activism and loves playing the saxophone. Maggie Simpson is a baby who, for the most part, simply sucks on a pacifier and doesn't speak.

四、练习

A 请将下列句子翻译成英文。

1. 我很喜欢这孩子，因为她总是那么开心，弄得我也禁不住跟着开心起来。

____

2. 跟毛毛在一起让我看到尽管我已不再是个孩子，要承担很多责任，但我也可以有一个良好的心态，仍然可以过得很开心。

____

3. 那样的话小孩子又有好身体，又能学着跟同龄人去交流和交往。

____

4. 在家里接受教育更加个性化，更能针对学生个体的需求。但在学校里接受教育的话，那种对个体的关怀就没有了，因为有太多其它学生。

____

5. 父亲忙于事业，很少在家，因此管教子女的任务就落到了母亲身上。

____

(☞ P267)

B 听 MP3 实战演练。

Topic 3 Celebrities 名人

一、考试说明

社会名流一直是雅思话题库中的重要话题，考生向考官描述完自己喜欢的明星后，在第三部分双方会围绕明星效应以及明星的苦与乐等话题展开讨论。“真题演练”部分描述的是中西方都很熟悉的篮球明星姚明。“话题相关材料”部分为考生提供了国外明星网站上对姚明的介绍，相信可以从中发现更多更为专业和漂亮的明星相关语言。

二、真题演练

CUE CARD
Describe a famous person (sports star, film star, etc.) whom you admire.
You should say:
who the person is
what the person does
why the person is famous
and explain why you admire this person.

点题	I admire Yao Ming. I know it sounds common, but I think he's a very interesting person, and I like him.
概括描述	Yao Ming is a professional basketball player. He's well over two meters tall, but unlike most tall players, he has a lot of skills, not just a height advantage. He's currently playing for the Houston Rockets.
成名原因	Yao is famous for two reasons. The first is that he is only the third Chinese player to play in the NBA, and the second is that he's the tallest NBA player — and very good, too. It's not just because he's Chinese that he's famous in China; he's also famous in the United States, for his skill, his **good sportsmanship** and his **warm personality**. For him, basketball is a passion and a career, but despite all his fame, he doesn't have **a big head**, and stays cool, both on court and in front of the camera.
感受	I guess that's why I admire him, because he's famous, but not **arrogant** or proud. He plays well without **playing mean**, and he is still just a simple man, even though his face is on **posters** and in advertisements everywhere. There are many stars who become famous and

	then fall in love with themselves. Fame is passing, so I really like Yao Ming's attitude. To him, it doesn't seem to matter whether he's famous or not, as long as he can keep doing what he loves: basketball.

重点词句

good sportsmanship 良好的运动精神
arrogant 傲慢的
warm personality 平易近人的性格
play mean 球风不好
a big head 头脑发热
poster 海报

Part 3

Celebrities in your country

1. What kind of people become famous these days?

   It's mostly musicians, singers, actors (and actresses) and athletes who become famous. That's because their careers are all about being seen by many people. They wouldn't have a job if no one watched, so if they do what they do well, they will be famous automatically. Politicians are also famous, but only the ones in top positions, or the ones who interact a lot with the press.

2. Is this different from the kind of achievement that made people famous in the past? In what way?

   When compared to the recent past, not really. Sports and the performing arts have always been the more public professions. But I think in times past, there were more political and military leaders who were famous in China. I think what has mostly changed is that more people **have access to** mass media, so fame has become a more cultural interest.

   have access to 可以获得，有获得…的途径

3. How do you think people will become famous in the future?

   Probably in the same ways they do today. As long as there is mass media, athletes and performers will become famous. Politicians will also always be famous, because power is something people pay attention to. But maybe the most important people will still be the least known.

Being in the public eye

4. What are the good things about being famous? Are there any disadvantages?

   Being famous can be useful. You can use it to do good, or for personal gain. But I think the disadvantages outweigh the advantages. You can never go anywhere in public without having crowds of people follow you, and you will always have cameras in your face. Whatever personal things happen in your life will often become common knowledge to everyone. And being famous isolates you from the real world, so that you can't see what's really going on in people's lives.

5. How do the media in your country treat celebrities?

I think it's similar to most places. If someone becomes famous enough, they become a national hero, at least until they do something that offends people. If they do something that is not **patriotic**, they will quickly lose their popularity. I think it's the same as most places.

patriotic 爱国的

6. Why do you think ordinary people are interested in the lives of celebrities?

I think it's because they are bored and feel unhappy and unsatisfied with their own lives. They try to comfort themselves by paying attention to things that happen to celebrities, especially the bad things. Then they can think about something other than their own problems and things they don't like.

7. Do you think celebrities should appear in advertisements?

I don't think so, but I don't think there's anything that can be done to change it. Companies want their product to become famous, so they pay famous people to support it or become associated with it. It's simple psychology. I don't think it's honest, but I also don't think it will change.

8. Some professional athletes are very well-paid. Do you think they deserve to be so well-paid?

No. Sports are just games, nothing special. I think it's really quite **pathetic** actually, but at least they are not doing something harmful and being paid for it, like being a gangster or a smuggler. I don't think they deserve it, but most people who are paid well don't deserve it either. That's life.

pathetic 悲哀的

三、话题相关材料

A 下面是美国一家名人录网站(www.askmen.com)对姚明的介绍和评价，请你看看他们的评价跟我们中国媒体的评价一样吗？

Why we like him?

The latest and greatest addition to the Houston Rockets has thrilled NBA fans with an offensive and defensive onslaught. Whether dunking on someone's head, draining a three-pointer off the glass, pulling down rebounds, or rejecting shots into another time zone, Yao Ming has skyrocketed during his rookie season in the NBA.

Why is he famous?

He was the No. 1 draft pick during the 2002-03 NBA season and has emerged as one of the Houston Rocket's most valuable players. His instant popularity in the NBA earned him enough fan votes to claim the starting center position on the Western team during this year's All-Star game. Due to his dominance as a defender down low and his 7′ 5″ frame, every NBA player and their grandmother want to dunk on him. What can we say? He's a popular guy.

Personality & talent

Since stepping into the NBA as the No. 1 pick in last year's draft, Yao Ming has put to rest much of the speculation concerning his skills as a pro basketball player. Before the big man joined the Rockets and helped transform them into a team worthy of playoff contention, fans and critics of the young superstar questioned his ability to compete in a league with dominant giants including Shaquille O'Neal and David Robinson.

After being put to the test, Yao managed to pass with flying colors by averaging 13.5 points, 8.2 rebounds, 2.8 assists, and 1.8 blocked shots per game. In addition to his trademark shot-blocking and in-the-key scoring abilities, Yao is equally as impressive as a sharpshooter from behind the three-point line. You won't see the big guy shy away from dropping three-point bombs from the outside. Whether serving up facials on his competition while inside the key or nailing treys from afar, the 7′5″ giant is an offensive threat from all areas of the court. And his abilities as a dominant defender are equally as impressive.

Whether on or off the court, Yao has proven to be a team player in every aspect of his game. While developing his skills as the star center for the Shanghai Sharks during his earlier years in the Chinese Basketball Association (CBA), Yao learned the true value of teamwork. The Chinese players were trained to focus on playing as a unit, instead of concentrating their efforts on their solo game. As a matter of fact, personal player statistics weren't even tracked in the CBA during its first few seasons.

Accomplishments & fame

During his earlier career in the Chinese Basketball Association, Yao dazzled fans at the center position while playing for the Shanghai Sharks. It was during this period that his skills as a dominant force were recognized and Yao was invited to play for the Chinese national team. The invitation to represent his country in the 2000 Summer Olympics in Australia allowed Yao to display his remarkable talent to basketball enthusiasts around the world. This exposure to the U.S. market introduced the 7′5″ Chinese sensation to NBA fans and talent scouts. At this point in time, Yao Ming-mania was beginning to unfold. Upon entering the NBA in 2002 as the No. 1 draft pick, Yao became only the third Chinese player in NBA history to play in the league, following in the footsteps of fellow countrymen Wang Zhizhi and Mengke Bateer.

His growing popularity has left many companies salivating at the chance to use him for endorsements and advertising. Various businesses ranging from software firms to athletic apparel companies are in competition to snatch up the young basketball star in an effort to gain recognition in markets outside of North America. Looking to capitalize on Yao's immense popularity in China, American businesses see him as a way to promote their products and services in the growing Chinese market, home to 1.3 billion people.

Yao has already been featured in television commercials for companies including Apple and Visa, and has endorsement deals with the likes of Gatorade, Nike, and U.S. computer game company Sorrent. He has also signed a high-profile endorsement deal in Asia for telecom company China

Unicom Ltd. In addition to all this hoopla, Yao has appeared on the covers of major sports magazines including Sports Illustrated, ESPN and Slam.

Coolness factor

If you've seen Yao in the latest TV commercials for Apple and/or Visa, you'd notice that he seems just as comfortable on screen as he is on the court. Although Yao's lines in these ads are very minimal, due to the fact that he's still trying to get a tight grasp of the English language, his onscreen charm is enough to make these commercials memorable. His potential as a product endorser and commercial phenomenon has led many marketing experts to believe that a combination of Yao's charisma and athletic ability could help market him as the next Michael Jordan or Tiger Woods of the advertising world. Of course, much of this speculation hinders on the assumption that Yao continues to evolve as a superstar in the NBA.

His appeal to the massive audience in China and his growing popularity in the U.S. and Canada have led advertisers to believe that Yao Ming may be the next biggest phenomenon in the sports world. But before we jump to any conclusions, let's wait and see how Ming fares in his second season in the NBA.

（注：以上材料选自 www.askmen.com 网站）

四、练习

A 请将下列句子翻译成英文。

1. 他有两米多高，但不像其他高个球员那样，他不光有身高优势，技术也很好。

____

2. 尽管已是名声大震，他并没有头脑发热，而是依然保持冷静。

____

3. 我觉得坏处多过好处。

____

4. 不管什么样的私事发生，往往会成为所有人的谈资。

____

5. 成名会把你跟现实世界隔离开，那样你就无法知道老百姓的生活到底是怎么样的。

____

（☞ P267）

B 听 MP3 实战演练。

人物类进阶级（Topics 4~6）

Topic 4　Adventurous People 有探险精神的人

一、考试说明

谈到“探险精神”，很多考生可能会想到那些敢于去攀登珠穆朗玛峰或者去挑战极限的人，但实际上“adventurous”不仅包括“not afraid of taking risks”，还包括“not afraid of trying new things”，这样的话选材的范围就会更加宽广。在“真题演练”部分外教以中国学生的口吻描述了一个非常有代表性和可模仿性的人物。第三部分通常围绕探险活动和如何培养孩子独立性展开。“话题相关材料”部分为考生提供了“极限运动”的定义，以及美国 Rice University 一位盲人大学生的探险经历。

二、真题演练

CUE CARD
Describe an adventurous person you know.
You should say:
　who the person is
　how you know this person
　what this person does that is adventurous
explain how you feel about the risks this person takes.

点题	I'd like to describe my cousin Liu Ying to you, who, in my opinion, is very adventurous.
表现	During the time she was studying at university, she was always **active in sports** and often **organized excursions** with fellow students to **go mountain biking, rock climbing**, swimming in rivers and so on. She even **backpacked in Tibet** for two weeks with only 400 RMB in her pocket.
具体事例	After she graduated with a degree in medicine, she decided that instead of joining a large hospital, which would have guaranteed her a high salary, she joined **a volunteer group** to Yunnan to help treat sick villagers. She often has to travel to remote mountain villages and is always in danger of having an accident, being caught in terrible weather, or catching the illness herself.
感受	I feel very proud of my cousin for taking these risks because it shows that she is selfless and cares more about those around her. Many people are concerned about those who need help

	but seldom sacrifice their own time, energy, and money to **reach out to** them. My cousin has sacrificed her own career to help others, and I believe her memory will live on in the hearts of those she helps. Daring to be different definitely makes my cousin adventurous.

重点词句

active in sports 积极参加体育活动
organize excursions 组织短途旅行
go mountain biking 骑山地车
rock climbing 攀岩
backpack in Tibet 在西藏背包旅游
a volunteer group 志愿者团体
reach out to 接近，亲近

Part 3
Challenging Activities

1. Are adventurous activities popular in China?

   Yes, as more and more people in China are looking for new and different ways to spend their free time. The Chinese youth wish to challenge themselves, which often leads them to extreme sports like **snowboarding**, **rollerblading**, rock climbing and **trick BMX**. The problem they face is that adventurous activities and extreme sports are not always available, or if they are, they're too expensive for the average Chinese to participate. If more facilities and opportunities were available then I believe these activities would **grow in popularity**.

   snowboarding 单板滑雪
   rollerblading 滚轴溜冰
   trick BMX 自行车特技
   grow in popularity 越来越受欢迎

2. Why do you think people like adventurous activities?

   I think it's for the **rush** and excitement that comes from challenging yourself and **pushing yourself to the limits**. Our lives are set in a routine of work or study. Going on an adventure or doing an activity requires risks, tests our strength and capabilities, and gives us a **thrill** and **feeling of triumph** as we conquer nature, **conquer our fears** and realize our own strength.

   rush 一阵激动
   push yourself to the limits 把自己推向极限
   thrill 心跳的感觉
   feeling of triumph 征服感
   conquer our fears 征服自己的恐惧

3. What do you think are the advantages and possible disadvantages of experiential training?

   The advantages and disadvantages all depend on the individual. Two people may do the same thing but come away from it with different views on the experience. Some of the advantages are greater self-confidence, more awareness of your capabilities and limits, and greater **physical dexterity**. On the other hand, if you don't **take proper precautions** you can have serious accidents or cause someone to get hurt. Some people can be overly confident and take too great of a risk which can end tragically.

experiential training 拓展训练
physical dexterity 身体灵巧性
take proper precautions 采取适当的保护措施

Children's development: Challenges

4. How do you think parents could bring up their children to be more independent?

Parents should give children more opportunities to make mistakes. If children are too **sheltered**, protected, or **pampered**, then they will not have the chance to be independent. Parents need to encourage their children to be responsible. If a parent does not give children the opportunity to do things themselves, even if they can't do them very well, then they will never learn. Everyone has to start somewhere and we're not born knowing how to take care of ourselves. This information should be taught to children in an environment where it's okay to make mistakes, and which encourages children to learn from them and to try new things.

shelter 庇护
pamper 纵容

5. Do children have more freedom today to do what they want than before?

That's hard to say. In general I would say yes they do. However in certain areas, such as education and deciding their career, I think it's the same. Children today have more things than before and definitely more opportunities to experience things that were not available in the past. So in a way, yes, they do have more freedom. But I think that proper education on how to wisely use that freedom is sadly missing. Children have more freedom but are not responsible so they often misuse it.

6. Do children today face more challenges than before?

In a way yes, they do. Today's society is more demanding and the pressure is greater than ever. Every parent wants their child to be the best and often they push their child too hard. Children today do not have time to be a child, but instead have the challenge, difficulty and pressure of getting high grades, having to go to many classes, and getting into good schools. The challenges children face and experience today are very different from the past, but it's hard for me personally to say if they are greater than before.

三、话题相关材料

A “真题演练”部分提到了很多种极限运动，**An extreme sport**（also called **action sport**, **adventure sport**, and **adventurous sport**）is any sport featuring speed, height, danger, a high level of physical exertion, highly specialized gear, or spectacular stunts. 下面这些极限运动你感兴趣吗？

skydiving 跳伞运动
parkour 街头攀爬跳跃
scuba diving 潜水
whitewater rafting 漂流
paintball 彩弹射击运动
zorbing 山坡悠波球

B　Alysha Jeans 是美国 **Rice University** 大学的新生。她患有先天眼疾，视力丧失。但她从不向命运屈服。正如她自己的座右铭中所言“**I refuse to be held back**”，她到底做出了什么连常人都很难做到的事情，大家可以读一读这篇从该大学网站上节选的文章。

No Boundaries

Rice freshman lets nothing corral her adventurous spirit

BY ARIE WILSON

Rice News staff

Baker College freshman Alysha Jeans may have been born blind, but she certainly sees more potential in the world than most people.

Maybe that's because the 18-year-old has a simple motto: "I refuse to be held back." That motto has helped take her around the world and will soon make her a minor celebrity.

Jeans traveled to Peru this past summer with Global Explorers, a nonprofit organization that specializes in international immersion experiences for students. The trip paired students with visual disabilities with able-bodied counterparts and was led by athlete Erik Weihenmayer, the first blind person to scale Mt. Everest. It was an experience the most visually gifted individual would have trouble describing.

On the final day of the trip, Jeans finally made it safely across rocky terrain and ancient trails to some of the most famous ruins in the world. As she reached the top of Machu Picchu, Jeans was overwhelmed by her surroundings. Using her other sensations — hearing, touching and smelling — and relying on the visual descriptions of her sighted climbing partner, Jeans was able to formulate a mental picture of the ancient Incan city, nestled in the mountainside. She said it was certainly a trip worth taking.

"Machu Picchu was wonderful," Jeans said. "It was truly an amazing thing to be a part of."

But Peru wasn't the first adventure for Jeans, a graduate of Wichita West High School in Wichita, Kan. She has been scuba diving, rock climbing and parasailing. For her 18th birthday this past July she went skydiving for the first time.

Jeans was born with Leber's congenital amaurosis, an inherited degenerative retinal disorder characterized by a severe loss of vision at birth. Some may think that the daring activities she has undertaken might be difficult for someone with vision loss, but Jeans doesn't believe so — and neither do those who have met her.

"The most difficult thing is overcoming stereotypes, and there are a lot of stereotypes out there," Jeans said. "A lot of people have never met someone who is blind and don't understand that being blind is just a part of life."

Jeans said she learned early on that she can do anything a person with sight can, just in a slightly different way.

四、练习

A 请将下列句子翻译成英文。

1. 她上大学的时候就积极参加体育活动，经常跟同学组织郊游。

____

2. 有一次她甚至在西藏背包旅游了两个礼拜，口袋里只揣着400块钱。

____

3. 像单板滑雪、攀岩这样的极限运动在中国越来越受到年轻人的喜爱。

____

4. 去探险或参加一些需要冒险的活动可以考验我们的力量和能力，并能给我们一种心跳的感觉和征服感。

____

5. 今天的孩子所面临和经历的挑战跟以往的很不一样。

____

（☞ P268）

B 听MP3实战演练。

Topic 5　Leaders 领袖人物

一、考试说明

领袖话题是人物题中的新题，2006 年底首次出现。雅思的话题卡往往会给考生很宽松的发挥余地，比如关于此话题，考生便可以从政界、商界和体育界中任意选择。当然对大部分考生而言，商界和体育领域内的领袖人物更容易谈，或者以前准备过的名人题也可以拿过来用。第三部分会围绕领袖所需的能力以及如何培养领袖等话题展开讨论。在"话题相关材料"中，考生可以看看世界商业领导培训界大师 Warren Bennis 总结出的六大领袖素质。

二、真题演练

CUE CARD

Describe a leader who you admire (for example, in sports, business or politics).

You should say:

who this person is

what this person did (has done) that you admire

how you know this person or know about this person

and explain how this leader's qualities impressed you.

点题	One leader that I admire is Bill Gates.
事迹 + **崇拜原因**	Well, what do I admire about Bill? He's really rich! No, just kidding. But that is one of the reasons that I admire him. I think that if you are going to make money and that is your goal then he is the best role model. His is a **success story** that you don't see too often. Of course I use his software and I know that it is not the greatest, but you know what, it is the first and that says something to me. I also admire him for not staying in school just to stay in school. Once he saw what he wanted to do, he didn't wait around until graduation, but instead **grabbed the opportunity** while he could and **took off** with it. Another thing that I admire about him is that he is not **content with** what he has **accomplished**, but is still looking for ways to get his product to the world. Now I know that he has enemies and people that say this and that about him, but so has every other **visionary** that has stood out from the crowd. I hear now that he is giving a lot of his money to **charitable organizations** and this just makes me want to say, "**Bravo** to him!" He's a modern day hero.

重点词句

success story 成功范例

grab the opportunity 抓住机会

take off 成功

be content with 满足于

accomplish 实现

visionary 目光远大的人

charitable organizations 慈善组织

bravo 好样的(感叹词)

Part 3

Being a leader

1. Would you like to be a leader?

   I would like to because I know that being a leader requires something great of people. Being a leader will help to **bring out the best in someone,** and I want my best qualities to be **apparent** in my life. I wish to have children some day, and I know that raising children will require the best leadership. Also, my parents expect me to get a good job, and a high position means having many others working under your **authority**. I believe this world needs more leaders and a higher standard of leadership.

   bring out the best in someone 调动起某人最大的潜能

   apparent 明显的

   authority 权威

2. Why don't some people want to be leaders?

   The answer to this question has become very clear to me recently as I must deal with it every day. To be a good leader, one must be a good follower, and there are very few people who can and wish to follow. It is very hard to take orders from others when you are excited about your future and when you have many personal dreams. But we have to learn from others to be able to lead them, and that is the hardest part to learn.

3. Why do we need leaders?

   We need leaders because without them, life would be **chaos**. I know when I was a child, if my mother did not teach me lessons, I would have caused many terrible problems. Many people are **ignorant** when they are young, but many are just as ignorant when they are older. We can see when a society is **lacking in** leadership, how quickly it falls. Being a good leader is a **priceless** quality.

   chaos 混乱

   ignorant 无知的

   be lacking in 缺少

   priceless 珍贵的

Leadership Qualities

4. What are the qualities of a leader? (or what abilities are needed to be a leader?)

   I would say a leader needs a lot of **dedication** and **passion** for what he is doing. He must be able to **convey** this in his work. He needs patience to handle people. This leader must also understand those he leads, and like I said above, he must understand what it is like to follow. A leader should be a good example of what he is trying to teach, and should follow his own advice.

dedication 奉献 | convey 表达
passion 激情

5. Is it possible to be a good speaker in front of others and to be a good leader but at the same time not be a good person at the personal level?

   Yes, of course. Every day I watch a little TV and sometimes when I have free time I will watch movies. Every person that I see on TV knows what he is doing and acts his part. But maybe, inside, he is not at all the character I see him as. My boss at work may lead me and my workmates, and treat us well, but does he treat his family well? Do I know for sure that he treats people on the street well? No, I do not know.

6. What are some differences between current leaders and leaders of the past?

   The leaders of the past are as **varied** as they are today. But I think before, there was more to being a leader. A long time ago people could not treat each other badly without suffering themselves or being tried by the law. But these days I often see very bad **occurrences** between bosses and their workers, or even governments and their people. In many ways, things should be done as they were before.

   varied 不同的 | occurrence 事情

Training Future Leaders

7. How do people become leaders?

   By **perseverance** and **willpower** I think. I also believe that a person who wants to be a good leader must be **focused** but not stressed. He should know what he wants and give his all for it. But he should never stop caring for those around him, because who would want to follow someone who shows no interest in or **appreciation** of others? I certainly wouldn't.

   perseverance 毅力 | focused 执着的、专注的
   willpower 意志力 | appreciation 欣赏

8. What can parents do to encourage the development of leadership abilities in their children?

   Be a good example. Try their best to understand and not order children around. Never **spoil** them but **reward** them for hard work. The parents should never stop learning from their children. A child who feels **ignored** by his parents will never grow to full **maturity.**

   spoil 溺爱 | ignore 被忽视
   reward 奖励 | maturity 成熟

9. How do you think leaders of the future will be different to current leaders?

   I think they will grow less powerful. The more independence people have, the more they see their own potential, and the harder it will be for them to accept their leaders. Each person in China is pushed to succeed, to **reach their full potential**, and I think it will be very hard for them to live their life following rules and orders. I think many Chinese will realize that they could be anything, and will **be discontented with** living to serve their leaders.

reach their full potential 实现最大潜力　　be discontented with 不满

三、话题相关材料

A 补充语汇

Warren Bennis（沃伦·本尼斯），美国南加州大学马歇尔商学院商业管理教授，商业领导培训界的大师，总结出了领导应具备的六大素质，看看是不是符合你对领导素质的定义。

Warren Bennis, widely known as a modern leadership guru, has identified six personal qualities.

Integrity 正直

Integrity means alignment of words and actions with inner values. It means sticking to these values even when an alternative path may be easier or more advantageous.

A leader with integrity can be trusted and will be admired for sticking to strong values. They also act as a powerful model for people to copy, thus building an entire organization with powerful and effective cultural values.

Dedication 敬业

Dedication means spending whatever time and energy on a task is required to get the job done, rather than giving it whatever time you have available.

The work of most leadership positions is not something to do "if time". It means giving your whole self to the task, dedicating yourself to success and to leading others with you.

Magnanimity 宽宏

A magnanimous person gives credit where it is due. It also means being gracious in defeat and allowing others who are defeated to retain their dignity.

Magnanimity in leadership includes crediting the people with success and accepting personal responsibility for failures.

Humility 谦逊

Humility is the opposite of arrogance and narcissism. It means recognizing that you are not inherently superior to others and consequently that they are not inferior to you. It does not mean diminishing yourself, nor does it mean exalting yourself.

Humble leaders do not debase themselves, neither falsely nor due to low self-esteem. They simply recognize all people as equal in value and know that their position does not make them a god.

Openness 开放心态

Openness means being able to listen to ideas that are outside one's current mental models, being able to suspend judgement until after one has heard someone else's ideas.

An open leader listens to their people without trying to shut them down early, which at least demonstrates care and builds trust. Openness also treats other ideas as potentially better than one's own ideas. In the uncertain world of new territory, being able to openly consider alternatives is an important skill.

Creativity 创造力

Creativity means thinking differently, being able to get outside the box and take a new and different viewpoint on things.

For a leader to be able to see a new future towards which they will lead their followers, creativity provides the ability to think differently and see things that others have not seen, thus giving reason for followers to follow.

四、练习

A 请将下列句子翻译成英文。

1. 一旦他发现自己想要做的事情，他没有等到大学毕业，而是马上抓住机会，并且做成功了。

____

2. 成为领导之后会把我们的最大潜能调动起来。

____

3. 给孩子们做个榜样，试着去理解他们而不是把他们呼来喝去。

____

4. 正直的领袖值得信赖，他们执着于自己的信念，并因此而受人爱戴。

____

5. 创造力指的是以不同的方式思考，能够打破常规，以崭新的角度来看待事物。

____

（☞ P268）

B 听 MP3 实战演练。

Topic 6　Neighbours 邻居

一、考试说明

"邻居" 话题是雅思中的古董级题目了，但它仍然活跃在现在的雅思考场。对大部分考生而言，这个题目属于那种看似简单、实则很难的类型，因为在现代社会邻里关系越来越淡薄，可能有不少人连自己的邻居叫什么、做什么都不知道，更别提去描述他们了。好在人物题有共性，考生也可以把其他人物话题做蓝本，使用"调包计"。在"真题演练"部分，native speaker 向我们讲述了一位非常热心肠的邻居阿姨，让人觉得非常亲切。第三部分围绕邻里关系展开。在"话题相关材料"部分，考生可以看到国外"eHow"网站上列出的关于如何建立良好的邻里关系的建议。

二、真题演练

CUE CARD

Describe one of your neighbours.

You should say:

how long you have known this neighbour

what sort of person they are

how often you see them

and explain what kind of relationship you have with them.

点题	I would like to talk to you about a neighbor that lives next door to me.
交往	I just **moved into** a new apartment so I didn't know anyone. But this neighbour is an old woman and she was very friendly when I first met her. She saw me **move** in all my things and I think she felt sorry for me or something because she **offered to buy me some vegetables** at the market. She said that she gets them very cheap and that I would have to pay a lot in the store. At first I told her not to buy anything for me as I didn't want to bother her but she insisted and kept **assuring** me that she wanted to buy vegetables for me. So finally I agreed. I was so surprised when she **showed up** at my door later as I was arranging my new apartment. She had an **armful** of onions! She told me that they are very healthy, so I gave her some money for the onions. Then she went home and I continued cleaning and unpacking. **Later that day** or the next day, I don't remember, she knocked on my door again. She had made a special dish from her hometown and she brought me a little **bowlful**. I thanked her and she seemed very happy that she could do things for me.

评价	I think she is **a very motherly type of person** and it makes me feel good that even though I live away from my family, I have a **caring** person like her as a neighbour.

重点词句

move into/in 搬入

offered to buy me some vegetables 提出帮我买蔬菜

assure 保证

show up 出现

armful 一抱之量

later that day 那天晚些时候

bowlful 一满碗

a very motherly type of person 像妈妈般慈爱的人

caring 关爱的

Part 3
Neighbours

1. Do you think neighbours are important?

   I think neighbours are very important because they are some of the people that you are around every day. If you ever have a problem you may need to ask a neighbour for help, since they are right nearby. If you are new in a place, you can always ask a neighbour where to find something. And they are also right there if you are in danger and knowing they are there might make you stronger or less afraid.

2. What are the qualities of a good neighbour?

   I think the most important quality of a good neighbour is friendliness. For example, saying "Hello" when you see each other is a good quality. I often speak to my neighbours and try to be friendly because one day I might be lonely and sad, and if I have been friendly to my neighbours they will be friendly to me and cheer me up. I also like for my neighbours to be patient and honest. If I make noise and disturb them I would like them not to get angry but to just tell me that the noise is bothering them. I also think neighbors should be polite and not disturb each other unnecessarily.

3. Now that most people watch a lot of TV, how do you think this has affected relationships with neighbours?

   I think TV watching has had a very bad effect on relationships between neighbours. In the old days people would go out for a walk in the evening or sit outside their houses. They would make friends and keep up with what was happening in their neighborhood. But now, many people just **plop** down in front of the TV in the evening and are "**couch potatoes**." Having this kind of habit keeps people from being able to **build close relationships** with their neighbours and even members of their own family.

   plop 扑通一声坐下

   build close relationships 建立紧密的关系

   couch potatoes 电视迷

4. Do you think it's important to teach children how to have good relations with neighbours?

I think it is important for children to be polite to neighbours. If your children offend your neighbours then it is hard for you to have a good relationship with your neighbours because they will be upset by what your children have done. One thing that is important for children to learn in life is how to **relate to** others. It is actually a good opportunity for them to learn this in their interactions with the people they live close to.

relate to 理解

5. How has the relationship between neighbours changed over the last 20 years?

I think that 20 years ago people cared more about each other. I think that neighbours saw themselves as a kind of group to help each other. But now with so much violence and dishonesty in the world today, I think many people are afraid to get involved with others. They don't know if they might be taken advantage of or get in trouble in some way. However, I think that inside, people want to find friends and they want to love. As Mother Theresa said, "Everyone, no matter what color or **creed**, wants to love and be loved." I believe that even though we may not be perfect, I think we all would like to live **harmoniously** with our neighbors and others around us.

creed 信仰

harmoniously 和谐的

Community

6. What are some of the qualities of a good community?

I think the most important quality of a good community is to be unified. That doesn't mean that every single person has to think exactly the same thing, because that is not possible. But I think they should all have the same **ideals**. In other words, to be **compassionate** and **concerned about** each other, to want to be honest and **trustworthy**. I know this sounds **idealistic**, but if you only want to better yourself and live to make yourself rich or more comfortable, you soon find that nothing makes you happy anymore. But if you can **incorporate giving into your lifestyle** then you do not lose the joy of living.

ideal 高尚的道德情操

compassionate 富于同情心的

concerned about 关心

trustworthy 可信赖的

idealistic 理想主义的

incorporate giving into your lifestyle 将给予融入到你的生活方式中去

7. In China, are there any facilities for improving relations between neighbours?

Well, there are some but not very many. In the old days, the people in China simply had time, and this helped to facilitate relations between neighbours. Spending time really means the most in almost any relationship. If you spend time to talk or listen, that goes far to **build good neighborly relations**. Of course having a place to go to mix and mingle with **people your own age** also helps, you can see these facilities **springing up** here in China.

build good neighborly relations 建立良好的邻里关系

spring up 开始出现

people your own age 同龄人

三、话题相关材料

A 邻里关系是中西方社会和宗教中一个重要的话题。犹太教和基督教历史上的摩西“十诫” **Ten Commandments** 中就有3条戒律是跟邻里关系有关的。“**Thou shalt love thy neighbour as thyself**”更是圣经中被人们广为流传的一句话。在中国也有句古话“**A close neighbour is more helpful than a distant relative**”。下面是国外“**eHow**”网站上列出的关于如何建立良好的邻里关系的建议，看里面有没有你所需要的更多词汇。

Instructions

STEP 1: Welcome new neighbours with an introductory note or a friendly chat.

STEP 2: Maintain the area around your home so that it's neat and attractive.

STEP 3: Be conscientious about noises that might disturb your neighbors, such as vacuum cleaners, music, loud talk and barking dogs.

STEP 4: End parties at a reasonable hour. While you're at it, invite your neighbours to come, too.

STEP 5: Return anything that you borrow from your neighbor, such as tools or appliances, as soon as possible. Express your gratitude when you do so.

STEP 6: Replace anything that belongs to your neighbor that you, your children, or your pets break or soil.

STEP 7: Respect your neighbor's privacy.

STEP 8: Offer to collect mail, water plants and watch the pets while your neighbours are away on a trip.

STEP 9: Learn from neighbours with cultural backgrounds different from your own.

STEP 10: Invite your neighbour over for a leisurely cup of coffee to discuss any problems you may have, or to share good news.

STEP 11: Throw a house party once a year on a weekend or holiday to socialize with your neighbours.

四、练习

A 请将下列句子翻译成英文。

1. 她做了些家乡特色菜，给我盛了满满一碗。

____

2. 我觉得她是那种特别有妈妈般慈爱感的人。

____

3. 尽管我远离父母，但身边有个像她这样会关心人的邻居，心里还是感觉很温暖。

____

4. 我觉得邻居很重要，因为他们是你每天低头不见抬头见的人。

____

5. 生活中小孩子要学的很重要的一件事就是如何去理解别人，而跟他们住的最近的人的交往实际上为他们学习这种能力提供了很好的机会。

____

____

（☞ P268）

B 听 MP3 实战演练。

地点类核心级(Topics 7~8)

Topic 7 A Building in Your Hometown 家乡建筑物

一、考试说明

关于建筑物的话题是雅思口语中的经典老题，但2007年初出现了一个难度较大的新题——“modern building”。在“真题演练”部分描述的是哈尔滨的索菲娅大教堂；在“话题相关材料”部分，考生可以看到对2008年北京奥运会标志性建筑物“鸟巢”和“水立方”的描述。这样无论新、旧建筑物，考生都可以从容处理了。第三部分通常围绕建筑物保护和住房等问题展开。

二、真题演练

CUE CARD

Describe an important building in your hometown.

You should say:

what it is

what it looks like

what it is used for

and explain why it is important.

点题	Ok, I will tell you about a building in my hometown, Harbin. In a square in downtown Harbin, there is an old Russian **Orthodox** church. It's called the Sophia Church, probably named after a saint Sophia.
描述	Anyway, it's in a nice square about 100 meters long and 50 meters wide. The church is about 30 or 40 meters high, not very big. It is made of red brick, and the architecture, as I said before, is in the old Russian style. If you've ever seen pictures of the famous church in Moscow—I cannot remember its name—you'll know what it looks like. Of course it's smaller and less **fancy**. There is only one large **domed roof**, and there are maybe 5 or 6 **bell towers.** I think there are more **pigeons** inside than people. They charge a lot of money to see the inside. I never went inside, so I don't know what it looks like.
用途	I heard that the church was once going to be **demolished**, but it was built so strong, the workers gave up and left it there. Now it is a very famous **tourist attraction**, and visitors from around China and the world go to see it and take pictures.

重要性	I think it's important because it is a **historical relic**, and a little peaceful place in the busiest part of the city. It's also part of the city's image. Harbin is an interesting mixture of both old and new. No matter how many **skyscrapers** and tall apartment buildings are built, it still has an **old and friendly flavor**, like a visit to your grandparent's home. I hope the church stays there.

重点词句

Orthodox 东正教
fancy 华丽的
domed roof 穹顶
bell tower 钟楼
pigeon 鸽子
demolish 推倒，拆除
tourist attraction 旅游胜地
historical relic 历史遗迹
skyscrapers 摩天大楼
old and friendly flavor 古老和友善的味道

Part 3
Old Buildings

1. How do people in China feel about protecting historic buildings?

   I think people are beginning to understand the principle that old buildings are sometimes—I don't say always—treasures to be preserved. Today, most people agree that if a building is an important part of history, then it should be well taken care of. But I think what's missing is the protection of the building's atmosphere. It's not enough to just keep the bricks and mortar from falling apart; you also have to be careful you don't ruin its appeal to visitors by having it **overly** "**touristy**". The Forbidden City here in Beijing is a good example. It's an amazing place, but it's really boring now, because it has no atmosphere. It's so crowded with sellers, tourists, tour guides, and **shop vendors**, that you feel like you are just in a shopping street, not an ancient seat of **imperial power**.

   overly "touristy"过分商业化
   imperial power 皇权
   shop vendors 店铺卖主

2. Is it important to preserve old buildings?

   Well... sometimes. Some old buildings are good to keep as **reminders of the past**, as long as they remind people what was right or wrong, not just that they existed. Some old buildings are just wasted space. If the building is a symbol of something good or important to remember about the past, then it should be kept. If it's ugly or in a place where something more useful to the people could be built, and it is not very unique or special, then I would say it's better to get rid of it.

   reminder of the past 让人们牢记过去的东西

3. Do you think an area can benefit from having an interesting historic attraction?

   For sure. Most historically important places are tourist attractions. That can be good, as tourism benefits the local economy. Also, attractions can give locals something to be proud of, and a reason to live and work there. If the historic building—or natural wonder—is not a major focus, or is too neglected and out of touch with the present, then such historic places lend a kind of **dignity** to an area. They show the past and present are **well integrated**, which suggests **a vision and plan for the future**.

out of touch 脱离

dignity 尊严，尊贵

well integrated 和谐的

a vision and plan for the future 对将来的展望和规划

4. What do you think will happen to historic buildings in the future?

I think there will be less of them, but the ones that remain will be **well-preserved**. I think a lot of old buildings will become like little islands of the past in an ocean of a modern world. At least that's what I think will happen here in Beijing. I really don't know how historic buildings in other places around China will **hold up**. Probably a lot of them will lose their uniqueness and beauty to over-tourism. Others will simply fall apart and no one will even remember what they were or what importance they held. That's what time does.

well-preserved 保存完好的

hold up 支撑下去

Housing

5. Compare old houses and modern houses. Which do people prefer to live in?

That's easy. Nearly everyone wants to live in a new house. Whatever appeal old houses have to the artistic or **nostalgic** mind, that appeal is not as strong as **running water**, electricity, central heating, and a **well-functioning management**. It's mostly the older generation, or my parent's generation, that prefers old houses to new. Among my own generation, if we can, nearly all of us will choose to live in a modern apartment.

nostalgic 怀旧的

running water 自来水

well-functioning management 井井有条的管理

6. How has housing in China changed, compared to your parents' time?

Housing today means tall apartment buildings if you live in a city. In the countryside, I think it's mostly unchanged; only the objects inside of the houses are different. But the conveniences widely available in modern urban housing are many: better electricity, **plumbing systems** and heating. Many of these were rare before.

plumbing systems 各种管道系统

7. What changes do you think will occur in the future?

If the current trend continues, **residential contractors** will keep building the same style of buildings, until some creativity enters the business. Modern housing in China is all the same: tall, **identical** apartment buildings around a central garden or courtyard, sometimes with a smaller building **adjacent** or built into the foundation of a few of the taller buildings. It will probably be many years before this trend is **reversed**. That's too bad, because a lot of what is being built today is wasting space and materials. But I'm hopeful that it will change, even if it takes awhile.

residential contractors 建筑承包商　　adjacent 临近的

identical 相同的　　reverse 扭转

8. What factors do people consider when deciding where to live?

Scenery, convenient transport, availability of stores and restaurants, noise or pollution levels nearby; the list goes on and on. Then of course, there are the actual attributes of the apartment complex they choose, whether it has hot water and central heating, and what ventilation system is used. But in the end, the cost of living is the biggest factor. If one's income is high enough, then he can afford to be **choosy** about the other factors.

choosy 挑剔的

9. How do you think the climate of a place effects the way buildings are constructed (the design)?

I don't think climate affects it that much. The outer design of a building can be pretty much the same, whether it's in a **temperate**, cold, or hot climate. It's more the structure of a building that matters. Buildings that are further north are generally built with more **insulation** and **double-paned glass**. Although, if the architect is really good, he will design a building that is in harmony with its surrounding nature, and one which makes use of materials and the sun's light to keep the building naturally temperate. This is also good for the environment, as it uses less energy to keep it cool or warm.

temperate 温和的　　double-paned glass 双层玻璃

insulation 隔热

三、话题相关材料

A 2007 年初雅思口语出现了新话题——“你见过的现代建筑”。考生可以看看下面对 2008 年北京奥运会标志性建筑物“鸟巢”和“水立方”的描述，从里面可以找到更多描述建筑物的词汇。

The Beijing National Stadium, also known as the bird's nest, was the main track and field stadium for the 2008 Summer Olympics and was host to the Opening and Closing ceremonies.

The stadium is conceived as a large collective vessel, which makes a distinctive and unmistakable impression both when it is seen from a distance and from close up. It meets all the functional and technical requirements of an Olympic National Stadium, but without communicating the insistent sameness of technocratic architecture dominated by large spans and digital screens.

The structural elements mutually support each other and converge into a grid-like formation almost like a bird's nest with its interwoven twigs. The spatial effect of the stadium is novel and radical and yet simple and of an almost archaic immediacy, thus creating a unique historical landmark for the 2008 Olympics.

The National Aquatics Centre, known as "The Water Cube", was one of the most dramatic and exciting venues to feature sporting events for the Beijing Olympics in 2008.

Being one of the three landmark buildings for the 2008 Beijing Olympic Games, the Centre is located inside the Beijing Olympic Park. Covering a total floor space of 50,000 square meters, it has 17,000 seats. It was a venue for swimming, diving, synchronized swimming and water-polo games during the period of the Olympic Games. After the games, the center became a recreational water park open to the public.

The building's structural design is based on the natural formation of soap bubbles. To bring the design to life, the individual bubbles are incorporated into a plastic film and tailored like a sewing pattern. An entire section is pieced together and then put into place within the structure. There are interior and exterior films, which are inflated once in situ. They will be continuously pumped thereafter.

In Chinese culture, water is an important natural element. It creates a calming atmosphere and inspires happiness. Taking full consideration of the functions of water in recreation and bodybuilding, designers have explored many ways for people of different age groups to appreciate its function. Many creative designs have been employed in the creation of the swimming pools at the Centre. Other high-tech facilities including optical devices used to define positions of athletes, and multiple-angle, three-dimensional screening systems are provided to help spectators enjoy competitions.

四、练习

A 请将下列句子翻译成英文。

1. 教堂高约三四十米，并不很大。由红砖砌成，整个建筑属于古俄罗斯风格。

____

2. 现在它成了著名的景点，吸引着国内外游客来参观拍照。

____

3. 我觉得它很重要，因为它是历史的印记，而且它也为闹市提供了一处安静的地方。

____

4. 不管盖起了多少高楼大厦，这城市仍保留着一种古老和友善的味道。

____

5. 可能要很多年后这个趋势才能逆转。

____

（☞ P268）

B 听 MP3 实战演练。

Topic 8 Your Childhood Room 童年房间

一、考试说明

关于房间的话题是雅思口语中的老话题，考生向考官描述小时候住的房子或者现在自己喜欢的房间，在第三部分里会围绕房屋和住宿与其展开讨论。在“真题演练”部分 native speaker 描述的是小时候家中的一个“landing”。严格地讲，这并不是一个房间而是一小片区域，在那儿做作业或者上网。在“话题相关材料”部分，考生可以看到外国人在谈自己最喜欢的房间，答案五花八门，但真实自然。有位妈妈还提到自己孩子最喜欢的房间，猜猜看是什么，读完之后看你是否猜中了。

二、真题演练

CUE CARD

Describe a room you lived in when you were a child.

You should say:

what it looked like

what was in it

what you did in the room

explain what you liked about the room.

点题	My favorite room was the study room in my house. It had been a **landing**, but we made it into a study and that is where I used to do my schoolwork or any kind of project.
房间描述 + 活动	The room was not so big, about 5 square meters. It had a **bookcase**, a table with four chairs, a **filing cabinet**, an entertainment center with a TV, a large window, and a door leading to our balcony. Because of the window and door there was **plenty of light and fresh air**, which made it a very nice place to work. During the school year that would be my study room; during vacation and after I finished high school, I would use it for reading and other projects. There was also a computer in the room which I often used to go online and do research. Sometimes I would also chat with my friends on the computer.
感受	I liked this room because it was quiet and very sunny. There was a large **mango tree** outside the window that was very nice to look at. I always felt very relaxed and calm when I used that room. I also liked to practice on my keyboard in that room.

重点词句

landing 楼梯平台
bookcase 书架
filing cabinet 档案橱柜
plenty of light and fresh air 光线充足，空气清新
mango tree 芒果树

Part 3
Rooms and Individuality

1. Do you think children should have their own rooms?

   I think that it is good for children to have a chance to share rooms with other **siblings**. Once they get a little older many children like to have their own rooms and learn how to take care of them. I think it's good for them to have a chance to have both their own room and a shared room. They learn many good things from each situation.

   sibling 兄弟姐妹

2. How do children benefit from sharing a room with others?

   They learn how to get along with the people they share a room with, and they learn to share their toys, which is very important later in life. They learn to share responsibility in keeping the room clean and neat. They have someone to play with and don't have to be lonely; someone who can be a close friend. I think that it is more beneficial for children to share a room than to be by themselves.

3. Do you think people have enough privacy today?

   Privacy is often very important. To those people who like privacy, it seems they can never have enough and they will always want more. Others would rather exchange privacy for more protection. They don't mind having less privacy if they know that in exchange they don't have to worry about theft or being in danger.

4. What do you think of people who decorate their houses in a very **flamboyant** manner?

   I think that they want to **make a statement** of their status when they decorate in a colourful and **showy** way. This may not always be so, as some people may just like that **décor**. Often the decoration is to show their artistic tastes. Because it is difficult to make a colourful décor match well, having a well arranged and well decorated house shows a lot of taste **on the part of** the owner.

   flamboyant 浮华的，华丽的
   make a statement 向外界显示
   showy 炫耀的
   décor 装饰风格
   on the part of 就…而言

5. Have the rooms in houses changed much compared to the rooms of your parents' youth?

   The **layout** of houses and rooms are pretty standard and stay almost the same. One thing that does change is the material that the furniture is made out of. When my parents were young almost everything was made out of wood, and sometimes metal. There was rarely anything plastic. Today much of our furniture is made out of plastic, metal and other **man-made materials**.

layout 布局　　　　man-made material 人造材料

6. How do you think the climate of a place affects the way buildings are constructed (the design)?

Well, in my view climate has quite a lot to do with the way we design and build our houses. For instance, in places where it snows a lot, you find houses built with a steep roof so that the snow can't settle on and damage it. But in warm climates the houses are often built with a **verandah** to keep the sun out of the rooms and to provide a cool place to sit.

verandah 阳台

7. How do you think rooms will change in the future?

I think that in the future, rooms will change to use more natural materials. There is a great demand for **genuine wooden furniture** and it is very stylish to use furniture that looks like the furniture used in the past. I think it's a good change. Other than that I can't see that much of a change in rooms really.

genuine wooden furniture 实木家具

Places for Public Use

8. What kinds of public places does your hometown have?

In the place where I grew up there were quite a few small parks and places to **stroll around**. There were not many playgrounds for children to play in, but my siblings and I liked to run and play games. We were very happy to play in the **open area** in front of our apartment. There was also a nearby field where we could play football and a track to run around.

stroll around 散步　　　　open area 开阔区域

9. Do you think it's important to have facilities such as public parks and playgrounds?

I think that it is important to have places that are safe and clean for children to play in. It's good to have large open areas where both children and grown-ups can get good exercise outdoors in a safe environment. If nothing but skyscrapers are being built then of course children are going to suffer. It is more important to have parks and playgrounds than some of the other facilities that are being built nowadays.

10. Compare public facilities (such as parks) in China today to those of the past.

In the old days there were not many parks or public facilities, and the ones that were around were often **small and unkempt**. The plants were not taken care of and the ground was often **dirty and littered.** Today more efforts are put into keeping the parks clean and the area free from litter. The plants are well taken care of and emphasis is put on making the parks look pretty.

small and unkempt 小而乱　　　　dirty and littered 脏而且有杂物的

11. In your opinion, how will public facilities change in the future?

I think that there will be larger and nicer parks made in the future. I think the parks will be made available to more people and easier to reach. I also think that there will be more playgrounds and better equipment. You know in the future there might even be transportation to and from the playgrounds that would include free refreshments.

三、话题相关材料

A 补充语汇

What Is Your Favorite Room in the House and Why?

封闭阳台

I love the sunroom. I have a panoramic view of the mountains, and can see all the birds and squirrels in the trees outside. I also grow most of my plants in that room. It gives me a sense of being outdoors, which is very soothing for me.

卧　室

My bedroom, just because it is the only place that is totally mine. It really reflects who I am, what I am all about and what I like. My bedroom always gives me a sense of peace and it is the perfect place for me to go whenever I need to be alone or just want to relax. Everything I could possibly need is there and there is really no reason to leave.

书　房

My study/office/what ever you want to call it, it is way cooler than my bedroom. I have records （all Rolling Stones）hanging on one of the walls. On another wall, photocopies of all of my sketches/artwork. On another wall, I have a large collection of comics from the Sunday newspaper stapled to a large corkboard. I can sum the rest up in one word: sixties（beanbag chair, lava lamp, Formica table）. It's a totally awesome place to hang out, daydream, take a nap in the beanbag chair （which is actually pretty comfy), and my favorite, draw. Sometimes, I even use the room for what it's intended for—doing homework.

厨　房

The kitchen, because that is where I can be creative and please my family. I love a big airy kitchen with lots of room to move around. When we have parties, people seem to congregate in the kitchen too. I guess I like it because I like to cook.

卫生间

My daughter seems obsessed with the bathroom. If I don't keep the door closed my ten-month-old daughter is always in the bathroom beside the toilet. I always know that when it gets really quiet, that is where I will find her. Yesterday she pulled all the toilet paper off the roll and quite merrily sat beneath the huge pile. Fortunately I found her just in time, with her mouth full of paper! I really need to remember to close the door.

四、练习

A 请将下列句子翻译成英文。

1. 地方不大，5平米左右。

____

2. 由于挨着窗户还有阳台的门，这里光线充足，空气新鲜，因此很适合在这儿工作。

____

3. 他们学着跟住同一个房间的人去相处，跟他们分享玩具，这些对今后的生活都有很重要的意义。

____

4. 屋子和房间的布局非常固定，基本保持不变。有一点的确变化了——制作家具的材料。

____

5. 以前没有很多公园和公共设施，即使有也是又小又乱。花草没人管，地上很脏，还有很多杂物。

____

（☞ P269）

B 听MP3实战演练。

地点类进阶级(Topics 9~11)

Topic 9 A Leisure Centre 休闲健身中心

一、考试说明

关于休闲健身中心的话题是雅思口语考试中的新话题，内容涉及的是生活中的新时尚。但“新”未必难，由于这样的话题属于比较现代的生活方式，因此更容易找到最地道最时髦的英语资源。这个话题的难点在“Leisure Centre”上，很多人会照字面意思把它翻译成“休闲中心”，但实际上它在英文中的意思是“(British English) a place where people can do many different sports and activities, and take exercise classes”(摘自《朗文当代英语词典》)，也就是指中文中的“健身房”，“休闲中心”这个翻译肯定不是很准确了。所以建议考生在准备雅思口语和写作考试题目的时候，一旦遇到不熟悉的词语，应尽量查英-英词典确认一下。

二、真题演练

CUE CARD

Describe a leisure centre you often go to.

You should say:

what it is and when you go there

what facilities it has

what you do there

and explain why you like this place.

点题	One leisure centre that I really enjoyed going to was located in Tianjin. It was in Teda actually. It was in a hotel and it was quite nice.
设施 + 活动	One of the facilities that I enjoyed using was the swimming pool. It was indoors and heated and very relaxing. There was also a **bowling alley**, which along with bowling had some nice **shuffleboard tables** that were clean and not too busy. The restaurant was quite nice with good food and wonderful service. I loved to go to the **Karaoke bar** that they had there and sing **to my heart's content**. I even practiced some English songs like, “Sounds of Silence” and “My Heart will go on” from the movie *Titanic*. If I felt tired after studying or working all week, I would go to the **massage** center and after just an hour there I felt **on top of the world**. Then of course there was the **Jacuzzi** and the **sauna**—to just lay back and let the heat and the water take away the pressures and tension **out of this world**. Some nights at the restaurant, they would have **floor shows** with dancing and singing. If I wanted to go out and meet someone, or just enjoy a drink, I would go to the disco that they had there and **boogie** to **the wee hours** of the morning.

重点词句

bowling alley 保龄球馆
shuffle board tables 沙壶
Karaoke bar 卡拉 OK 歌厅
to my heart's content 尽兴地
massage 按摩
on top of the world 〈口〉幸福到极点
Jacuzzi 水力按摩
sauna 桑拿浴
out of this world 〈口〉太棒了
floor shows 夜总会节目表演
boogie 情不自禁(跟着迪斯科乐或摇滚乐)跳起舞来，蹦迪
the wee hours 凌晨

Part 3
Healthy lifestyle

1. How do Chinese people like to relax?

   I think that one of the most common ways that Chinese people like to relax is to go out to a restaurant with their friends or family and enjoy a good meal together. Another way to relax for them is to simply go out for a walk and enjoy the evening or morning atmosphere. It's an excellent way to **relieve stress**. Chinese also like to read books and the youth enjoy going to Internet cafés and playing computers games.

   relieve stress 减压

2. Do you think most Chinese people lead a healthy lifestyle nowadays?

   To be honest it seems to me that we don't lead a very healthy lifestyle. We work a lot, are **under stress** and often have to travel on crowded buses or subways. Sometimes the Chinese men in particular drink a little too much and end up with **health problems**. The way that we eat is not so good, with many foods being fried with a lot of oil.

   under stress 感到有压力
   health problem 健康问题

3. What do Chinese people think about daily exercise? Is it considered important?

   If you ever go by a health club and see all the **sophisticated machinery** there, one of the most outstanding things you will notice is that it is almost empty. Most Chinese people just don't use that equipment, they don't consider it very important. Now of course things are changing a bit and you do see some Chinese people out **jogging** or **working out**, but it is a slow change. With the younger generation exercise is changing, as you will see lots of young guys out on the basketball court **for hours on end**.

   sophisticated 精密的，复杂的
   machinery 机械
   jogging 慢跑
   work out 锻炼
   for hours on end 一连好几个小时

Leisure and Work

4. Do you think employers should provide recreational facilities for their employees?

   It would be a good idea to do this. It would increase **productivity** because it would increase **stamina** and **mental alertness**. Exercise is good for you and sometimes people working just get

weary sitting at their desks for hours at a time. The employers don't have to provide facilities but it would **be in their best interests to do** so and help to **lift the spirits** of their employees.

productivity 生产力

stamina 持久力，精力

mental alertness 头脑灵敏度

weary 疲惫的，无聊的

be in one's best interests to do sth. 做某事符合某人的利益

lift one's spirits 鼓舞士气

5. Should employees be paid overtime for working on the weekend?

Well if they didn't get paid there might be a mini revolution. The weekends are very special to most people and to have to work is a sacrifice as it is, and not to get paid would **add insult to injury**. On the other side of the coin, if the reason that they are working is they didn't get the work done during the week, then they should come in **of their own accord** to finish this work, and the company shouldn't have to pay for this.

add insult to injury 伤口上撒盐

of one's own accord 自动地，自愿地

6. How do you think a person can find a balance between the time spent at work and the time spent on leisure?

They say, "All work and no play makes Jack a dull boy." Well the same holds true in reverse: all play and no work makes Jack a very poor boy. Each has to be in its own place, a time to work and a time to enjoy life. Even if you enjoy your work you should pull yourself away from it in order to have the proper balance in your life. Sometimes you just have to stop whatever you are doing, whether work or play, and do the opposite to have a healthy life. Many people these days are literally dying of over work, while other people are wandering around day after day with nothing to do. It is a tough thing to do, but you have to discipline yourself to work and then play.

三、话题相关材料

A 下面是新西兰 Christchurch 市一些 Leisure Centre 的网页介绍文字，请从里面找出更多有关健身中心的词汇。

Welcome to the Christchurch City Council Leisure Centres

Christchurch City Council would like to welcome you to our Leisure Centres. The Centres offer a fantastic range of recreation and fitness activities from sports training through to family recreation. Leisure for life—experience it! It is the philosophy and vision that we, at Christchurch City Council, live by. It is about leisure throughout your life, leisure for all ages and it is about getting out and participating at all levels.

The benefits of leisure are extensive and these are foremost in our minds when we are looking at designing programmes for the facilities. Being active gives us more energy, reduces stress and makes us feel good. It's easy to be active at our facilities and we would like to encourage you to find more about our classes and centres by reading through this website.

Welcome to Pioneer Leisure Centre

Pioneer Leisure Centre is a suburban centre that was transformed in 1999 into a modern recreation and aquatic facility. The centre features a fun leisure pool with a wave machine, spa, sauna and steam room all poolside, along with a separate 25m, 5 lane lap pool. The fitness centre is well equipped with a side rage of cardio and weight gear, with an aerobic studio and circuit room. There are 2 squash courts available for hire, as well as a large indoor sports stadium that can cater for sports training, major competitions and large display or trade show events.

Each term a fantastic variety of popular exercise and recreation classes for babies through to adults are available, such as Jazz dance, swimsmart (learn to swim), basketball, pre school gymnastics, gymnastics, aquafit, aerobics, pilates, yoga and much more.

B 中国传统健身方式

太极是中国文化的瑰宝，也是传统的健身方式，下面是国外某健身中心对中国太极的介绍，你认为这篇介绍讲得是否地道？

Tai Chi

According to Chinese legend a man named Zhang Sanfeng founded the art of Tai Chi about eight hundred years ago after observing the movements of a snake and a magpie in combat. Zhang created a wondrous style of martial art that focused on the powerful element of softness. Today Zhang's principles and methods of training have been handed down as Tai Chi.

What Is Tai Chi?

Tai Chi involves a series of gentle movements and techniques that are performed in what appears to be slow motion. Tai Chi is practised by 20% of the world's population and is fast becoming the most popular exercise in the world today. Tai Chi is excellent for strengthening the body on many levels. The slow paced, gentle movements help the body strengthen bone mass and connective tissue and improve the natural functions of the internal organs.

Regular Tai Chi practice reduces stress, increases breathing capacity and improves balance and co-ordination.

Who Can Do It?

Because of its gentle nature Tai Chi is accessible to people of all ages and physical abilities. Many people with mobility problems and ailments practice Tai Chi as therapy. Tai Chi is particularly suited to older adults and those new to exercise. Its gentle and supple movements promote good health and total well-being.

About This Style

Conventional forms of Tai Chi consist of 80 or more movements. These forms take a considerable amount of time to learn and perform. China's Physical Culture & Sports Commission created a shorter form called “Simplified Tai Chi” based on the contemporary Yang Style which traces its origins back to Master Zhang. Christchurch City Council Tai Chi Classes are the revised form which involves 13 techniques within 24 moves.

四、练习

A 请将下列句子翻译成英文。

1. 我喜欢去卡拉OK歌厅唱歌唱个痛快。

____

2. 工作或者学习了一个星期，如果我感觉累，我就会去按摩，一个小时后马上就会觉得自己幸福到了极点。

____

3. 中国人最常见的放松方式之一就是跟朋友家人下馆子好好吃一顿。

____

4. 有时候中国人喝太多的酒，最后导致很多健康问题。

____

5. 多做运动能让我们精力充沛，帮我们减压，让我们有个好心情。

____

（☞ P269）

B 听MP3实战演练。

Topic 10　A Hotel 旅馆

一、考试说明

关于旅馆的话题是06年底才出现的雅思口语话题。很多考生面对这道新题时都有些手忙脚乱，第一是由于生活中的确很少接触旅馆，第二是由于语言资源的缺乏。而实际上本话题很容易跟旅游、房间、健身中心等题目建立联系，从而找到基本的语言资源。第三部分一般围绕旅游业和旅馆的发展等话题展开。“话题相关资料”中收录了旅店业星级分类的标准和国外旅客对住过的酒店的评价，考生可以通过它熟悉有关饭店业更专业的语言资源。

二、真题演练

CUE CARD
Describe a hotel you stayed at or have seen.
You should say:
　　what the name of the hotel was
　　where it was
　　what facilities it had
and explain your impressions of this hotel.

点题	There was a very nice hotel that I used to **frequent** called the Victory Hotel.
位置	It **was located** in Tanggu, Tianjin on the way to TEDA. It was close to a market so if you felt like making yourself something to eat instead of going to the cafeteria, then you could just **take a stroll**, buy what you want and go back to your room and eat it.
房间和其他设施	Each room at the hotel had a nice kitchen that contained a stove and other **basic utilities** needed for a **homey** kitchen. The hotel also had excellent swimming facilities. The **swimming pool** wasn't very large but it was kept clean **all year round** and was **heated** to perfection in the winter. This was one of my favorite places in the entire hotel. The hotel also had a very good **bowling alley**. This was another of my favorite places to **hang out**. On one floor there was even a **disco** and a **spa**. This hotel had **virtually** everything. Although I never got a very good look at the **cafeteria** I was always told that it served good food and that all of the waiters and waitresses were very kind and helpful.
感受	I personally liked this hotel and enjoyed staying there. All of the **maids and cleaning staff** were very cheerful and the hotel **carried an air of** joy and happiness. I would recommend this hotel to everyone, even more than The Hilton or Holiday Inn.

重点词句

frequent 经常光顾
be located 位于
take a stroll 溜达
stove 炉子
basic utilities 基本设施
homey 像家一样的
swimming pool 游泳池
all year round 常年
heat 加热
bowling alley 保龄球道
hang out 打发时光
disco 迪斯科舞厅
spa 水疗馆
virtually 事实上，差不多
cafeteria 餐厅
maids and cleaning staff 女服务员和清洁工
carry an air of 洋溢着…气氛

Part 3
Tourism

1. Is tourism an important industry in China?

   In my opinion, tourism is very big in China. I believe that it is very important to the Chinese economy. If it weren't for tourism, China would have to look for other ways to bring money into the country. Tourism not only helps to bring in money, but also helps to influence and **modernize** China.

   modernize 使现代化

2. How has tourism contributed to the development of your hometown (or the place where you live now, or China)?

   Tourism has helped by making people more **aware of** the value of old buildings and famous places. Because of the attraction of these places **there is more of an effort to preserve** and improve them. There is also more development to make tourists and travelers more comfortable. The hotels and hostels are improving their standards, and the restaurants are learning to **cater to** westerners.

   aware of 意识到
   there is more of an effort to do sth. 投入更多努力去做某事
   preserve 保存
   cater to 迎合

3. Has tourism had any bad effects on your hometown (or the place where you live now)?

   Because of the rapid development and the expansion of cities, tourism will force many people to move out of their old, lower-priced homes. These people will have to find new, often more expensive apartments and houses. This may be difficult for them and they may not be able to afford the new housing. Also, the construction workers who build new buildings and roads will be out of work when they are completed. This will cause a rise in unemployment.

Accommodation When Traveling

4. When people are traveling away from home, what choices do they have for places to stay? (What kinds of hotels does China have?)

   There are many very nice hotels all around China. Almost every city will have at least one of the more well-known **international hotels**. There are also **local hotels** that are cheaper and economical. Then there are **hostels** and **dorms** where you can stay for a very low price for a longer time.

   international hotel 国际旅店　　hostels 招待所；客栈
   local hotel 本地旅店　　dorm 外租房间，宿舍

5. How have hotels changed (improved) in recent years (or, compared to the past)?

   I think the standard of hotels has risen in general. The standard hotel has nicer facilities and often more options as far as rooms and prices go. They are now put in more convenient places and also well-distributed around the city. Hotel service has also gotten much better as employees are aware of how important it is to treat guests well.

6. What facilities should a (good) hotel have?

   I think a good hotel should have everything that people need to stay for a while. It should have a restaurant or some place where the people staying there could get food easily. It should have a few places for **recreation and exercise,** such as a **gym**, swimming pool, and sports equipment room. It should also have **a business center** with **Internet access**, international phone service, fax, printer, photocopier, and computer.

   recreation and exercise 休闲和锻炼　　a business center 商务中心
   gym 健身房　　Internet access 网络连接

7. What could be done to improve the environment (e.g., the appearance) in some hotels?

   The hotels should be **nicely and tastefully decorated**. They should have a simple, efficient **layout** that does not confuse the guests. The outside should be clean and the outside appearance should match the **inside décor**. It also would be an improvement to make sure that there are plenty of plants and trees.

   nicely and tastefully decorated 装饰得美观而有品位　　layout 布局
   inside décor 内部装饰格调

8. What kind of people (what kind of personal qualities) are best suited to work in a hotel?

   The most important qualities for working in a hotel are friendliness and consideration. When the staff of a hotel is friendly and considerate the guests are well taken care of and happy. It is also important for the staff to be neat and clean. This will help them to make their work area and the hotel clean for the guests.

9. What can hotel service people (hotel employees) do to help tourists?

The most important thing is for the hotel employees to be able to understand the tourists and guests. Efforts should be made to make sure that most of the hotel personnel have at least a basic knowledge of English. It is also nice to have a few people who speak other common languages or languages that are spoken by people who frequent the hotel. It is good to also be able to give directions to nearby **tourist spots** or have a service to help tourists get to more distant ones.

tourist spot 景点

三、话题相关材料

A 补充语汇——旅馆分级标准

摘自 www.answers.com

Stars are often used as symbols for classification purposes. In particular, a set of one to five stars is employed to categorize hotels.

* (**one star**)	—	low budget hotel; inexpensive; may not have maid service or room service.
** (**two stars**)	—	budget hotel; slightly more expensive; usually has daily maid service.
*** (**three stars**)	—	middle class hotel; moderately priced; has daily maid service, room service, and may have dry-cleaning, Internet access, and a swimming pool.
**** (**four stars**)	—	first class hotel; expensive (by middle-class standards); has all of the previously mentioned services; has many "luxury" services (for example: massages or a health spa).
***** (**five stars**)	—	luxury hotel; most expensive hotels/resorts in the world; numerous extras to enhance the quality of the client's stay (for example: private golf courses or even a small private airport).

B 如何评价旅店

下面几段文字是国外游客对北京某大酒店的评价，看是不是可以从中得到点启发。要想知道对更多酒店的评价，也可以登陆 www.tripadvisor.com 网站，上面有各国旅客对世界各地酒店的评价。

1. Hotel was absolutely incredibly beautiful, **tranquil** gardens and the **cuisine** was **awesome**. The rooms were **stunning** too—very well decorated and very clean and modern. The staff are, **without exception**, polite and helpful without being **pushy**. My overall impression of the hotel and staff was nothing but excellent. The only drawback is that the hotel is quite far off the city center and bearing in mind the traffic conditions during weekdays, it can take well over an hour to reach downtown if your work requires so.

2. Upon arrival, until departure the staff were professional and **courteous**. In particular, the girls at the Tour Desk were very efficient and booked some last minute excursions for us without any problems. Our room was comfortable, attractive and clean with no detail overlooked. The **lobby** and the **adjacent** bar area were stunning and the Chinese garden extremely well kept and attractive. The prices for food and drinks were very expensive... but this was a five star establishment.

tranquil 安静的；祥和的
cuisine 食品
awesome 〈口〉极好的
stunning 惊人地好
without exception 无一例外
pushy 热心过头的；逼迫的
courteous 有礼貌的
lobby 大厅
adjacent 临近的

四、练习

A 请将下列句子翻译成英文。

1. 就个人而言我很喜欢在这个旅馆住，在那儿工作的小姑娘和清洁工都很热情，整个旅馆洋溢着一种快乐的气氛。

___

2. 旅游业不仅为中国带来了财富，也影响着中国，改变着中国。

___

3. 一个好的旅店应该有休闲和锻炼的地方，比如说健身房，游泳池，和其他体育设施。

___

4. 最重要的就是旅馆员工要理解入住的宾客。

___

5. 房间棒极了，装饰得很好，既干净又时髦；员工待人礼貌，无一例外，热情而不让人生厌。

___

（☞ P269）

B 听 MP3 实战演练。

Topic 11 A Library 图书馆

一、考试说明

关于图书馆的话题总体来说难度不大，考生向考官描述完自己常去的图书馆后，在第三部分里会围绕图书馆的作用和未来与其展开讨论。在“真题演练”部分 native speaker 描述的实际上是一个虚拟的图书馆（这一点从地址上可以看出来），语言平实易懂，举的例子很有普遍性。在“话题相关材料”部分，考生可以看到对大英图书馆和纽约公共图书馆的介绍，相信从中能发现更为专业和漂亮的语言。

二、真题演练

CUE CARD
Describe a library that you often go to.
You should say:
what library it is
where it is /what the library looks like
what you do there
and explain why you like this library.

点题	I like to go to a library called the Peoples' Library near my home.
地点 + **介绍**	It is located on First Avenue near Main Street in a very new building that has some beautiful urban sculptures standing on the grounds around it. The library has many floors, and each floor has different sections.
活动	The first time I went there I needed a lot of help to find books but now I feel like it is my second home. When I go to the library I feel like I am leaving a lot of my worries and cares behind, even if I have to go there to research or study. I think that is because I know I can always find a quiet, private place to read or do my work. And if I want to travel to a different place or a different time, I can do that at the library by finding a book or computer that will take me into another world.
感受	I am particularly interested in this library because it has a lot to offer. Besides having a good stock of books, it also provides **office equipment** such as a good copy machine, a **book binder**, many computers and printers, and much more. And it has very good service too. If you need a book in another library it will obtain that book for you by either shipping it from the other library or purchasing the book.

重点词句

office equipment 办公设备

book binder 装订机

Part 3
Libraries

1. What kind of people go to libraries most often?

   I think people of all ages use the library. However, I think students use the libraries more often than older people. I often see young children in the library, but I think university students use the library the most frequently. In my opinion, the older generation use libraries the least. Some are too busy and others have no interest in books.

2. Why do you think a library is a good place for reading?

   I think that the atmosphere in the library **is conducive to** reading because number one, it is one of the quietest places you can go. Also if you start reading something and you find you are not interested in it, it is one of the best places to find another book. Nowadays many people read from computers. It is very convenient therefore to be able to **access** materials on the Internet at the library.

   be conducive to 有益于

   access 接近，使用

3. Even though it might cost a lot to maintain a library, do you think the government should open more public libraries?

   On one hand, I think that it is very worthwhile to have plenty of libraries. On the other hand, with the way technology is improving practically each day, it may be wiser to invest in making computers more accessible to more people. It is possible to go to an Internet café and go online, but much of this time is spent on worthless computer games and watching movies. Establishing computer libraries and teaching people how to use them beneficially might be a good idea.

4. Do you think public libraries should be free of charge?

   It would be nice if libraries were free, but usually you have to pay a fee or put down some kind of **deposit**. I don't think this is too unreasonable as people often do not **appreciate** things they get totally for free. If people know they can get their deposits back if they do not damage any books, then it makes them more careful. Of course the government should **subsidize** libraries so that people do not have to pay **exorbitant** costs.

   deposit 押金

   subsidize 资助

   appreciate 珍惜；欣赏

   exorbitant (价格)过高的

5. How do you think libraries will change in the future?

   I can picture a future where computer technology will enable us to have easy access to all the resources a library provides. People may not even have to read. They could just listen to texts. It may sound like **fantasy**, but with all the progress in technology I think it is very possible.

fantasy 幻想，白日梦

Improvement

6. What kind of skills do you think library staff should have?

I think library staff should always be very well informed as to where things are located in the library. This will enable them to help people to save time in finding what they need, which is a very big help in our busy times. I think they should also be very **courteous** as people who are using the library can often be under a lot of pressure and often need a lot of help. Library staff should also be efficient and have **organizational skills**. They may have to take care of a lot of details and it would make things very difficult for those using the library if items were lost or difficult to find. Last but not least library staff should be patient. They may be faced with **a myriad of** requests each day and those using the library will be unhappy if the staff are frustrated, impolite or upset.

courteous 谦恭有礼的　　a myriad of 无数的

organizational skill 组织能力

7. What can be done to make libraries more attractive?

I am interested in **interior decorating** and one thing I would recommend for libraries is to **incorporate** more **neutral colors** into the **décor**. I believe that nowadays libraries are decorated to use maximum space and reflect maximum light. Browns and other **muted colors** can create a warm atmosphere. Comfortable and attractive seats can also make the environment more inviting. Also I am in favor of having works of art in libraries. Not necessarily **originals** but good quality copies of famous works are attractive as well as **educational**.

interior decorating 内部装饰　　muted color 柔和的颜色

incorporate 包含，吸收　　original 原作

neutral colors 中性色　　educational 有教育意义的

décor 装饰之格调，装潢

8. How has the Internet affected the popularity of libraries?

Certainly the Internet provides easy access to sources of information, although their **validity** should be **suspect**. However, there is nothing on the Internet that replaces picking up an actual book and reading it. Reading a book is a **tactile** experience. Books can be carried everywhere and read at any time. Although I use the Internet for a number of things, I have in my personal library about 300 **reference books** and I find things in them that I do not find on the internet. I **augment** this library with books from the public library.

validity 正确性，有效性　　reference book 参考书

suspect 值得怀疑的　　augment 扩大

tactile 触觉的

三、话题相关材料

A 下面两段文字分别是对大英图书馆和纽约公共图书馆的介绍。对前者的介绍比较平实，大家可以找到很多描述图书馆的专业语句；对后者的描述比较艺术化，大家可以看到西方人对图书馆的评价。

British Library

The **British Library** （**BL**）is the national library of the United Kingdom. It is based in London and is one of the world's most significant research libraries, holding over 150 million items. The Library's collections include around 25 million books, along with substantial additional collections of manuscripts and historical items dating back as far as 300 BC. As of March 2004 the Library held 11.2 million monographs and received more than 41,500 regular serials. As a legal deposit library, the BL receives copies of all books produced in the United Kingdom and the Republic of Ireland, including all foreign books distributed in the UK. It also purchases many items which are only printed abroad. The British Library adds some 3 million items every year.

The New York Public Library

Libraries are the memory of humankind, irreplaceable repositories of documents of human thought and action. The New York Public Library is such a memory bank par excellence, one of the great knowledge institutions of the world, its myriad collections ranking with those of the British Library, the Library of Congress, and the Bibliothè que Nationale de France. Virtually all of the Library's many collections and services are freely available to all comers. In fact, the Library has but one criterion for admission: curiosity.

The New York Public Library comprises simultaneously a set of scholarly research collections and a network of community libraries, and its intellectual and cultural range is both global and local, while singularly attuned to New York City. That combination lends to the Library an extraordinary richness. The research collections （for reference only, and organized as The Research Libraries, with four major centers）resemble the holdings of the great national and university libraries, and the community circulating libraries （organized as The Branch Libraries）resemble classic American municipal libraries.

All these features, taken together, make The New York Public Library a unique and complex institution, wonderful to use but not always easy to grasp. A useful way to understand the Library is to consider its beginnings and subsequent evolution. It has been very much a creature of time and place, bearing the imprint of its origins but always, like any living organism, coping with struggles and problems while adapting to an ever changing environment.

B 图书馆不只是读书的地方，它也可以提供很多服务。下面这些服务你想到过吗？

The Library offers hundreds of **free programs** and many **exhibits** each year, which are attended by thousands of people. For adults, these include **concerts, author readings, films, plays, lectures, musicals**, and **operas**. **Special exhibits** highlight **photography, artwork, crafts**, and **new books**. The newly refurnished **auditorium** seats 263 people and includes **wheelchair seating**. The Central Children's Room and Teen Central present programs and exhibits for children and teenagers throughout the year. These include films, **puppet shows, story hours**, and **talks by popular authors**.

The library offers **laptop docking**, giving users the opportunity to connect laptop computers to the Internet and to connect to many of the **electronic information resources** available at the library.

四、练习

A 请将下列句子翻译成英文。

1. 那是一个很新的建筑物，周围还立着美丽的城市雕塑。

   ____

2. 除了有很好的藏书外，这个图书馆还提供像复印机这样的办公设备。

   ____

3. 我觉得图书馆的气氛很适合阅读，因为首先它非常安静。

   ____

4. 这听上去像是白日梦，但随着技术的进步我觉得这些都是很有可能的。

   ____

5. 我也主张在图书馆里放置一些艺术品，当然不一定非得是原作，一些名人名作的复印品也可以，它们同样既美观又有教育意义。

   ____

（☞ P270）

B 听 MP3 实战演练。

喜好类核心级（Topics 12~14）

Topic 12　A Film 电影

一、考试说明

关于电影的话题是雅思口语考试中的十大经典话题之一。该题对考生最大的挑战就是要把电影的基本情节用简练的语言表达出来，并加以评论。第三部分一般围绕电影在中国、电影与社会、言论自由等话题展开。本单元除了为考生提供了 native speaker 样板答案之外，也列出了该话题中最常用的词汇和句型，并附有几个最受欢迎的国内外电影评论网站，供考生搜索之用。考生也可以把中西方对同一部电影的评价进行比较来感受中西方的审美差异。

二、真题演练

CUE CARD
Describe a film that you have recently seen.
You should say:
what the film was
when and where you saw it
what the film was about
and explain how you felt about this film.

点题	A film that I saw recently was called *The Passion of the Christ*. I was in my hometown of Chongqing when I saw it when it first **came out** a few years ago.
电影内容	The film was about the last 24 hours of Jesus' life on earth. It showed when he was in the garden before he was captured and brought before a trial all the way up to when he was crucified and rose up again from out of the grave. It was actually quite **moving** because the director, Mel Gibson, actually put his own money into making the picture, so he was able to just **do it the way that he wanted it done**. This movie caused quite an **uproar** when it **was released** as some people really loved it and others hated it. It was in the news for a long time with a lot of debating going on over it. It ended up making quite a bit of money for Mel Gibson.
感受	Everything about it was very beautiful, from the **cinematography** to the **actual scenery**. The **acting** was **top notch**. I think the main actor deserved an **Academy Award** but anyway I enjoyed it very much. One of the hardest scenes for me to watch in the movie was where Jesus gets whipped before he is crucified. It was so **realistic**; I had to hide my eyes.

重点词句

come out 上映

moving 感人的

do it the way he wanted it done 按照自己的想法处理

uproar 哗然，骚动

be released 上映

cinematography 拍摄

actual scenery 实景

acting 表演

top-notch 〈口〉极棒

Academy Award（特指）奥斯卡奖

realistic 真实的

Part 3
Films

1. What kinds of films are most popular in China?

   Well **Hollywood blockbusters** are very popular here, films like *Titanic* and *Saving Private Ryan*. Also Hong Kong films are very popular because the stars are well known here. **Kung fu films** are popular because this art form **originated** here. Of course **love stories** are very popular as well as Chinese **historical films**.

   Hollywood blockbuster 好莱坞大片

   Kung fu film 功夫片

   originate 起源

   love story 爱情片

   historical film 历史片

2. Do old people and young people like to watch the same kinds of films?（Compare the differences.）

   Well I think that old people like to watch stories about their country since they were so **involved** in this time period. They also like to watch **variety shows** that show the native singing and dancing from different parts of China. Young people on the other hand **go for** the foreign films, as I already mentioned. There are some films that both young and old like to watch such as Chinese historical movies.

   be involved in 参与，涉及

   variety show（歌舞、杂技和滑稽短剧的）联合演出

   go for 喜欢；选择

3. What do you think people can learn from watching films? （Or should films be considered as entertainment only?）

   Oh I think that people can learn so much from films. You know there is an old saying that goes "A wise man learns from his mistakes, but a wiser learns from the mistakes of others." Just by watching a movie and seeing what a character does **in certain circumstances** can help you to know what to either do or not do. You can feel what the characters feel if the actors are really good. You can see sights that you might not be able to see **if it were not for** movies, so definitely you can learn from watching films.

   in certain circumstances 在某些情况下

   if it were not for 如果不是因为…（对现在的虚拟）

4. To what extent do you think films reflect real life?

Well that is a big argument that has **been around** for a long time: Does art **imitate** life or does life imitate art? I believe that each **reflects on** the other. Sometimes films **observe life** and **comment on** it and sometimes life observes film and imitates it. Film is **a powerful medium** and **brings many parts of life to the public for observation**.

be around 存在
imitate 模仿
reflect on 反思，思索
observe life 观察生活
comment on 评论
a powerful medium 一种强大的媒体
brings many parts of life to the public for observation 把生活的方方面面呈现在大众面前供人们审视

5. Do you think that film stars deserve the large incomes that some of them receive?

Absolutely not! I think film actors' salaries have just gotten **way out of hand**. I know that some of them are very good actors and do the job that they have to do well, but when I think of all that money and what else could be done with it I just can't seem to **justify** it. When you pay people this much money, it absolutely makes them **larger than life** and reality can become a little **blurred**.

way out of hand 极为失控的
justify 证明…为正当
larger than life 光彩照人，有传奇色彩
blurred 模糊的

Censorship

6. What do you think about **censorship**?

I believe in it. I think that some of the stuff that is available to the public is just pure garbage. Not censoring would be like allowing garbage to be strewn around your living room. I believe in **freedom of speech** and having the right to say what you think, but I believe that also goes along with **a sense of responsibility** of who would be around to hear it. Some things are just not **fit for** all **audiences**. I think that maybe censorship can **go too far** but if you **have a good balance** in what is censored it is not such a bad thing.

censorship 审查制度
freedom of speech 言论自由
a sense of responsibility 责任感
fit for audiences 适合观众
go too far 某事被做得过分，超过正常
have a good balance 保持平衡

7. Should films be classified before release?

Of course this goes along with my previous answer. Although really with today's films some of them could be classified as junk one and garbage two. I hope that you don't think that I am being too negative on this subject but **realistically speaking** expanding these **ratings** or **classifications** would not be a bad idea. I think that the rating system is too simplistic and many more **guidelines** and ways to classify movies **are long overdue**.

realistically speaking 现实角度来讲
rating 分级
classifications 分类
guideline 指导原则
be long overdue 某事早就该做但没做

三、话题相关材料

A 补充语汇

film genre 电影风格
mainstream studio film 主流电影
independent film 独立电影
avant-garde film 先锋电影
action film 动作片
martial arts film 功夫片
spy/espionage series 间谍片
disaster film 灾难片
crime/gangster film 警匪片
drama film 现实题材片
horror films 恐怖片
fantasy film 魔幻片
war film 战争片
New Year film 贺岁片

B 经典评论句型

1. I really enjoyed the movie from start to finish.
2. ...really has it all. It makes you laugh, moves you, makes you cheer, makes you gasp and lets you feel smart.
3. He seemed completely natural in the role and brought a depth and realness to the character.
4. She brought a special quality to the character, and many, many men and boys will walk out of the theater in love with her.
5. I'm afraid I'm not eloquent enough to describe just how much I loved this movie. While not perfect, the sum total of the parts created a great, memorable experience.
6. I truly think this is the best comic book movie ever made and I'm not exaggerating. It was very funny at points, it was very heart rending at other points. Dramatic, intense and exciting.
7. The director displays an amazing vision. Believe it or not, the acting is superb and the dialogue is rich.

C 电影评论网站

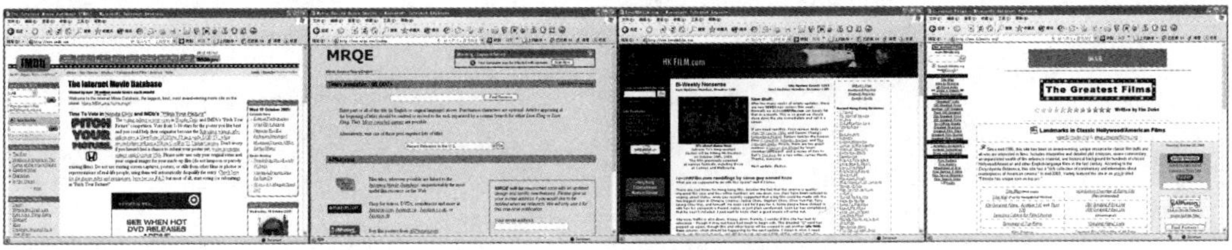

自左至右
www.imdb.com 全球电影网上数据库
www.mrqe.com 全球电影评论搜索引擎
www.lovehkfilm.com 香港电影爱好者网站
www.filmsite.org 美国经典电影评论评估网站

四、练习

A 请将下列句子翻译成英文。

1. 电影上映时引起一片哗然，人们褒贬不一。

____

2. 从某种程度上讲，看电影、看里面的角色的活动可以让你知道什么可以做，什么不可以做。

____

3. 电影是个很强大的媒体，它把生活的方方面面呈现在大众面前，供人们审视。

____

4. 我认为现在的分级体系太过简单，我们早就应该设立更多的指导原则和分类方式。

____

5. 自始至终我对这部电影欣赏有加。

____

B 猜一猜下面所列英文名称是哪些中文电影的英语翻译。

1. Curse of the Golden Flower
2. Confession of Pain
3. Crazy Stone
4. Raise the Red Lantern
5. House of Flying Daggers
6. A World without Thieves
7. Farewell, My Concubine
8. Chungking Express

（☞ P270）

C 听 MP3 实战演练。

Topic 13　An Outdoor Activity 户外活动

一、考试说明

关于户外活动的话题总体来说难度不大，考生向考官描述完自己喜欢的户外活动后，在第三部分双方会围绕户外活动的变迁和环境展开讨论。在“真题演练”部分讲叙的是慢跑，很常见的一项活动。“话题相关材料”部分为考生提供了更多户外活动的类型，相信会对考生有所启发。

二、真题演练

CUE CARD

Describe an outdoor activity that you like doing.

You should say:

what this activity is

when you do it

where you do it

and explain why you like it.

点题	I really enjoy running. Not the fast **sprinting** kind of run, but rather the more **drawn-out** jogging kind of run.
时间	I usually like to run when the weather is warm but not too hot, because if it's too hot then I'll be sweating like a camel, and will be so thirsty and red from the heat that I can't function for about a half hour after that. Somewhere between 21 and 28 degrees **Celsius** is a good temperature for running.
地点	I extremely dislike running on a **track** or in wide open spaces, because it makes me feel like I'm not getting anywhere. I think that the best place to run is on a smaller, not-so-busy street in a nice **residential area**. But if there isn't a place like that to run near my house, I'll run anywhere—even on a track.
解释	One reason that I enjoy running is it's faster than walking and cheaper than taking buses or taxis. Also, running is good for your health; the more you run the stronger your legs, back and lungs get. I also like the **rush** that you get when you push yourself farther than you've ever gone before, where you feel like collapsing and keep on running until you don't even feel your legs anymore and it's just mechanical.

重点词句

sprint 疾跑

drawn-out 持续很久的

Celsius 摄氏的

track 跑道

residential area 居民区

rush 身体的一阵感觉，快感

Part 3

Outdoor Activities

1. Would you say people spend more time outdoors today than they did, say, 20 years ago?

   I don't really think so. Now with so many modern conveniences there's less need to work outdoors. There are so many offices and indoor jobs now that it's almost considered "low class" to do manual labor or work outside. Most middle-class working people do not get sufficient amounts of exercise, and as a result **are** weak and more **prone to** sickness.

   be prone to 易于

2. Are there any outdoor activities that many people used to do but which most people don't do now?

   One of the main ones that I can think of is walking. People still walk, but not in the same proportion that they used to years ago. Walking used to be the main source of travel, unless you could afford a horse, donkey, or mule. But now with cars, buses, and the Internet, people do a lot less walking to get to work, the store, or wherever they need to go.

3. What are the most popular outdoor activities in China?

   Many Chinese enjoy playing badminton, riding bicycles, performing Tai Chi, and walking. Some sports that have been adopted from other cultures are also popular, such as basketball, tennis, and track sports. One outdoor activity that most Chinese both old and young like is table tennis, it is a national sport here in China so it's not really surprising that so many people enjoy playing it.

4. Do old and young people like doing the same kinds of activities outdoors?

   It really depends on the people playing sports, because some old people are very fit and can keep up with the younger ones quite well. But for the most part old people generally don't **exert themselves** physically as much as the younger ones do. They'd much rather take a walk or play badminton than climb a mountain or play a **full-court** game of basketball.

   exert oneself 努力做某事

   full-court 全场

Working Outdoors

5. What do you think are some of the differences between working outdoors, compared to say, working in an office?

   If you're always indoors then you'll get weak and sick easier; whereas if you work outside then you're getting fresh air and sunshine, which are two things that everyone needs to stay healthy. If you're working outdoors, then you'll probably be much more physically fit and a whole lot stronger than if you're sitting at your desk all day. Of course if you don't have a balanced life then you're bound to have **complications**, and if you don't spend at least a few hours on your computer every day you might not be able to sleep at night.

complication 复杂情况

6. Do people in China prefer to work indoors or outdoors?

Most Chinese prefer working inside over working outside. They've had to work outdoors for so many years that it's a relief to work inside. I think that **a common mentality** is that if you work outdoors you're low class and can't do anything else. This might be true in some cases, but I'm not sure that it's true with everyone.

a common mentality 一种普遍心理

7. If you had to choose an outdoors job, what would you choose to do?

I would probably choose a job where you have to exert yourself physically. Maybe I'd work on a farm or some job like that, although I'd like to learn **carpentry**. Oh, I know I'd work at a zoo cleaning the monkey cages. And when I'd have time off I'd go to the elephant cage and feed them peanuts.

carpentry 木工手艺

Outdoor Environment

8. How do you think climate and the environment affect what activities people do outdoors?

If it's really cold, then you can't do some of the things that you can when it's really hot. If you try to play basketball, the ball won't **bounce** so well because the cold makes it flat. That's why they have indoor basketball courts; they keep it warm so that the ball can bounce and the teams can play without freezing. In the cold climates you can skate, ski and snowboard, and in hot climates you can surf, swim, and play football or basketball.

bounce 弹起

9. Do you think the air quality in your hometown has improved or worsened in recent years?

Improvement as far as air pollution is concerned is an impossibility, if the air has steadily gotten worse at an alarming rate. Over the past few years more people have gotten cars, more factories have been constructed, and the air has just gotten worse. The sad thing is that it's slowly killing us all, and in a matter of years we'll all have **bronchitis**, or maybe **tuberculosis**—not a very pleasant thought if you ask me.

bronchitis 支气管炎　　　　tuberculosis 肺结核

10. Do you think it will be easy for the government to solve environmental problems?

It won't just be hard, it'll be almost impossible. As far as air pollution, the government is fighting a losing battle: every time they pass new regulations or set the standards higher something nasty happens. Like when the Russians were conducting the safety tests at the Chernobyl Nuclear Power Plant, it blew up in their faces. But they should definitely try to do their best to solve these problems.

11. How do you think the environment in your hometown should be changed?

If we had more trees and plants around the city then the air would be a lot fresher. There needs to be some kind of quality control on vehicles that are going around the city, some of those farm tractors are blowing out black smoke that **suffocates** anybody who's nearby. The sad thing is that people in my hometown are so accustomed to the environment being bad that they don't really care about changing it; they just want to do what's easiest, even if it means ruining their health and slowly killing themselves.

suffocate 使窒息

三、话题相关材料

A 下面是国外网友眼中最喜爱的户外活动。

What's Your Favorite Outdoor Activity?

1. Well I don't know if it will beat boredom but for me I go fishing when I can. It's relaxing, I can clear my mind and get fresh air. I can sit there for hours just holding that rod, doesn't matter if I don't catch anything but it's a bonus if I do. I let the fish go and start all over again.

2. I play tennis. It is a good sport. You can play in a public place and there are cheap rackets too. You exercise, meet people, maintain your shape, and relax.

3. Kayaking!! I was about 9 when I tried it in the ocean. I've been hooked ever since, although I prefer whitewater kayaking now.

4. Scuba diving...you could see a whole new, different world down there, serene and yet invigorating for the busy mind. You could also join group activities that support cleaning the environment.

5. Backpacking, most definitely. Being one with nature is the best feeling in the world. You're away from all the hustle that you're faced with every day. It just gives you a break and refreshes everything that seems to overwhelm you during the average work week.

6. We like to get together to barbecue and play games. Games like Taboo, Cranium and Guesstures are some of our favorites.

四、练习

A 请将下列句子翻译成英文。

1. 我喜欢跑步，不是那种短跑式的，而是那种时间更长一些的慢跑。

   ____

2. 我通常喜欢在天气暖和但又不是特别热的时候跑步。

   ____

3. 我也喜欢那种超越自己的极限后的快感。

   ____

4. 大部分中产阶层得不到足够的锻炼，因此身体较差且容易得病。

   ____

5. 如果你老待在室内，身体就会虚弱，而且容易得病；但如果你在室外工作，就可以享受新鲜空气和日晒，这两者是保持身体健康所必需的。

   ____

   ____

（☞ P271）

B 听 MP3 实战演练。

Topic 14　Favorite Time of the Year 喜欢的季节或月份

一、考试说明

关于季节的话题是雅思口语考试中的老话题。考生向考官描述完自己最喜欢的季节后，在第三部分会围绕季节和气候变化等话题与其展开讨论。在"真题演练"部分描述的是春天。在"话题相关材料"部分，考生可以看到国外网友对四个季节的评价。

二、真题演练

CUE CARD

Describe your favorite season or time of the year.

You should say:

when this time is

what the weather is like at this time

what you usually do at this time

and explain why it is your favorite time of the year.

点题	I think my favorite time of the year is spring. The main reason I like it is because it's not too cold and not to hot.
气候	In some places I've lived, such as Hangzhou and Shanghai, it rains most of the spring. But I was mainly thinking of when I lived in Kunming, it's so beautiful all spring. The sky is blue and the weather is nice and warm. The flowers start to bloom and the leaves on the trees turn green.
活动	Since Kunming has many parks, my family and I would often go for **picnics** in the parks where we would **play badminton**, eat, rest, and look at all the plants and flowers. Our favorite park was the Kunming Botanical Garden. It had so many different kinds of plants, trees, flowers, ferns, you name it. Another thing I like to do during springtime is to get up early and climb mountains. There was one mountain near our house called Chang Chong Shan, it wasn't so high but there were no steps, only a few **rough trails**. Another thing I like about spring is that's when all the animals are born. That's when you can see all of the little baby squirrels, dogs, cats, snakes, and spiders.
感受	The air always seems fresher in the spring, the sky is bluer, the grass greener, and the people friendlier—or at least I think so.

重点词句

picnic 野餐

play badminton 打羽毛球

rough trail 崎岖的小路

Part 3

Seasons

1. How do the different seasons affect the lifestyles of Chinese people?

   In places like Guangzhou, Shenzhen, or Xiamen where it's always hot, there aren't many **extreme weather changes** to worry about. But in other places in China such as Beijing, Shanghai, Tibet, or Harbin the weather changes so **drastically** from summer to winter that it affects lifestyles. During the winter the weather may go **below zero**, and in the summer it may get as hot as 40° **Celsius.** That means you have to have different kinds of clothes for each season. Also, in the winter you might need heating and in the summer you'll most likely have to use a fan or an air conditioner; one friend of mine uses both.

   extreme weather changes 极端的天气变化

   drastically 激烈地

   below zero 零下

   Celsius 摄氏的

2. How do different seasons affect the way people feel?

   One of the things that weather affects is the kind of food you eat. I don' t know about other people, but when it's really hot I don't usually feel like eating a lot, just some fruit or quick and easy food, like sandwiches, cold noodles, or McDonald's, whereas in the winter I usually feel like eating lots of filling hot food, such as soups, rice, noodles, and other things like that. Also when it's hot I just feel like sleeping, but in the winter I'm naturally colder, so I have to move around to keep warm.

Weather / Climate

3. How does the climate of a place affect the kind of buildings that are built there?

   Well, if the climate is hot then the builders will construct the buildings to stay as cool as possible. But if you're in a cold climate then you might find **double insulation** on the windows, or the houses will be built to **retain heat** as much as possible. It's quite common to see a house with a bunch of open **porches and verandas** in a hot climate. And probably every room will have a hole for an **air conditioning vent**. But colder climates will most likely have central heating.

   double insulation 双层隔热

   retain heat 保持热量不散失

   porch and veranda 走廊和阳台

   air conditioning vent 空调通风口

4. Do you think fighting global climate change is a governmental responsibility or the responsibility of individuals?

   As the saying goes, **many hands make light work**. If the governments and individuals work together on the climate problems, there will be many changes and more progress will be made. Of course more responsibility should fall on the shoulders of the government because they have the means to do more than the average citizen. But that shouldn't stop ordinary people from doing their part.

Many hands make light work. 众人拾柴火焰高。

Vacations / Holidays / Tourism

5. What are the major public holidays and festivals in China?

There is of course Spring Festival, **the Lantern Festival**, and the **Dragon Boat Festival**. There's **Grave Sweeping Day**, Labor Day, the Moon Festival, and National Day Holiday. I think that's about it.

the Lantern Festival 元宵节　　Grave Sweeping Day 清明节

Dragon Boat Festival 端午节

6. What do people in China do when they have holidays?

Most of the time they will party with their friends, but it really depends on the holiday. Take Grave Sweeping Day for instance. Chinese usually burn fake money, clean graves, and place flowers on them. Or at the Dragon Boat Festival they either watch the races or participate in one. But at Spring Festival everyone will party and eat and drink all night.

7. Why do Chinese people like the Spring Festival?

The Spring Festival is a time for family, a time for everyone to get together and party, eat, give presents and enjoy each other's company. It's in a sense like Christmas, at least as far as the partying and gift giving is concerned. It's the celebration of a new year, giving thanks for the last one and hoping and wishing that the next year will be prosperous. Also, it's a time off from school and work to relax without having to worry about meeting a deadline.

8. How can people benefit from visiting new places?

The more extensive and comprehensive your knowledge of other peoples and cultures is, the easier it'll be for you to **relate** to them. You'll have more in common with them and will better understand them. If you never leave your home, your understanding of other people will be very minimal. You'll most likely be **narrow-minded** and **bigoted**. Although this isn't always the case, most of them are this way.

relate 适应，和睦相处　　bigoted 顽固的，偏执的

narrow-minded 思想狭隘的

9. When many people visit a particular place, what effects can that have on this place?

An American friend of mine once told me that about 150 years ago some people found gold in California and people came by the thousands to look for it in the water. Because there were so many people and they all needed food, shelter, and supplies, some of the more **industrious pioneers** started building hotels, restaurants, and stores. Now, more than 100 years later, those towns are some of the biggest and most **thriving** cities on the west coast. What I'm trying to say here is that if there are enough people they can greatly change a place either for better or for worse.

industrious pioneers 勤劳的开拓者　　　　thriving 兴旺繁荣的

三、话题相关材料

A 春夏秋冬，各有所爱。下面是很多国外网友对四季的感受，看看是不是跟你想的一样。

春 Spring. Everything starts to come back to life again. The grass turns green, trees grow back their leaves, flowers grow and bloom, the weather is nice and the temperature is perfect! It just doesn't get any better than that!

夏 Absolutely love the summer! I am a teacher, so I get the summer off. I spend the entire summer swimming, lying in the sun, shopping, and relaxing.

秋 The fall is the prettiest, and I love the crisp cool air, sweater weather, blankets, I love the way the leaves crunch under your feet, and the way the air smells when people are starting to light their fireplaces. But then comes winter...

I love the fall because the leaves are changing and falling. It's so beautiful. And it's nice and cool. I wish it was fall all year around. There's so much to do because it's not too cold but not too hot. The fairs all come into town where I live. You can actually go for walks at the lake without feeling like you are going to die. You can go out and play with your kids and dogs. It's just a fun and beautiful season.

Autumn. Because of the trees turning colors, traveling at that time of year is awesome. I get some beautiful pictures then. It is cooler out and I like planting flowers that will last until mid-January. I will be skating more, camping, and hiking because of cooler weather. And I can turn off the a/c and smell the air from outside, sleep better and listen to all the crickets and birds do their thing.

冬 Winter. It's cold and grey and you can go for a walk in the frost and wrap up warm with your coats and scarves, and snow is fantastic. The air is so fresh in the winter. And then you can go inside the house with a mug of tea and watch the snow falling outside the window or watch a movie. The trees look so great in the winter, too, and everything is so still and quiet at night.

四、练习

A 请将下列句子翻译成英文。

1. 天很蓝，天气温暖舒适。

____

2. 春天的时候我喜欢做的另外一件事是早早起床去爬山。

____

3. 春天的时候，空气总是显得更新鲜些，天也更蓝，小草更绿，连人也更友善。

____

4. 到了冬天气温可能降到了零下，夏天最高温度可以到40摄氏度。

____

5. 政府应该承担更多的责任因为他们有资源去做更多的事情。

____

（☞ P271）

B 听MP3实战演练。

喜好类进阶级(Topics 15~17)

Topic 15　A Walk 经常走的一段路

一、考试说明

散步在近几年好像忽然成为人们追捧的锻炼方式。也难怪，毕竟散步是最省钱但效果却最好的健身方式之一，因此也就顺理成章地成了雅思口语中的常考话题。考生需要向考官描述自己经常散步(或走过)的一段路，第三部分会围绕散步的作用和健康的生活方式等话题展开讨论。在"真题演练"部分讲述的是自己在南京时从家到单位那段路。"话题相关材料"部分补充了国外有关研究散步的益处的文章。

二、真题演练

CUE CARD
Describe a walk you take regularly.
You should say:
　where and when you walk
　who you walk with
　what you see on this walk
and explain why you walk.

点题	I remember when I was in Nanjing last year, there was one walk I took extremely often.
具体描述	The walk was from my apartment to my work, about two and a half kilometres away. I did it every Sunday, there in the early morning, and back in the early afternoon. It was the best walk ever. In the mornings, since it was a Sunday, the streets were empty, so it was a really peaceful time. In the summer, I would get to see the **sun rise** over the city hall; and in the winter, I got to walk in my favorite kind of weather, cold **pre-dawn** darkness. Every time, I would **wear my iPod** and listen to music that fit the mood of the walk and weather. Then, in the afternoon, since Nanjing is such a big **tourist draw**, I would walk by many, many happy people on vacation seeing the sights in town. It made me really pleased to walk by all these people, because they were always really excited to be in Nanjing, and many had their small kids, who were always laughing and playing.
感受	It was really great to see people enjoying life.

重点词句

sun rise 日出

pre-dawn 黎明前

wear my iPod 戴着我的 iPod 随身听

tourist draw 吸引游客的地方

Part 3

Walking and Health

1. Do many people in China go for walks?

   Yeah, lots of Chinese people go for walks. Any time I walk by a park late at night, I always see people taking a stroll and looking pretty content. I think they do it for the same reason people worldwide who live in big cities walk: **it feels good to** get outside when they have been stuck inside all day. Also, walking in parks gives people a taste of nature in **a concrete world**.

   it feels good to 做某事感觉不错

   a concrete world 钢筋混凝土的世界

2. How do you think walking is beneficial to health?

   Walking does lots of things for your health. First, and perhaps most obvious, is the physical benefits. Walking is exercise, which is important for everyone. Just as important is the good walking does for your mind. For me at least, when I can walk somewhere, it gives me a good opportunity to think about things and not feel stuck inside. I get to feel the sun and the fresh air.

3. Do you think that playing sports is better for your health than walking?

   Walking and playing sports are both good for your body. They both improve your physical health, though sport does a better job at that. When playing sports, you are more active and your heart rate increases, so your body has to work harder, which makes the exercise more beneficial. But, walking does a lot of good for your mental health. It provides a great escape from the working world, and gives the mind a good opportunity to just wander. So if measuring just physical health, sports are better for your body, but if you look at mental as well, they are equally good for your health.

Walk and Leisure

4. Do you think people in the past walked more than people today, or less?

   I think that yes, people in the past did more walking. People today have many more **distractions** that occupy time that was once spent walking. They go on the Internet, or watch TV, or play video games. In the past, there was less to do, so people walked a lot more. Whether it was walking somewhere or walking just to walk, I think they did it a lot more.

   distraction 分心的事物

5. What is the relationship between standard of living and the amount of walking people do?

   I think that it is not really the standard of living that affects how much people walk. As long as you are talking about walking for pleasure, I think the main **variable** is how people value their time. For instance, rich, busy people and poor people that have to work really hard to **scrape by** probably don't have that much time to walk. But people that value life more than money probably walk more often because they want to enjoy themselves every once in a while. If you are talking about all kinds of walking, though, rich people walk less, obviously, because they can afford other modes of transportation.

variable 变量，易变的东西　　　　scrape by 勉强过活

6. How do you think the government could encourage people to walk more?

In my opinion, the best way to get people to walk more would be to build more places where people would enjoy walking. Parks or nice **tree-lined streets** would be a good way to start. People are much more likely to walk in places that are nice as opposed to places that feel **grimy**. Other than that, I think most Chinese cities are pretty walker-friendly. Lots and lots of people walk, and that is a really good thing.

tree-lined street 林阴道　　　　grimy 污秽的

7. Can you think of any examples where people walk a lot while doing their jobs?

Well, obviously, many postal workers must walk their routes in order to deliver the mail. As far as other jobs where people walk a lot, though, I can't think of many: Different kinds of deliverymen and waiters and waitresses are the two best examples of these kinds of jobs. Other than that, I don't think companies need employees to walk. It's more efficient for them to either stay in one place or to get around by other modes of transportation.

三、话题相关材料

A 散步是最简单的运动方式之一，但好处却很多。下面的文章讲述的便是散步对身体、心理和环境的益处。读完之后你会发现看似再平常不过的走路居然有那么多的好处。

Walking for Health

"I have two doctors, my left leg and my right."

George Trevelyan, 1913

"Walking is the nearest activity to perfect exercise."

Professor J. Morris and Dr. Adrianne Hardman, 1997

There's no doubt about it, walking is good for you. It's good for your heart, it's good for your lungs, it's good for the muscle and bone growth of your children and it's good for your feeling of well-being! Whether you want to walk to improve your general health, to keep fit, to control your weight, or perhaps to recover from a period of ill-health, walking can help. It is something that can be done with children or older family members, it need cost you nothing, and can fit in with any lifestyle, income bracket, culture or domestic circumstance.

Health Benefits of Walking

Studies show that walking can:

- Reduce the risk of coronary heart disease and stroke
- Lower blood pressure
- Reduce high cholesterol and improve blood lipid profile
- Reduce body fat
- Increase bone density, hence helping to prevent osteoporosis
- Reduce the risk of non-insulin-dependant diabetes
- Help to control body weight
- Help flexibility and co-ordination, hence reducing the risk of falls

Walking for Mental Health

Walking has been shown to improve self-esteem, relieve symptoms of depression and anxiety, and improve mood. Walking, particularly in pleasant surroundings, and with other people, offers many opportunities for relaxation and social contact.

Environmental Benefits

Motor vehicles create a substantial amount of air pollution. In fact, transportation is responsible for nearly 80 percent of carbon monoxide and 50 percent of nitrogen oxide emissions in the U.S. Not surprisingly, many metropolitan areas do not meet the air quality standards specified in the 1990 Clean Air Act Amendments. Although individual cars are much cleaner today than they were in earlier years, if total traffic continues to grow, overall air quality will deteriorate. Moreover, cars and trucks burn millions of barrels of oil, a non-renewable energy source, every day.

Keep it Steady

A steady routine is the most important factor in getting the most out of your exercise program. Walking for 30 minutes, 5 times a week is recommended.

Use these tips to keep you on track:

- During your walks, you should be able to maintain a conversation. If you're breathing too lightly, increase your pace. If you can't catch your breath, slow it down.
- Walk around the local area after lunch or dedicate 15 minutes to walking up and down stairs. Climbing is an excellent way to strengthen your heart.
- At night, trade a half hour of TV for a brisk stroll around the block. Take a friend with you for company or get the whole family involved.

四、练习

A 请将下列句子翻译成英文。

1. 每次我都带着随身听，听着跟我当时走路时的心情和天气相一致的音乐。

   ____

2. 在公园里散步也能让人们在钢筋混凝土的世界里亲近大自然。

   ____

3. 散步对精神健康大有益处。它让人们暂时逃离工作的世界，给我们的思想以遐想的机会。

   ____

4. 更看重生命而不是钱的人可能会花更多的时间散步，因为他们想时不时地享受一下生活。

   ____

5. 在我看来，鼓励人们散步的最好的办法就是建造更多吸引人们去散步的场所。花园和林荫道是不错的开始。

   ____

（☞ P271）

B 听 MP3 实战演练。

Topic 16 Sporting Events 体育赛事

一、考试说明

有关体育的话题在雅思考试中屡见不鲜，体育赛事题可以看作是体育题和体育明星题的延伸，但难度要比其他两题略高，因为它需要把有关的资源融合到叙事中去。第三部分无非还是围绕体育和生活展开。在“话题相关材料”部分，考生会看到一些世界顶级赛事的英文名称，国外对 NBA 某场比赛的报道以及一个讲述体育赛事的框架，考生可以把自己想到的体育赛事嵌入进去试一下，这也不失为短期备考的一条捷径。

二、真题演练

CUE CARD

Describe a sporting event that you enjoyed watching.

You should say:

what the event was

where you watched it

who watched this event with you

and explain why you enjoyed watching this event.

点题	A few years ago my father took me to a basketball game that was being played at a university.
赛事介绍	The teams were the Shanghai Sharks and another university team. I can't remember what the team's name was but they were all dressed in purple and looked quite funny. The game was quite short and only had 2 **halves** (instead of 4 **quarters**). I can't remember who won, but it was obvious that the Sharks were **playing very soft on** the other team.
特写	At halftime some of the Shark team members started throwing **signed jerseys** into the crowd, I think there were about 10 **in all**. I really wanted one but we were so far back that they never reached us. A friend of mine got one though and I got to try it on.
感受	The **atmosphere** in the stadium was so exciting. Everyone was shouting, **whistling**, **cheering**, and just making noise. I was cheering for the Sharks and my dad was whistling so loudly that people started looking at us. I was kind of embarrassed, but he didn't care. After the game we stopped at a **snack shop** and got some drinks and a snack. I don't think I'll ever forget that game.

重点词句

half 半场
quarter 一节(篮球比赛)
play soft on sb. 让着某人
signed jersey 签名的球衣
in all 总共
atmosphere 气氛
whistle 吹口哨
cheer 欢呼
snack shop 快餐店

Part 3
Sports in General

1. What are the benefits of sport (or exercise)?

   Exercise keeps you healthy. **It's been proven that** people who exercise more **get sick** less. When you exercise it helps **build your strength** to **fight sickness**. I have a friend who has a bad back and if he doesn't run, play basketball, or exercise in some way then his back will go out and he'll have to stay in bed until it is better.

   It's been proven that 经证明
   get sick 生病
   build one's strength 增强体力
   fight sickness 对抗疾病

2. What kinds of sports facilities exist in your community?

   I live near a university and my friends and I often go there to exercise. It has **football fields, tracks, badminton, volleyball**, and **tennis courts**, and other kinds of exercise equipment. There is also a **weight room** and **taekwondo** lessons. So I think that my community has quite a good **assortment** of sports facilities available.

   football field 足球场
   track 跑道
   badminton court 羽毛球场
   volleyball court 排球场
   tennis court 网球场
   weight room 力量器械室
   taekwondo 跆拳道
   assortment 多种多样

3. Do men and women play the same kind of sports?

   It really depends on the person, because I know some girls who are a lot more athletic than most guys are. But **for the most part**, girls generally don't play most of the **rougher**, **aggressive** sports. An American friend of mine told me that many of the men there like to play American football and even though some girls will join the game, most of them will just sit on the side and watch or do something else.

   for the most part 大体上
   rough 粗野的,粗犷的
   aggressive 有进攻性的

4. How do you think the government could encourage more people to exercise and participate in sport?

   Advertisements are some of the biggest ways people are influenced either for or against something.

If the government would air some very **catchy**, **appealin**g ads on TV or maybe even hold a public competition where the winners get a **monetary** prize, that would work, for me at least. I can't really think of anything else that would work, but that would be their **best shot** because that's what most people will respond to.

catchy 容易记住的　　monetary 金钱的

appealing 吸引人的　　best shot 尽力能做的事

5. Do you think children should be encouraged from a young age to participate in competitive sports (or team sports)?

I don't really think that it's good if children are taught at a young age to be competitive. If you can teach the child how to play competitive sports without stressing that winning is the only way that you can have fun then I guess it's okay. But personally I think that's a bit **unrealistic** because everyone wants to win, and if kids don't win their natural reaction is to cry or get mad. This doesn't really help them in life. When they grow up they'll find that you don't always win **the first time around**, you just have to keep trying and keep going on with your life.

unrealistic 不现实的　　the first time around 第一次

Live Sports Events

6. Do you prefer to watch sports events on TV at home or to watch them live? (Why?)

I prefer watching sports on TV, because sometimes you're watching a game that looks like it'll be **loads of** fun but it turns out to be super boring where your team **gets creamed** and you feel like crying. If you are at the **stadium** watching the game there's nothing you can do but cry, but if you are at home you can just change the channel to something fun. Watching sports at home is also more **economical**, you can be watching 3 or 4 games for just a few mao an hour.

loads of 很多的　　stadium 体育馆

get creamed 惨败　　economical 省钱的

7. What are the advantages and disadvantages of going to see a live sports event, such as a football match, compared to watching the event at home on TV?

Like I said before, if you go to a sports event you have to stay and watch the whole thing, **whereas** if you stay at home you can change the channel or turn off the TV. Also you can see the game **close up** whereas if you're in the stadium then you'll see a faraway view of the game. One advantage of going to a sports event is that you can experience the excitement of the game. The game is so much more alive and real than if you were just watching it. You feel like if you **yell** louder then your team might actually have a greater chance of winning. Also if someone decides to **streak** at halftime then you won't have to worry about the sports channel switching to the **anchors** who talk about the game.

Like I said before 如我刚才所说 close up 近地，仔细地
whereas 但是 yell 吼
streak 飞跑 anchor 主持人

8. Does the ticket price to live sporting events affect decisions to attend?

Yes, I think the price is an extremely big **deciding factor**. Take the World Master's Cup in Shanghai for instance. If the **admission fee** was only 100 RMB, more than half of Shanghainese could've attended the game.

deciding factor 决定因素 admission fee 入场费

三、话题相关材料

A 大型国际体育赛事英文名称

篮球

NBA 美国职业篮球联赛
The Eastern Conference 东部联队
The Western Conference 西部联队
Playoffs 延长赛
NBA Draft 美国职业篮球联赛选秀赛

足球

FIFA World Cup 世界杯足球赛
FA Premier League 英格兰足球超级联赛
European Championship 欧洲冠军杯
Asian Cup 亚洲杯
UEFA Champions League（European Cup）欧洲俱乐部联赛
Serie A, Italian Football League 意大利足球甲级联赛
La Liga 西班牙足球甲级联赛

综合赛事

Olympic Games 奥运会
Asian Games 亚运会
Hurdling 跨栏
IAAF World Championships in Athletics 世界田径锦标赛

其他

World Table Tennis Championships 世界乒乓球锦标赛
Uber Cup 尤伯杯赛（世界女子羽毛球团体锦标赛）
Thomas Cup 汤姆斯杯赛（世界男子羽毛球团体锦标赛）
F1 一级方程式赛车
Australian Open 澳大利亚网球公开赛
The Wimbledon Championships 温布尔登网球公开赛

B 2006年圣诞前夜，NBA休斯顿火箭队以97:78客场战胜西部联队冠军圣安东尼奥马刺队。下面是美国体育有线电视台ESPN对这场比赛的概括(略有删剪)，考生可以感受一下西方体育报道的语言风格。

Rockets, without McGrady, Dominate Spurs on the Road

SAN ANTONIO （AP)—The Houston Rockets hope Friday night was the start of a new era against the San Antonio Spurs.

Yao Ming scored 22 points and the Rockets beat the Spurs 97–78 for their first victory in San Antonio in over nine years.

San Antonio had won 17 straight home games against the Rockets and seven in a row overall. Houston's last road win against the Spurs was a 103-94 decision on April 20, 1997.

Manu Ginobili had 23 points for the Spurs, who finished with a season-low point total. Tony Parker followed with 21 and Tim Duncan had 14 points and 11 rebounds.

"My teammates did a great job, a huge job in the second half," Yao said. "They showed a lot of energy. They put the life into the game."

Parker said his team did just the opposite.

"We were definitely flat, had no energy," he said, "and they just came out very strong, played more physical and made shots."

Yao's performance wasn't on par with his recent games, the last four of which he scored more than 30 points, but he did enough to lead the Rockets. He scored 14 of his 22 points in the first quarter but had four fouls about midway through the third.

He sat out the rest of the period and played just about 4 minutes in the final quarter, when he picked up his fifth foul.

The Rockets took a 30–21 lead into the second quarter, with Yao scoring 14 points in the first. They extended the advantage with an 8–0 run in the second. The Spurs missed five straight shots during the second-quarter surge.

At the end of the third period a visibly angry Duncan was given a technical for complaining about his third foul in the quarter. The Rockets led 74–59 after three.

The Rockets were again without Tracy McGrady, who has missed six games because of back spasms. The Rockets are 2–4 without him in the lineup.

C 下面表格中是一个描述体育赛事的小模板，考生可以把自己喜欢的赛事套进去试一下。

运动、赛事综述	**As my favorite sport** is ______, **I'd like to talk about** __________. I guess **it's one of the greatest shows on earth** and it attracts so many people from so many countries.

时间、大体情况、跟谁看、感叹	You know, the __________ comes ___________. I watch it faithfully every ________. Thirty-two teams compete for the ____________, I watched this year's game ________, with _______________. They're also _______________ fans but we support different teams, which made the watching more fun.
突出转到明星	**The best match** was of course the final, between ____________ and _____________. It was absolutely **incredible**. My favorite player is _______________. **He's sort of my hero**, and he is handsome too. In the end, ______________scored ______________ and defeated ________________________.
为什么喜欢运动、喜欢明星，体育无界限	**Speaking of the reasons why I like this event**, I think **first of all**, when I watch a game, I feel excited and happy to see all these players and also a bit nervous. It's so beautiful and **I feel attached** to the game. **Secondly**, ____________ brings people together, it transcends politics and social classes. It is a sport that unites the world in the most unique way. Anyone can play it, from the richest to the poorest of people.

四、练习

A 请将下列句子翻译成英文。

1. 体育馆里的气氛很好，有大喊的，有吹口哨的，有欢呼的，有弄出其他声音的。

____

2. 锻炼让你保持健康，有人曾证明多锻炼的人得病的几率要小很多。

____

3. 如果小孩子没有赢，他们的自然反应就是哭或者恼怒，而这样对他们将来的生活不会有任何帮助。因为当他们长大后，他们会发现我们不可能做什么事情都一次成功，最重要的是要不断去努力，生活也要继续。

____

____

____

4. 比赛比你在电视上看到的要更加火爆和真实。你觉得好像你吼的声音再大一点，你喜欢的球队获胜的机会可能就会更多一分。

____

____

5. 而且(在现场看时)如果有人在半场的时候飞跑，你也不用担心镜头马上会转向解说比赛的主持人。

____

(☞ P272)

B 听 MP3 实战演练。

Topic 17 Foreign Cultures 外国文化

一、考试说明

针对本话题卡，考生要向考官描述自己感兴趣的外国文化，第三部分会围绕文化交流和全球化展开讨论。在“真题演练”部分 native speaker 讲述的是自己在哥斯达黎加的经历，的确让人羡慕。在“话题相关材料”部分，考生可以看到国外网友大谈自己感兴趣的文化，意大利、埃及、印度、日本，你喜欢哪一种文化呢？

二、真题演练

CUE CARD

Describe a foreign culture that you are interested in.

You should say:

what this culture is

how you learned about this culture

what you know about this culture

and explain why you feel this culture is interesting.

点题	I have spent most of my time learning Chinese and Chinese culture, but I did have an interesting experience about a year and a half ago that **inspired** me to learn about Costa Rican culture.
了解途径	One of my friends spent a semester abroad in Costa Rica in early 2005, and I spent two weeks at the beginning of the summer visiting him there. **Prior to** visiting, I knew almost nothing about the culture, but staying there, even for such a short time, really **opened my eyes.**
特别之处	Costa Rican culture is extremely different from either American or Chinese culture. Two of the phrases most often used in Costa Rica are **a good illustration** of their culture: *pura vida* and *tranquilo*. *Pura vida* translates as “pure life” and *tranquilo* means “calm”. Both are used in situations where the level of stress is rising. When Costa Ricans say this phrase, they are telling themselves or others “Don’t worry. **Chill out**.” It’s an extremely **laid-back**, relaxed culture. Their main goal in life is to be happy. Workdays tend to be shorter, and since the country is so small and borders both the Atlantic and Pacific Oceans, it is really easy to go to the beach, so many do just that. When I was there, it was routine to see people getting up around 6 am, go to the beach and surf for two or three hours, work from 10-4, go home and eat, then go back to the beach.
感受	It was great to see a culture with such a different **outlook on life**.

重点词句

inspire 激发

prior to 在…之前

open one's eyes 开阔眼界

a good illustration 很好的例子

chill out 放松

laid-back 松弛的

outlook on life 对生活的态度

Part 3
Learning about Other Cultures

1. Do you think it's important to know about other cultures?

   I do think it's extremely important to learn about other cultures. Not only can you find out interesting things, but it makes it easier to interact with those people if you ever come in contact with them. Also, it makes it a lot easier to do business with those cultures. It's important to be educated about the world and not just **shut yourself into** your own country.

   shut oneself into 封闭自己

2. How can we benefit from learning about other cultures?

   Several ways that people can benefit from other cultures are in business, personal relationships, and just in self-improvement. In business, it is necessary to know a little bit about whatever culture you plan to work with. For instance, I think in Muslim cultures, shaking hands with your left hand is considered extremely rude. If you didn't know that, it could hurt your chances of doing business. Also, it's important just to improve yourself by learning as much as you can, and culture is a good subject.

3. What do you think is the best way to learn about another culture?

   Obviously, the best way to learn about a culture is to go there and experience it. If you can get a feel for the culture **firsthand**, it will be a lot easier to pick things up. But I also believe that you can learn a ton about other cultures just by reading books about them. Reading about people's experiences in foreign lands is the **next best thing** to being there.

   firsthand 直接地

   next best thing 紧次于最好的事情

4. Do you think that learning foreign languages can help us understand foreign cultures?

   I'm not sure that just learning the language is a good way to learn about a culture, but most places where you would learn a language would help you learn about the culture, so indirectly, yes. The language alone isn't great for understanding culture. For instance, German is a really **harsh** language, but Germans aren't harsh people. You really need to study more than the language if you want to get to know a culture.

   harsh 粗糙的，刺耳的

5. Do you think it's better to go overseas to study a foreign language or to study it in your home

country?

I think it is better to study a language in its native country. When you do that, you are **engulfed** in the language and forced to encounter it outside of the classroom. Otherwise, your only **exposure** to the language is when you're studying or in the classroom. I know firsthand that when learning a foreign language in your home country, it is easy to lose what you have learned.

engulf 吞没　　exposure 接触

Globalization

6. What is your understanding of the term "globalization"?

Globalization, in my mind, is the idea that the world is becoming smaller, so societies can interact and exchange culture more easily and more efficiently. Unfortunately, because some countries are richer and have more influence than others, certain cultures get spread around more than others. On the whole, however, globalization is a good thing because it is not only culture that gets spread, but things like information and medicine that can help people.

7. Do you think globalization is a good thing?

Yes, globalization has its problems, but for the most part, it is good for most people involved. Some people have different opinions because they are really concerned with the loss of culture, but for me, the benefits outweigh the drawbacks. People have access to more information, so diseases can be better treated, food can be made more efficiently, and goods that make people's lives easier are now available.

8. Do you think it's easier to learn about other cultures today than it was before?

Yes, of course it is. All you have to do is to look at art from long ago about foreign cultures and you can see the lack of knowledge people had. Today, with the Internet and the number of books available, it is almost impossible to be ignorant. It is so easy to learn about anything you want.

三、话题相关材料

A 补充语汇

language learning 语言学习	exposure 暴露；接触
academic skills 学术技能	communication skills 交流技能
rote learning 死记硬背	cross-cultural communication 跨文化交际
memorise 记忆	cultural background 文化背景
positive effects 积极作用	cultural difference 文化差异
intellectual growth 智力发育	cultural identity 文化特性
broaden horizons 开阔视野	

B “真题演练”中的拉丁文化的确让人着迷，还有什么其他文化让你特别向往吗？下面是国外网友的答案。

Is There a Specific Foreign Culture Which Fascinates You?

意大利

Hmmm...all cultures interest me because they are all different. I've been blessed enough to travel to three different countries besides my own which were France, Switzerland and Italy. While all three were down right gorgeous and had something different to offer, I fell in love with Italy so much that I am going there for a year after graduation. We visited three cities... Rome, Assisi, and Florence...it was like a dream. It had everything I've ever wanted. Italy has been the birthplace of many things for thousands of years so there is a lot of history, art, and culture. And the people are just fantastic...or in general they are at least. A friend and I stopped in some sort of deli in Assisi to get a sandwich...we ended up talking to the owner and his daughter for hours...he did not speak much English and we didn't have a clue about the Italian language so it was an experience. I had so much fun and I can't wait to go back!

埃 及

I love Egyptian culture. I just think it's so fascinating and so wonderful. I want to go to Egypt one day. Then I also love Asian cultures, their customs, fashion, and art is pretty amazing. And I think Mayan culture was very impressive in knowledge and architecture. So basically I'm fascinated by many cultures. Greek, Roman, Celtic and Latin American cultures are very warm and interesting too.

印 度

I have met several people from India, and they have such gracious manners, and the ones I have met were very intelligent. I also find Hindu art and stories fascinating, as I am a polytheist myself. I also think the modern India, with its rapid development in the high tech world, is interesting and deserves attention.

日 本

I'm a big Japanese fan! I utterly love it. It's totally where I want to go to one day. I think the people and culture are amazing. It's just very attractive to me. One thing I don't like though is the whaling. But otherwise I think the West could learn a lot from the Japanese.

I see Japan as a blend of highly advanced technology meets environmentalism because although it is so technologically advanced there is a respect for nature there. Also there isn't really Christianity or Islam there, there is Shintoism and Buddhism, both of which I have zero problem with at all. The language is complex and hard to learn（for a foreigner）but I want to learn. Crime is rare and violent crime isn't really existent there. I think Japan is rated second in the world for the least amount of murder. Unlike the West, sex isn't advertised so in-your-face there, and they uphold traditions, which is very important. The people are polite, friendly, respectable, honourable...

四、练习

A 请将下列句子翻译成英文。

1. 去之前，我对那儿的文化基本上一无所知；但是去了那儿以后，即使是待很短一段时间都让我大开眼界。

   ____

2. 那是一种非常悠闲、非常放松的文化，他们生活的主要目标就是要活得开心。

   ____

3. 了解这个世界是很重要的，而不应该只是把目光局限在自己的国家。

   ____

4. 读一读别人在国外的经历也很棒，仅次于自己去那些地方。

   ____

5. 有些人有异议，因为他们很关切文化的消亡。但对我来说，全球化的好处要多于坏处。

   ____

（☞ P272）

B 听 MP3 实战演练。

物品类核心级(Topics 18~20)

Topic 18　Clothing and Fashion 服饰和时尚

一、考试说明

关于服装时尚的话题是雅思口语考试中的老话题。考生向考官描述完自己喜欢的服饰后，在第三部分里会围绕时尚和传统等话题与其展开讨论。大家可以看到在“真题演练”部分 native speaker 描述的是自己买的靴子。针对话题卡中前三个问题，她只用了寥寥数语。然而在回答最后一个问题“为什么”的时候却讲出了一大段原因，看似有点比例失调，但这才是最自然的答案，因为考生在自己准备答案的时候没有必要非得把每个小问题都回答得很充实，4 个问题中找到自己最能“侃”的跟考官说，其他几题稍微涉及，这也是保证自己能够说 1-2 分钟的重要技巧。

二、真题演练

CUE CARD
Describe an item of clothing that you recently bought.
You should say:
what it is
when and where you bought it
what it looks like
and explain why you bought it.

点题	The last item of clothing that I bought was a pair of boots. I bought them when I went to the Silk Market **on my day off**.
描述服饰	They are black, tall, and soft. They also look very smart. This pair caught my eye because they were simple and **matched** my clothes and **accessories**.
购买原因	I chose them because boots can be worn on many different occasions and still be appropriate. Also in the winter it's very cold here in Beijing and it's good to have some warm shoes to wear when you go out. It is popular to wear shoes that have **pointy** or **tight** toes, but to me this style looks silly and is very uncomfortable. My boots give my feet plenty of room to be comfortable without looking **clumsy** and bulky. I'm a little bit short, so I like these boots because they have a high enough **heel** to make me look **average** without being **awkward** or difficult to walk in. Now of course one of the most important things for me besides the style is the price and that is what attracted me to these boots. My friends all tell me that if I went to Europe or America, my boots would have **cost me an arm and a leg**. **No pun intended**. Here in China my boots are very **reasonably priced**. I guess that would be the final reason why I bought them.

重点词句

on my day off 在我休息日的时候

match 搭配

accessories 配饰

pointy 尖的

tight 紧的

clumsy 笨拙的

heel 鞋跟

average 中等的

awkward 不舒服

cost (sb.) an arm and a leg 极贵的

No pun intended. 没开玩笑。

reasonably priced 价格合理的

Part 3
Buying Clothes

1. What type of clothes do you like?

   I mostly like older styles, such as those during the 60s. I also like newer styles like some kinds of **punk** clothes. I like skirts and dresses best. **Loose** types of clothing are most comfortable. I like to have nice, neat, stylish clothing, too.

   punk 朋克(如破衣服、铁链、染发)

   stylish 时髦的，漂亮的

   loose 宽松的

2. How do people choose what style of clothing to buy?

   Many people buy clothing because it's a new style or it's a colour that they like. Often people will buy something because it looks like what a favorite movie star or singer wears. Other people buy clothes that suit them, or that they will wear most often. Other people just buy clothes because they are **functional**.

   functional 实用的

3. Do you think the brand of clothing is important?

   Personally I don't really care about the **brand** of clothing as long as what I buy is **good quality**. Famous brands are usually too expensive for me so I will rarely buy them. Often I can find inexpensive brands that are just as good a quality and very nice. Of course here in China you can get **brand name** clothes at a very cheap price.

   brand 牌子

   brand name 品牌

   good quality 好质量

4. Why do some people buy brand-name clothes?

   Many people buy brand name clothing because they like the style. However, some people simply want their clothes to last a long time, so they buy a certain brand of clothing that is known for its good quality. Other people buy brand name clothing because they feel it makes them look more stylish and **hip**. Some people just like to have that name on their clothing. I think it might make them feel important.

   hip 时髦的

5. Compare the materials and fashions of today's clothing with those of the past.

In my opinion, older fashions changed more slowly and gradually from one to another. They **faded** into each other. Fashions of today change **drastically** in a very short period of time. Often certain clothes will only **be in style** for one year or so before another, very different style is in. Of course there are more choices to choose now.

fade 逐渐褪变　　be in style 正在流行

drastically 急剧地

6. Do men and women have the same shopping habits when they buy clothes?

No, they have very different **shopping habits**. Often men will shop less and only because they need new clothes. They often do not buy much, and they will spend less money on what they buy. Actually I think that they **dread** shopping and probably would rather go to the dentist. Women buy clothes more often and usually pay more for their clothing. Often they will buy new clothes because they want to be in style. I think women also don't mind spending money as long as it's their boyfriend's or husband's.

shopping habits 购物习惯　　dread 怕，担忧

7. Sometimes factory workers and very often school students have to wear uniforms. What do you think of this?

I think it helps reduce competition in the work or school area. When the workers or students don't feel that they have to **keep up with** someone else's clothes or style, they are able to **concentrate on** work or study. The bad side to it is that if the uniform is uncomfortable or does not look very smart or stylish, it makes work or school unpleasant for some people. Also it can make people feel that they have no **individuality** and are just like everyone else.

keep up with 跟上　　individuality 个性

concentrate on 集中注意力于

Fashion

8. How much do overseas fashion trends influence China?

Overseas fashion treads, **especially** the Korean styles, greatly affect the styles in China. For young people, dressing like the young people do overseas is very important. Often a style will come into China a bit later than it does to the rest of the western world, but when it **catches on** in China it spreads very quickly. When you travel to cities such as Shanghai or Dalian you can really see the influence of foreign fashion here in China.

especially 特别　　catch on 变得流行

9. Do you think it is good that people in China follow foreign fashion trends?

I think many Chinese feel better about themselves if they dress more fashionably. Especially for young people, the way they dress is like their status, though dress is very important in all levels of society. With TV and fashion models and more money here in China, it is a lot easier to follow these trends.

三、话题相关材料

A 补充语汇

jacket 夹克	bra 胸罩
sweater 毛衣	scarf 围巾
long-sleeved 长袖的	sportswear 运动衣
short-sleeved 短袖的	jersey 球衣
close-fitting 紧身的	hoodie 带帽子的外套
V-neck V 领的	wedding gown 婚纱
round neck 圆领的	Cheongsam（Qi Pao）旗袍
T-shirt T 恤	Mao suit 中山装
high-heeled shoes 高跟鞋	sweatshirt 厚汗衫
pajama 睡衣	cotton 棉
underwear 内衣	wool 羊毛

B 实用语句

What Is Your Favourite Item of Clothing?

1. Years ago, I moved into a new house, and someone had left behind an old red and black flannel shirt. I am wearing it now. It is too big, full of holes, but so warm and comfy. I use it as a robe, a coat, a blanket on the couch. Handy old shirt!
2. My hooded sweatshirt...I live in this thing, man. Sleep, eat, and go to school in it. Most comfortable thing ever...
3. Mine isn't clothing. It's jewelry. A dolphin necklace I have had since I was 14. It turned out to be my good luck charm so I wear it every day.
4. I like everything comfortable and stylish, but not too vulgar of course. I carefully pick my clothes and outfits, but at the same I don't want to look like I spent hours putting it all together. I love skinny jeans, turtlenecks, hoodies (not the oversize ones), cute jackets, tweed coats.
5. I have a pair of grey fleece sweatpants that I am actually wearing now. They are so soft and comfortable! I put them on as soon as I get home from work.

四、练习

A 将下列句子翻译成英文。

1. 我一眼就看到了这双鞋，它们简单漂亮，很容易跟我的其他衣服相配。

____

2. 我之所以选这件衣服就是因为我在很多场合都可以穿，而且都挺得体的。

____

3. 宽松的衣服穿着很舒服，同样，我也很喜欢干干净净很时尚的衣服。

____

4. 如今的时尚变化太大太快，往往一种款式也就流行一年左右，紧接着，另一种完全不同的款式又开始流行起来。

____

5. 只要是舒服和漂亮的我都喜欢，当然不能太过恶俗。我很精心地选配衣服，但同时又不想让人感觉自己属于那种花上几个钟头搭配衣服的人。

____

B 将服装类型跟它们的具体描述匹配起来。

A. Punk

B. Hip-hop

C. Cheongsam

D. Kilt

E. Mao suit

1. baggy jeans, baggier sweatshirts, gleaming white sneakers
2. A long dress with a high collar and slit skirt, traditionally worn by Chinese women
3. knee-length skirt with deep pleats, usually of a tartan wool, worn as part of the dress for men in the Scottish Highlands
4. the style of male attire known in China as the Zhongshan suit, named after Sun Zhongshan The Western name comes from its popularization by Mao Zedong.
5. brightly-colored hair, chains and pins and torn clothing.

（☞ P272）

C 听 MP3 实战演练。

Topic 19 Wild Animals 野生动物

一、考试说明

口语考试中与动物相关的话题卡有两类：一为描述一个小动物或宠物，一为描述自己喜欢的野生动物。接下来的第三部分问题通常围绕人与动物的关系、物种保护、动物权利等展开。此类题目虽然出现频率低，但由于所涉及的语言资源对绝大部分考生而言都比较陌生，因此成为了雅思口语中的难题。在"真题演练"部分外教描述的是东北虎。在"话题相关材料"部分，考生可以看到对金丝猴和藏羚羊的介绍，相信从中能发现更多语言资源。

二、真题演练

CUE CARD

Describe a wild animal in China.

You should say:

what the animal is

what it looks like

where it lives

and explain how you feel about this animal.

点题	I'll describe an endangered animal in northeastern China. It's called the **Manchurian or Siberian tiger**.
描述	Manchurian tigers are very impressive animals. Like all tigers, they have orange and black **stripes** and a white **underside**, and powerful **claws** and teeth. The largest are nearly 1.5 meters tall, and can weigh between 300 and 400 kilos of muscle! They're the largest of the cat family, and the most effective and dangerous hunters. They're found all over Siberia and in a few places in northeastern China. They usually hunt and live alone, and only meet other tigers during the **mating season**. I think there are less than 50 of them in the wild in China. There are more kept in **captivity**, in zoos or special parks. There is one wildlife park in Harbin that is famous for its many Manchurian tigers.
感受	Most Chinese admire the tiger as a symbol of strength and **fierceness**. Tigers have had a place in Chinese culture for thousands of years. They are found in Chinese literature new and old, and are the subject of many famous paintings. But I don't think many Chinese know that this special **breed** of tigers is **all but wiped out** in the wild. I hope more efforts will be made in the future to protect the tiger's environment. Without the forests they live and hunt in, Manchurian tigers can only exist in captivity.

重点词句

Manchurian / Siberian tiger 东北虎
stripe 条纹
underside 底面
claw 爪子
mating season 交配季节
captivity 囚禁，束缚
fierceness 凶猛
breed 品种
all but 几乎
wipe out 消灭

Part 3

Pets

1. Do many people in China like to have a pet?

   I think the number of Chinese who like pets is less than half the total population. Many Chinese are afraid of common pets. I think it's very funny, but some are really scared of animals, even very tiny and harmless ones. This may be because of something in their childhood, I don't know. There are many people in China who like pets, but not the majority, for sure.

2. What kinds of pets are most popular in China?

   Dogs and cats are by far the most common. I think the single most common pet is either the **Pekingese dog** or the **Pug dog**. I think they are both quite ugly, but sometimes they're so ugly they're cute. A lot of people also keep guard dogs to protect their property.

   Pekingese dog 京巴犬　　pug dog 哈巴狗

3. What are some of the advantages and disadvantages of having a pet?

   A pet can be a good friend; sometimes the best friend. Pets are also great playmates for children. I think it's very good for kids to have a pet when growing up. The disadvantages are that pets are expensive to feed and care for, and require a lot of time, depending on the kind of pet.

4. Do you think there should be laws to protect the welfare of pets and farm animals?

   I don't really know. I guess there should be laws, but we really shouldn't need them. People should be responsible enough to treat pets and farm animals well. But since many people are too selfish to care, we must have some laws. But the laws shouldn't become so important that they nearly equal laws protecting the welfare of human beings.

Protection of Wild Animals

5. Are there any wild animals in China that are not found in any other country?

   Yes. The **giant panda** and the **Tibetan antelope**. There are probably also some birds and other animals that are only found here, but I don't know anything about them. It's sad, but the animals that are found only in China are the ones that are the most endangered. I think that's the same for other countries, though.

giant panda 大熊猫　　Tibetan antelope 藏羚羊

6. How do Chinese people feel about the protection of wild animals?

Many Chinese are only now beginning to learn about the importance of protecting wild animals, as well as the environment they live in. The new generations are being taught to respect wild animals. But people never even see them except on TV, so they only have a vague idea of the need to protect them. I admire the many brave people who have made sacrifices to protect wild animals, like the Kekexili mountain patrol. There was a recent movie made about them.

7. What do you think are some of the benefits to humans of protecting wild animals?

I'm not sure what benefits there are, but I know that everything in nature is there for a reason. If one species dies out, it can upset the balance of nature and do a lot of damage **in the long run**. Wild animals don't always directly affect people, but often, they fill a special role in the balance that we are also part of, and affect other species or plants that we are directly dependent on. So we should protect them, because we may be protecting ourselves without knowing it.

in the long run 长期来看

8. What is the purpose of having zoos?

Zoos are really a **compromise**, I think. They are a way for people who live in the city, especially children, to see wild animals. But I think that unless the zoos are the best quality, they shouldn't be operated, as it's cruel to keep wild animals in small cages or dirty surroundings. High standard zoos can be good, as they educate the general public about the world around them. But I still think it would be better if people could learn about animals straight from nature, not seeing them in zoos.

compromise 妥协

9. How do you think zoos in China could be improved?

Many zoos in China are poorly equipped, due to lack of funding. Zoos are not so popular or common. I think that they could be improved by more cooperation with other zoos in the west that are well-operated and have good techniques and facilities we can learn from.

三、话题相关材料

A 补充语汇

动物的外貌

horn 角　　muscular 强健的

large ear 大耳朵　　natural habitat 自然栖息地

动物的品性

loyal 忠诚的　　intelligent 聪明的

faithful 忠实的　　cuddly 令人想拥抱的

affectionate 充满爱的，温柔的　　brave 勇敢的

obedient 顺从的	easy to train 容易驯养的
easy to care for 好养活的	
动物的作用	
good company 好伙伴	food chain 食物链
a rich source of pleasure and fun 愉悦和乐趣的源泉	gene pool 基因库
drive off one's loneliness 驱走孤独感	animal rights 动物权利
nurture a love for nature 培养对大自然的热爱	animal welfare 动物福利
Olympic mascot 奥运吉祥物	poach 偷猎
extinction 灭绝	die out 灭绝
ecosystem 生态系统	safari park 野生动物园（游客可驾车观看动物）
endangered species 濒危物种	conservation 保护

B 金丝猴和藏羚羊也是我国的珍稀物种，下面是有关它们的英文介绍。

金丝猴

Chinese children are very familiar with the legend of a magical monkey called "Sunwukong"（Monkey King）, who helps the weak with kindness, and fights evil with justice. But the real monkeys are fighting mankind for their own survival. There are three species of Golden Monkeys who all live in the forests of China, with some species in the mountains. Golden monkeys live in large groups into the hundreds. They seem to have a hierarchical society, like baboons, and inhabit the bamboo jungles, coniferous forests, and rhododendron thickets found in the high mountains of central and western China. This area is snowbound in the winter. To adapt to the cold, golden monkeys have developed robust bodies and long thick fur, particularly over their shoulders.

Golden monkeys are rare and obscure, and they're just beginning to be studied. They are highly endangered, so it's a race to study them before they disappear. The monkeys are killed for their beautiful fire-orange fur and also their bones, which are believed by Asians to hold special medicinal powers. State-run nature reserves were set up, but illegal hunting continued because the monkey's brain is considered a delicacy in some local cuisines.

藏羚羊

The Tibetan antelope is a medium-sized bovid which is about 1.2 metres（4 feet）in height. It is native to the Tibetan plateau including China's Tibet Autonomous Region, Qinghai province, and Xinjiang province. The Tibetan antelope is also known commonly by its Tibetan name "chiru." The coat is grey to reddish-brown, with a white underside. The males have long, curved-back horns which measure about 50 cm（20 inches）in length.

Chirus are gregarious, sometimes congregating in herds hundreds strong. Chirus live on the high mountain steppes and semi-desert areas of the Tibetan plateau such as Kekexili, where they feed on various forb and grass species. The average life span is about eight years.

Chirus are listed as endangered by the World Conservation Union and the United States Fish and Wildlife Service due to commercial poaching for their underwool, competition with local domesticated herds, and the development of their rangeland for gold mining. The Chiru's wool, known as shahtoosh, is warm, soft and fine. The wool can only be obtained by killing the animal; Chiru numbers have dropped accordingly from nearly a million (estimated) at the turn of the 20th century to less than 75,000 today.

The Chiru was selected as one of the five official mascots for the 2008 Summer Olympics in Beijing, China. The mascot, named "Yingying," was one of the "Five Friendlies" of the 2008 Olympics and represented the blessing of health.

四、练习：

A 请将下列句子翻译成英文。

1. 它们通常独自捕猎和生活，只有在交配季节才与其他老虎相会。

   ____

2. 几千年来，虎一直在中国文化中占有一席之地。古今文学中都有它们的影子，它们也是很多名画的主题。

   ____

3. 我希望将来人们能做更多的是事来保护老虎生存的环境。

   ____

4. 很多中国人现在才开始了解保护野生动物以及它们生存的环境的重要性。

   ____

5. 野生动物不一定会直接影响人类，但他们总会在人类所生活其中的生态平衡中扮演特殊的角色，影响人类所赖以生存的动植物。

   ____

   ____

（☞ P273）

B 听MP3实战演练。

Topic 20 Electrical Appliances 电器

一、考试说明

平时人们离不了家用电器，在雅思口语考试中关于电器的话题也是个传统话题。很多考生可能会像“真题演练”中的 native speaker 那样描述自己的计算机，因为毕竟计算机最常用，而且也容易描述。但很明显这样的选材有点太落俗套，考生也可以考虑参考“话题相关材料”部分提供的词汇和补充材料，选择更具时代特色和新意的电器去描述，效果可能会更好。

二、真题演练

CUE CARD
Describe a useful electrical appliance (e.g. a mobile phone or computer) that you use at home or at work.
You should say:
what it is
where it is
how you use it
and explain why this item is important to you.

点题	The most useful piece of equipment is my computer. I use it for both my work and for **recreation**.
描述	It is a **laptop**, so I can take it with me wherever I go. I usually keep it on the **dresser** at the end of my bed, though when I use it, I am usually on my bed or in my armchair.
用途 + **评价**	I use it for my research, and to read assignments that I have been given. I also use it for my work and writing. It is important to me because I have all of my most important information on it. If I didn't have it my life would be so much more difficult because I would have many problems finding all the different things I need to do my work. I also use it to listen to music so I would have a hard time listening to music if I didn't have it. Often my mother will ask me to type something up for her and I like to use my laptop for that because **I'm accustomed to** using the keyboard on it. Then I can type faster because I don't have to get used to a new keyboard, and I make less mistakes.

重点词句

recreation 消遣

laptop 笔记本电脑

dresser 梳妆台

be accustomed to 习惯于

Part 3
Electrical Appliances

1. Have computers (the items you chose to talk about) changed much over the years?

   Yes, computers have changed so much since they first **came out**. The first computer took up a whole, huge room. Today, computers are so small you can put them easily into a **shoulder bag**. Some are even small enough to fit into your pocket.

   come out 问世

   shoulder bag 肩挎包

2. What kinds of electrical appliances are used most?

   I use computers every day and they are used in almost every area of my life. I also use printers often to print out the information that I have put together on my computer and give it to someone else. In my kitchen there are also some electrical appliances that I use every day like **toasters**, microwaves, and refrigerators. A **coffee maker** is an appliance not used much here in China, but probably is used more in the U.S. and Europe.

   toaster 烤面包机

   coffee maker 咖啡机

3. Do you think we can live without electrical appliances?

   I think it is possible for people to live without electrical appliances. However, people are so used to having them and living with them that I think it would be very difficult, especially if the change is very sudden. I think that it's not good for people to be so dependent on machines to do things for them. I think that people should learn how to live and do things without machines and appliances so that if there is ever a time when they don't have them, it will be easier to adjust.

4. Do you think science and technology will one day completely eliminate traditional skills and equipment?

   I think that it is very possible, but I don't think that this is good. Right now it's very hard to **keep up with** technology so what would it be like if it was all replaced? It is almost hard to **fathom**. Well you know if we ever run out of oil it seems to me that a lot of the technology would change.

   keep up with 跟上

   fathom 理解

5. How do you think electrical appliances will develop in the future?

   I think we will have electrical appliances that will do many of the jobs and duties that require less thinking. Jobs like cooking, cleaning, and repairing may soon be **taken over** by machines and very **intelligent** appliances. We may soon have appliances that can have dinner on the table by the time a mother and father have come home from work and the child has come home from school. We may have appliances that will clean the house and **make the beds**, **fix the sink** and paint the walls.

take over 控制，接管

intelligent 智能的

make the bed 铺床

fix the sink 修水槽

Office Equipment

6. What are some of the different forms of electronic communication that people use in offices today?

   The most common form of communication in the office is email. Even between people next to or near each other it is becoming more common to just type out an email or **memo**. Another very common form of communication is the phone. No matter where someone is they will almost always have an office phone or a cell phone.

   memo (供同一机构内不同部门间传阅的)通报字条；备忘录

7. What are the effects of using such electronic forms of communication?

   One of the main effects of using electronic communication is that the communications become less personal. There is a feeling of just communicating with machines and not talking to a human. Of course, it is much more convenient to be able to send an email to someone rather than going to where they are to ask them or tell them something. It is also much quicker to call someone than to find them and talk to them personally.

Inventions

8. Do you think people rely too much on machines nowadays?

   I think that many people rely too greatly on machines. They seem to forget that there are people around them. It is easy to become completely absorbed in computers or phones or **PDAs** or MP3 players. People will more often turn to their machines for entertainment rather than spending time with others or getting exercise.

   PDA(Personal Digital Assistant)掌上电脑

9. What are the advantages that we get from using modern home and office equipment?

   There are some advantages to using modern home and office equipment. One of the main ones is that more things get done and often we can complete projects and assignments very quickly. We are also able to do things that we wouldn't have been able to do before, like working at home. Also, because we are able to finish things quickly we have more time for other activities that we wish to do.

10. What do you think is the most useful thing that man has ever discovered?

    I think that the most important discovery was electricity. Without electricity we would not have any of the modern equipment that we have today. We would be unable to have phones, computers, lights, TVs, refrigerators, or music players. Electricity runs almost everything in our houses and work areas today.

三、话题相关材料

A 家庭和办公设备词汇

digital camera 数码相机	vacuum cleaner 吸尘器
PS（Play Station）电子游戏机	dish washer 洗碗机
MP3 player MP3 随身听	juicer 榨汁机
hair dryer 吹风机	humidifier 加湿器
water heater 电热水壶	steam iron 蒸汽熨斗

B 下面是国外顾客对某些电器用品的评价，很多语汇考生也可以使用。

Consumer Reviews of Domestic Appliances

Canon IXUS 700 

By **John Hutchison** from Scotland UK on 20th Feb 2006

Time Digital Camera Owned	6 – 12 Months
Image Quality	10/10
Battery Life	7/10
Features	10/10
Ease of Use	8/10
Value for Money	10/10
Overall Value	10/10

Good Points

Best outdoor camera I've had, and excellent indoor mid range to about 30 feet. "Zoom on Zoom" feature excellent for all the detail and ironing out the laugh lines afterwards. Superb quality pics.

Bad Points

Unless on continual shoot or video mode, seems to take just a wee bit too long to focus, and the "moment" can be lost.

General Comments

The Canon Ixus 700 is a super digital camera. It is lightweight, and takes excellent pictures. The only problem found so far is taking longish distance pictures inside gloomy buildings e.g. churches, and graduation halls, where the light is sort of "in between". I do manage to clean up pictures and enhance them, but it does take a bit of doing.

It is easy to use to start, but some features require a bit of practice. I'm still learning how to use all the features. Each new one enhances the previous pictures.

Philips Juicer

By AirScrew from Winchester on 9th Oct 2006

Good Points

Good juice.

Bad Points

Assembly.

Disassembly.

CLEANING!!!

General Comments

We have had the Philips HR1861 Pro Juicer for around 9 months. My wife used it daily for some weeks. It has not been used for months now, and I consider we are food and health conscious people. I tried to use it myself a few times in this last week, to take advantage of the quantity of apples in the garden. I am far from impressed. The assembly is fussy and illogical. The cutter refuses to be disabled by hand, and needs 2 screwdrivers (or spoon handles) to lever it out. Cleaning is a nightmare. It takes a full 10 minutes to disassemble, empty and then wash and rinse every piece.

The design team should be shot, or even better, be made to clean one every day for a month. And I say this as an engineer who does not know something about functional design.

四、练习

A 请将下列句子翻译成英文。

1. 计算机自问世以来变化很大。

____

2. 我觉得将来会有电器能执行一些不需要过多思考的工作和任务。

____

3. 电子通讯的主要影响之一就是沟通变得不像以前那样有人情味了。

____

4. 人们会从机器那儿寻求娱乐，而不是去社交或去锻炼。

____

5. 使用现代家庭和办公设备有一些优点。主要的一点就是我们可以做更多的事情，更快地完成一些工作和作业。

____

(☞ P273)

B 听MP3实战演练。

物品类进阶级(Topics 21~26)

Topic 21　An Important Letter 重要的信件

一、考试说明

本话题看似简单，但真正准备起来困难较大。随着 E-mail 的普及，手写的信件在生活中越来越不常见，所以考生还真得下一番功夫好好回忆有什么样的信件可以用来应对这个话题。当然家书、情书、job offer 等都是比较容易的选择。第三部分会涉及信件和电邮的区别、各自的优缺点以及科技对传统生活方式的冲击等。“话题相关材料”中列出了英国最常见的几种邮件寄送方式。

二、真题演练

CUE CARD
Describe an important letter that you received.
You should say:
who wrote it
when you received it
what the letter was about
and explain why it was important.

点题	A very important letter that I received actually came from my doctor believe it or not. I know that sounds a little strange coming from a young person like me.
信的来由	You see at the time I was in school and was working very hard and neglecting to take care of myself. I was so worried and stressed over my studies that, well, **number one** I wasn't eating very well. Then **on top of that**, I was spending so much time in the library that I wasn't going outside and getting any exercise. I noticed that I was starting to get sick easily and **kinda run-down**. It was really getting bad, even my friends noticed my lack of strength and energy and one of them **was** so **concerned about** me that he wrote and mentioned this to my parents, and my mom asked one of her friends who is a doctor to give me some advice.
信的内容	Well this doctor who I didn't even know wrote me a long letter and told me **flat out** that I really needed to have more balance in my life and make sure that I was getting all of the things that I already said I was missing.

重要性	So out to the **badminton court** I went whether I felt like it or not, eating a good healthy breakfast in the morning, slowing down and taking some time with my friends and then before I knew it I felt so much better. If this doctor hadn't taken the time to write me, I just don't know what would have happened to me. I think my life would be different and I might not even be sitting here talking with you.

重点词句

number one 其一
on top of that 除此之外，雪上加霜
kinda (=kind of) 〈口〉有一点
run-down 憔悴的
be concerned about 关心
flat out 直截了当
badminton court 羽毛球场地

Part 3
Letters

1. What are the different kinds of letters that the post office delivers?

   Well there are **bills** and things that you have to pay. Then there is a lot of **junk mail** and **advertisements**. The nice thing is when you get a personal letter from one of your friends. I suppose there would be some **credit card applications** and maybe **a bank statement. Birthday cards** and **Christmas cards** come through the mail, too.

   bills 账单
   junk mail 垃圾信件
   advertisements 广告
   credit card applications 信用卡申请
   a bank statement 对账单
   birthday cards 生日贺卡
   Christmas cards 圣诞贺卡

2. What can people do if they receive unwanted advertising in the mail?

   The best thing that they could do is simply drop it in the wastebasket. I suppose if they wanted to they could save them and tie them together and take them to the recycling center to make a little money. They could just put them in a corner and let them **stack up** and see if their friends are interested in them. If they have a pet they could use advertisements to line the inside of a bird cage or litter box, so it could **do its business** there.

   stack up 摞起来
   do its business 排便

3. Why do people write letters to newspapers?

   I think it is because people read newspapers and maybe something that they read affects them and they have something to say about it. Of course not everyone does this because some people are quieter in nature and would feel like writing and having it printed would be embarrassing. I really think that it depends on the nature of the person and what affects them. I don't know if I would do something like that unless an article really **got to me**.

get to sb. 惹恼某人

4. Do you think it is better to apply for a job by letter or by email?（Why?/Why not?）

Well, it really depends on the company, but a lot of companies do their business by email and so they might prefer that. If the company wanted a **hard copy** letter, well of course I would **oblige** them. I think because I am applying for the job, I would do whatever is convenient for the company.

hard copy 纸版的　　oblige 顺从，迁就

5. What do you think is the most difficult kind of letter to write?

I find it very difficult to write a letter **rejecting** someone. It's hard to tell them you don't want to date or whatever them and not hurt their feelings any more than you have to. You have to **word things carefully** and make sure they get the point, but be **subtle**.

reject 拒绝　　subtle 微妙的

word things carefully 仔细措辞

Emails

6. What are the advantages and disadvantages of emails compared to handwritten letters?

Well of course an obvious advantage is speed, getting it there quickly. Another advantage would be you don't need a paper, which would **save on the environment**, along with not needing a pen which again saves the environment. As to the disadvantages, well, a handwritten letter has a more **personal touch**, it shows that you took your time to sit down and gather all of the writing materials and also took time to go to the post office or put it in the mailbox to get it to the person on the other end.

save（on）the environment 保护环境　　personal touch 个人色彩

7. Do you prefer to write letters or emails?（Why?）

I really only write emails now. I haven't written a letter in so long, it is kinda hard to remember when. As long as I have a computer and the Net is there I will always prefer writing emails. Things are just moving too quickly for me to take the time and energy to write a letter. In a way I would have to change my whole way of thinking to write a letter. It might be fun to try it and see what it is like.

8. Do senior citizens in China write emails?（Why?/Why not?）

Well, unless they are very unusual senior citizens they don't write emails. You know that having a computer and more important knowing how to operate one is just not something that the older generation has a lot of experience in. In our culture and maybe even in the West, I don't know, senior citizens like to **get around** in their own **neighborhoods** and **mix and mingle** with their friends there, so the need to write emails and use a computer is not really there. I suppose that if an older person has a business, then they might write some emails, but **more than likely** they would have a secretary do it for them.

get around 活动　　　　　　　　　　mix and mingle 混在一起

neighborhood 小区　　　　　　　　　more than likely (=almost certain) 很大可能

9. What effects, if any, do you think the use of emails might have on traditional Chinese culture?

Well, as I was saying emails have had a big effect on Chinese culture already. We younger people want to **reach out to** not just the ones that are in our neighborhood or even in our city but to those that are all over the world. You know, for a long time China was closed to the West and Western culture, now that it has opened its doors there have been many changes, and writing emails is one of them. Emailing is more than just writing; it really is **a way of life**, and this way of life wasn't available here in China before.

reach out to 表现出兴趣，想了解　　　　a way of life 一种生活方式

10. Do you think handwriting will still be an important skill in the future?

Well in China right now the written characters are important for many things, such as billboards and small business signs. But now that computers are being made with Chinese character inputs, the actual writing out of them is no longer necessary. I think **there will come a time** in the future **when** writing the characters by hand will be a lost art, sad to say, as writing characters by hand is an art form here in China. Computerization is moving in and **taking over**, so **for the sake of** speed we will see the slower methods of communicating—such as handwritten characters—become a lost art and a **casualty** of modern times.

there will come a time when 迟早会有一天　for the sake of 鉴于…的考虑

take over 占领　　　　　　　　　　　　casualty 受害者

三、话题相关材料

A 下面列出了英国最常见的几种寄信方式，可以跟中国的方式比较一下。

头等信

First Class Mail 1ST

Prices start at 32p for letters and small items weighing up to 100g.

Most mail delivered the next working day.

Quick and easy to use.

二等信

Second Class Mail 2ND

Prices start at 23p for letters and small items weighing up to 100g.

Delivered by the third working day after posting.

Easy to use and affordable.

挂号信

Provides proof of posting, signature on arrival and online confirmation of delivery.

Just 68p plus First or Second Class postage.

Most First Class Recorded items arrive by the next working day.

航空信

Airmail can be sent virtually anywhere in the world.

Prices start from as little as 44p, economical.

Your mail is delivered in just three to five days, depending on destination, and possibly quicker.

特快专递

Guaranteed next day delivery before 1pm—or your money back.

Prices start at just £4.10.

99% of the UK covered.

四、练习

A 请将下列句子翻译成英文。

1. 如果当时那个大夫没给我写信，我真不知道我现在会是什么样。

____

2. 你得谨慎措辞，既要表达清楚又要表达得含蓄。

____

3. 手写的信有种让人见信如面的感觉，它比任何 E-mail 都更能反映写信人的情况。

____

4. 电子邮件不仅仅是写信给别人，也是一种生活方式，而这种生活方式以前在中国是没有的。

____

5. 计算机化正一步步走来并且攻城掠地，因此，鉴于对速度的要求，我们会看到像手写文字这样比较慢的交流方式会最终成为一门消失的艺术，从而成为现代生活的牺牲品。

____

____

（☞ P273）

B 听 MP3 实战演练。

Topic 22　Books 读物

一、考试说明

该话题要求考生向考官描述自己读过的一本书。第三部分会围绕读书和阅读习惯的变化展开。在“真题演练”部分 native speaker 描述的是《杰克·伦敦小说集》。在“话题相关材料”部分，考生可以看到更为熟悉的两本书的英文介绍——《红楼梦》和《鹿鼎记》，是不是很惊喜？

二、真题演练

CUE CARD

Describe a book that you enjoyed reading.

You should say:

what the title is

what it is about

why you read it

and explain what effect the book had on you.

点题	I am fond of reading *Selected Works of Jack London*. It is a collection of the writer's works including three novels and forty short stories.
简介	It is mostly about different characters in the Klondike region of Alaska during the **Gold Rush**, but also tells about people's struggles in different situations.
内容	I was given the book as a present, and I was immediately fascinated by the raw, beautiful but very real world the writer experienced and wrote about. One story in particular, *The Sea Wolf*, is about a man who was born into a comfortable life and is suddenly thrust into a dangerous, **harsh** and **pitiless** environment aboard a **seal hunting** ship under a cruel, **despotic** yet **charismatic** and **intriguing** captain. He is faced with a **moral dilemma**: whether he should fight to survive without regard for others, or hold on to values he grew up with in easy circumstances, such as **altruism** and self sacrifice. In the end he finds strength to stand against the merciless captain.
影响	When I first read the book I was most impressed with the exciting action and **imagery** in the stories, but as I grew older and read them again the most striking features to me were instead the deeper qualities of character hard to find and to define. It caused me to look further into people, both in books and in real life, for the qualities that made them truly interesting and enduring.

重点词句

Gold Rush 淘金热

harsh 残酷的

pitiless 无情的

seal hunting 捕猎海豹

despotic 专制的，暴虐的

charismatic 有个人魅力的

intriguing 迷人的

moral dilemma 道德上的两难选择

altruism 利他主义

imagery 影像

Part 3
Reading in China

1. Do Chinese people like to read?

   Like most countries it depends on individual preference, but I would say it is not so popular an activity as in countries where the pace of life is slower. Most readers in China are students who have to read technical subjects. But reading is becoming more common especially among the young. I imagine that as books find a wider audience, reading will become more common.

2. Do young and old people like to read the same books?

   No. The interests of young and old vary greatly. Young people mostly like **fantasy** and **fiction** best. Older people often prefer serious or historical works.

   fantasy 科幻小说　　fiction 小说

3. What kinds of books are most popular in China?

   I think **martial arts stories** are favorites. Some Chinese classics are famous and widely read as well. Of course, knowing what is the favorite of many people is difficult.

   martial arts stories 武侠小说

4. Compare reading habits today to those of the past.

   Today education is widely available so many people can read. Also, these days, printing is faster than it once was so many books of different kinds can be printed. In the past fewer people could read and there were fewer books so people enjoyed and appreciated reading more. Modern inventions have also made more time for reading.

5. How do you think reading habits will change in the future?

   I am not sure. Maybe reading will become more widespread. Maybe it will become less common as new technology, such as virtual reality, becomes more readily available. Of course people who like to read simply because they can get along with their thoughts will continue to read.

Children and reading

6. Do you think it's a good idea to teach children to read when they are very young?

Yes. They can learn more. Also they may be able to enjoy a new pastime. Many children, instead of playing games which develop social skills or doing things which promote good values such as reading good books, play computer games and watch TV, which often causes **anti-social behavior**.
anti-social behavior 反社会行为

7. What do children like to read?
Children especially enjoy reading stories. They also like reading books about nature. If a book has pictures, children will really enjoy it. Many children like reading stories with silly themes often because they were never given anything else. If parents or teachers introduce their children to a wider variety of choices, children will enjoy a broader range of books.

8. Do parents read stories to their children in China?
Some do and some do not. My parents read to me when I was a child, they were teachers. Some of my friends' parents did not read to them. In poor families the parents may not be able to read at all. Of course with their parents being so busy, to even have the time to read is a real challenge in this day and age.

9. How do you think these stories influence children?
Children are very much affected by the stories their parents read to them. These stories are sometimes the first education a child receives. I can remember many of the stories my parents first read to me. Values found in children's books will often affect the young readers. Because their parents are reading the stories, the children will listen more.

10. Why do you think people sometimes idealize characters in stories?
People need to have heroes they can look up to and learn from. Role models are very important in life, as many teachers can tell us. Children often imitate what their heroes or older people do. Idealistic characters in stories have a great effect on individuals; even whole societies have changed to imitate a famous character in a story.

三、话题相关材料

A 补充语汇

literature 文学	absorbing 引人入胜的
drama 戏剧	nonfiction 非小说类读物
short story 短篇小说	poetry 诗歌
biography 传记	picture storybooks 连环画
autobiography 自传	illustration 插图
best-seller 畅销书	fable 寓言
intriguing 吸引人的	folktale 民间故事
moral 寓意	bedtime story 睡前故事

B 下面是国外网站www.answers.com 对《红楼梦》和《鹿鼎记》的介绍，相当不错。

《红楼梦》

The novel is usually grouped with three other pre-modern Chinese works of fiction, collectively known as the Four Great Classical Novels. Of these, *Dream of the Red Chamber* is often taken to be the zenith of classical Chinese fiction.

The novel is conjectured to be semi-autobiographical, mirroring the fortunes of Cao Xueqin's own family. It was also intended to be a memorial to the women Cao knew in his youth: friends, relatives and servants, as the author detailed himself in the first chapter.

The novel is a detailed, episodic record of the lives of the extended Jia family, made up of two clans (the Ning-guo and Rong-guo houses) who occupy two large family compounds in the capital, Beijing. Originally extremely wealthy, with a female member who was made an Imperial Concubine, the family eventually fell into disfavour with the Emperor, and had their mansions raided and confiscated.

The novel is remarkable not only in its huge cast of characters—over 400 in all, most of whom are female—and its psychological scope, but also in its precise and detailed observations of the life and social structures of 18th-century China.

《鹿鼎记》

The Deer and the Cauldron is the last novel written by Jinyong, one of the most influential modern Chinese-language novelists. He is widely regarded as the finest Chinese wuxia ("martial arts and chivalry") writer.

This story centers on a witty, sly, illiterate and lazy protagonist named Wei Xiaobao, born in a Yangzhou brothel. Through a series of adventures—or misadventures—the teenage scamp makes his way from the southern playground of Yangzhou to Beijing, the seat of Manchurian imperial power. There, he is kidnapped and taken to the palace (the Forbidden City) where he impersonates a eunuch. Xiaobao bumbles his way into a fateful encounter with the young Kangxi Emperor and they develop an unlikely friendship. By sheer luck and clever but underhanded strategies, he manages to accomplish a number of seemingly impossible achievements.

Xiaobao plays a major role in disposing the cruel and power-hungry Oboi, rescuing Kangxi's father, Emperor Shunzhi, reuniting the father and son, destroying the Mystic Dragons Sect, weakening the uprising raised by renegade general Wu Sangui, and reaching a border treaty with Russian regent Sophia Alekseyevna and Fedor Golovin.

For his numerous accomplishments, he is rewarded with immense wealth and ever-rising titles of nobility by Kang Xi. In the mean time, he also earns respect from the Heaven and Earth Society, one of the anti-Qing resistance organizations, for his work against Wu Sangui and other foreign enemies, and also his help in rescuing people of the resistance who were captured by officials.

Like all conflicting identities, Xiaobao's separate lives come to an explosive end. Kang Xi reveals that he knew Xiaobao's relationship with the Heaven and Earth Society, and forces Xiaobao to choose between him and the society. In the finale of the novel, Xiaobao realizes that he would never be able to reconcile between the two opposing causes, and his divided friendships are tearing him apart. He chooses, instead, to walk out on it all—taking his seven beautiful wives for a life of peace and tranquility away from the Kang Xi and society.

四、练习

A 请将下列句子翻译成英文。

1. 这本书是作者作品的选集，包括3篇长篇小说和40篇短篇小说。

____

2. 这本书是别人送给我的礼物，读完后我马上被书中作者所经历的和描绘的那种自然、美丽而又真实的世界所吸引。

____

3. 像在其他国家一样，这取决与个人喜好，但我觉得在中国阅读不像在其他那些生活节奏较缓慢一些的国家那么受欢迎。

____

4. 这些故事有些时候就是孩子接受的初次教育。

____

5. 人们需要英雄让他们去景仰、去学习。

____

（☞ P273）

B 听MP3实战演练。

Topic 23　Furniture 家具

一、考试说明

关于家具的话题是雅思口语中的新话题，考生向考官描述自己经常使用的一件家具。家具的选择很多，不一定非要讲床和衣柜这些我们最熟悉的也是比较容易描述的东西，也可以谈谈CD架和茶几什么的。第三部分会围绕家具的选购、家具风格等展开讨论。在“真题演练”部分描述的实际上是一把折叠椅，语言平实易懂，举的例子较有普遍性。在“话题相关材料”部分，考生可以看到国外家具商对自己产品的描述。

二、真题演练

CUE CARD

Describe an item of furniture that you use often.

You should say:

what it is

where it is

what it looks like

and explain how or why you use it.

点题	A piece of furniture I use often is a small **folding chair**.
描述	It's made of green **canvas** and because it is a folding chair, I can easily **put it away** and **out of sight** when I'm not using it. It's convenient for me because my room is small and I don't have space for a lot of furniture. I also don't like **clutter**, so by putting the chair away after I use it, my room looks a little tidier. My bedroom is the only one place in the house that I have to myself so I spend a lot of time there either studying or working.
感受	I'm in my last year of university, so I have many writing assignments and individual research to do. I do most of my writing on my laptop so it's convenient and comfortable to sit in my chair with my computer on my lap either typing or reading or both. As I said the chair is made of canvas and of course the **frame** is **aluminum** so it's **lightweight** and easy to put away and take out whenever I need it. Surprisingly it is very comfortable for a folding chair, and that was the most important factor for me when I chose it. It was also inexpensive. It's not a very beautiful piece of furniture, but it has definitely been one of the most practical things I've bought in a long time.

重点词句

folding chair 折叠椅
canvas 帆布
put sth. away 把…收起来
out of sight 看不见
clutter 混乱
frame 框架
aluminum 铝
lightweight 轻的

Part 3
Buying Furniture

1. When (in what situations) do people in China buy furniture?
   Most people buy furniture at a few main points in their lives. Naturally when people are getting married is one of those times. Another time is when they buy a new flat.

2. How do people decide what furniture to buy for the home or office? What factors do they consider?
   Well, they will consider what kind of furniture is needed. They will also look at which room it will go in and how much space they have. The women especially will think about color and style and what design looks best to them. I'd say price is probably the deciding point. They might like something very much, but if it's too expensive they won't be able to buy it.

3. In Chinese families, who usually decides what furniture to buy for the home?
   I think it **varies from family to family**. Nowadays, couples are making more decisions together. In my family, my parents even ask me what I think or like. In the past, often the men made decisions that concerned money, but some of those things are changing now.
   vary from... to... 因…不同而不同

4. Do people in China prefer traditional or modern styles of furniture?
   That also depends on the people and the families. I don't think there is any **set preference**. From my experience though, I would say many younger couples prefer modern furniture. I think it goes along with other trends in our country. What I mean is that modern or foreign fashions are often more popular and interesting, especially for young people. Maybe I'm different in this way though because I think many pieces of traditional furniture in our country are very beautiful. They are also often made better than the modern things.
   set preference 固定的喜好

5. Have there been any recent changes in the kinds of furniture that people (in China) use?
   Well, as I said a lot of foreign influence has come into China and this is affecting what people buy, including furniture. A very popular furniture store right now in China is IKEA, this is a store from Sweden and its style of furniture is a big change from the recent and distant past. I think that if people have the money they may return to the quality furniture from years gone by. Over all, though, the predominant style of furniture that people in China use is modern.

Furniture Design

6. What factors should a furniture designer consider when designing a piece of furniture?
   The use of the particular piece would be the first consideration. A designer would also have to think of the market he is targeting. This would usually indicate the cost of the finished product. This **in turn** will influence what materials he can use within that **price range**.
   in turn 反过来 price range 价格范围

7. What are the qualities of a good furniture designer?
   I'd say he needs to be **artistic and imaginative**. At the same time a designer also has to have quite a bit of **practical sense**. It's generally no use to design something that is beautiful but impossible to construct. Or maybe the designer can figure out how to build it, but it ends up so expensive that no one can afford it. In any design field, there are people who design something more for art's sake: they don't really expect anyone to buy it or they hope to find a collector to buy it as a piece of art more than as something useful.
   artistic and imaginative 有美感和想像力的 practical sense 实用意识

Housing

8. What kinds of housing are there in China?
   There are many kinds of housing just as in other countries. There are flats and houses and also villas, but of course most people can't afford anything other than flats. That is at least the case in the cities. In the rural areas, there are many people who live in houses, but these are usually very simple houses and these people are usually farmers.

9. How do people decide on the kind of housing they choose to live in?
   In reality I don't think most people have a lot of choices. Unless they are very rich, and these people are few in number compared to the general population. Most decide on flats because that is all they can afford. Usually people will try to choose something as close to their workplace as possible. Unfortunately even in that there is not much choice and many people still have to spend a lot of time traveling to and from work.

10. For most Chinese people, what is an ideal house?
    I think if most Chinese people could choose any house they wanted, they would choose a private individual house rather than a flat. They'd also want something with a garden where they could have flowers and trees and even grow some vegetables. They would also want something big enough that they could have members of their family live with them or at least a place they could stay if they came for a visit.

11. How has housing changed in China?
    Nowadays people live in flats and often these are in tall buildings if in big cities. In the past most

lived in houses even if they were small. Some cities had courtyard houses where many family members lived together, and there was a garden in the middle where they could enjoy the outdoors together. You've probably heard of these. They are interesting to foreigners.

12. How will housing change in the future?

I can imagine there will be more flats in the big cities that will be in taller buildings and with more modern facilities and equipment built into them. I hope though that some designers will do something to see that there are more park areas in between the buildings. I think city planners are making a big mistake by cramming in so much concrete. More green areas would be an important change to make in the future.

三、话题相关材料

A 补充语汇——家具名称和描述用语

sofa 沙发	easy to assemble 装配简单
ottoman 无靠背沙发	contemporary 当代的
bench 长椅	fabric 质地
entertainment centre 家庭影院	removable 可拆洗的
TV stand 电视柜	varnished 涂漆的
CD storage CD 架	polished 抛光的
dining table 餐桌	exquisite 精致的
stool 凳子	delicate 精巧的
closet 壁橱	triangular 三角形的
bunk-beds 上下铺	rectangular 长方形的
wardrobe 衣柜	durable 耐用的
neutral colour 中性色	genuine leather 真皮

B 下面是国外某家具厂商网站上的商品描述，你喜欢这些家具吗？

1 Sensibly scaled and impeccably tailored, the Cambridge Sofa and Loveseat are designed for the way you live. The thick, luxurious seat cushions and back provide the comfort you would expect with much more expensive furniture. This sofa, made from durable, easy-to-clean microfiber, will be perfect for high traffic areas like your family room. Fits through narrow doorways. Easy to assemble. Durable 100% polyester microfiber in Butter or Dark Moss or a Cut Chenille in Victorian Mocha. Sofa: 79″W×35.5″D×37″H.

2 Pamper your overnight guests with one of the most comfortable sofa beds ever crafted. This luxurious 92″W×39″D×39″H sofa has a soft, pillow-top design and transforms into a full-size bed with just one click of a button. 640 pocket coils provide superior support for both sitting and sleeping. Stain-resistant microfiber fabric cleans up easily with mild soap and water. Assembly is required.

四、练习

A 请将下列句子翻译成英文。

1. 对我而言它很方便，因为我的房间比较小，放不了很多家具。

____

2. 这家具并不好看，但它肯定是很长时间内我买过的最实用的东西了。

____

3. 现在中国有一家很受欢迎的家具店，叫“宜家”，这是家瑞典的家具店，其设计风格跟古典的和近代的都不太一样。

____

4. 我认为一个设计师得有美感和想像力，同时他(她)还得有实用意识。

____

5. 现在人们大都住在公寓里，如果是城里，这些公寓都在高楼里。而以前人们大都住在独门独户的房子里，尽管有些房子很小。

____

____

(☞ P274)

B 听 MP3 实战演练。

Topic 24 Advertisements 广告

一、考试说明

广告话题是媒体话题中难度较大的一个题目，考生要描述出一个自己喜欢的广告。当然广告的选择其实很多，TV commercial, billboard 或 print ad 以及网络广告都可以谈。本节中样板答案是一个耐克运动鞋的广告，考生并没有过多地谈广告的细节，而是把重心放到了台词和自己的感想上。这样的“避难就简”是个对付难题的好办法。第三部分多围绕广告对社会的影响展开讨论。在“话题相关材料”部分提供了几个国外大学生对影响广告成败与否的因素的讨论，并附录了几个经典的广告台词供考生参考。

二、真题演练

CUE CARD

Describe an unforgettable advertisement that you saw or heard.

You should say:

where you saw or heard it

what kind of advertisement it was

what the contents of the advertisement were

and explain why this advertisement is so unforgettable.

点题	While waiting for my boyfriend to **pick** me **up** from work, I was watching advertisements on the TV in the lobby. That night I saw an advertisement that has forever **stuck in my mind**.
广告内容	It was a **commercial** for Nike shoes with Michael Jordan. In it he said, “I've missed more than nine thousand shots in my career. I've lost almost three hundred games. Twenty-six times I've been trusted to take the game winning shot but missed. I've failed over and over and over again in my life, and that is why I succeed.” I couldn't get that commercial out of my mind, not because I thought buying Nike shoes would make me as successful as Michael Jordan, but because of his **unflinching determination** and perseverance.
感受	Life is full of challenges and difficulties that test our level of **commitment**. I believe having determination divides the winners from the losers. Successful people are not ones who have never failed, but those who kept trying. As simple as this may sound, it is the one **ingredient** that separates the winners from the losers. The one skill that winners acquire is an understanding that growth is only possible if you have the courage to change what you have been doing, if it is not achieving the result you desire. Sometimes success is learning how to fall and recognizing that from that fall you will learn to grow. And growth is what a **fulfilling** life is all about.

重点词句

pick up 接

stick in one's mind 牢记

commercial 电视、电台广告

unflinching determination 坚定的决心

commitment 信念；许诺

ingredient 原料；要素

fulfilling 充实的

Part 3
The influence of advertisements

1. How do advertisements attract attention?

It all depends on what group of people the advertisement is aimed for. Young people look if it's cool, **hip**, or fashionable; whereas older people tend to be more practical-minded, so those in charge of advertising need to have a clear idea of who they will be **targeting** with their advertisement, and plan **accordingly**. If the advertisement **is geared to** the younger generation, then showing how the product can help kids be more attractive, confident, or successful is good. Catchy music also helps attract attention and helps listeners remember it. If you're trying to reach the older generation with your advertisement, explaining how the product will give them better health, or help them relax, or be happier may appeal to them.

hip 时髦的

accordingly 相应的

target 锁定

be geared to 针对

2. Do young and old people have the same attitudes towards advertisements?

Definitely not. Every individual has his own unique attitude toward advertisements and the advantages and disadvantages that advertising brings. Both old and young people **are inclined to** believe and think that advertisements tend to be **misleading**, dishonest, **phony**, shallow, and at times annoying, especially when they're not well made or **dorky**. On the other hand, if done well, they can be very creative, humorous, **artistic**, and enjoyable to watch. Those, however, are the exception, rather than the **norm**.

be inclined to 倾向于

misleading 误导的

phony 伪的，假的

dorky 愚蠢的

artistic 富有艺术性的

norm 常规

3. Do you think advertisements are a good or bad influence on children?

Looking at today's children, I would have to say advertisements have **predominately** had a negative influence on their lives and character. Ads create a **discontentment** with what children have and a desire to own more and to be like everyone else. Advertisements usually tend to be unrealistic and give a false impression of how the children should be or what will happen when they buy the product.

predominately 主要地

discontentment 不满

4. Do you think advertisements actually influence people to buy things? And How?

When seen a lot, advertisements make products more familiar and **ingrained** in people's mind, so when they want to buy something, they will take a brand that they recognize. In China, some people want to be like the West and so they buy what they see on TV that the Western people have. They think that if they have this Western product, they will be as cool as this person, which is totally **bizarre** to my mind.

ingrained 根深蒂固的　　　　　bizarre 奇怪的、荒诞的

Government control

5. Does the Chinese government control advertisements in any way?

Of course. All TV media is controlled in some way by the government, so advertisements must be as well. The government prevents advertisements from having inappropriate content or content that is not **in line with** government policy. That is common in every country. I'm sure that if the advertisement is within normal **bounds**, then the government wouldn't have much to say about it.

in line with 与…一致　　　　　bound 范围

6. Do you think there should be controls on advertising?

Yes, I do. Some things should not be advertised, such as cigarettes, which are harmful to people's health. Most people are aware of their existence, so they don't need to be promoted more. Children especially should not be shown advertisements that make harmful things look cool or interesting. Advertisements that have age-inappropriate content should also be banned.

7. Do you think that advertisements for products that harm the health, such as cigarettes, should be allowed?

Now you are getting into freedom of choice and whether it would be better to just **prohibit** something from being advertised to get people to stop using the product, but unfortunately this just doesn't work, as prohibition in the States found out. The best thing would be for the products just to not be **manufactured**, but this doesn't work either because then they would be produced illegally, becoming more dangerous.

prohibit 禁止　　　　　manufacture 生产制造

8. Can you think of any example of false advertising?

The biggest example that comes to my mind is McDonald's advertisements. Every time I go to McDonald's, I see pictures of happy, thin people with big smiles and perfect teeth holding hamburgers and **cartons** of French fries that are at least three times bigger than the real products. This advertisement clearly ignores three **glaring** facts. For one, if you eat at McDonalds a lot, you will not look like the people in the advertisement. Two, the hamburger and French fries are nowhere near the size pictured. Three, if you stand smiling holding a burger, nobody will think you are cool.

carton 硬纸盒　　glaring 显而易见的

9. What kinds of products are most often (most easily) promoted by false advertising?

Well, most products are really promoted by false advertising. I hate to sound so **cynical** but I have a friend in the advertising business, and a lot of so-called experts advertising their product know absolutely nothing about it. In the field of beauty care products, this happens a lot. The poor women sitting at home with nothing to do except watch TV are so **susceptible to** this kind of advertising.

cynical 愤世嫉俗的　　be susceptible to 容易受…影响

三、话题相关材料

A 补充语汇

brand loyalty 品牌忠诚度	telemarketing 电话营销
consumer decision-making process 消费者决策过程	public service advertisement 公益广告
	pop-up ad 弹出式广告
prospective customers 潜在消费者	internet banner 网络广告
product concept 产品概念	advertising slogan 广告宣传语
target market 目标市场	

B What makes or breaks an ad?

下面是几个大学生对衡量广告成功与否的标准的讨论，请你看看是否有更多的资源可以为你所用。

I like simple images, which at first glance, do not appear to have any link with the product or brand, and make people stop and think. Thought-provoking ads tend to be more successful, because they bring out the concept of the product in such a way that the message stays in people's minds. Creativity and marketability should be balanced in ads.

I think most ads with bright colours and those that make use of young celebrities do very well with a younger age group. These are normally fun-oriented and reflect current interests or the latest fad. Having good-looking models is always a plus while others add in a bit of sex appeal.

A bad ad would be one with too many things in it as it ends up looking cluttered. I've seen many ads that have big bright pictures, graphics and a lot of text. It looks very distracting, and you don't know what to focus on at first glance. Most of the ads I see today seem to make use of bigger images and fewer words. I still remember how a series of Guiness ads caused quite a stir in Malaysia with everyone trying to figure out who Adam King was. The fact that they made people talk about it showed how effective the campaign was.

C 广告宣传语（advertising slogans）可成为广告中的点睛之笔。下面列出几个经典例子，供考生体会。

"The toughest job you'll ever love."	—United States Peace Corps 美国维和部队
"Beyond Petroleum"	—BP 英国石油
"Like nothing else on Earth"	—Hummer 美国汗马汽车
"The world's local bank"	—HSBC 汇丰银行
"Because life is not a spectator sport"	—Reebok 锐步运动装
"Her kiss. Her smile. Her perfume."	—Chanel No. 5 香奈尔 5 号香水
"Buy it. Sell it. Love it."	—eBay 易趣网站

"St. Augustine founded it. Becket died for it. Chaucer wrote about it. Cromwell shot at it. Hitler bombed it. Time is destroying it. Will you save it?"

—Canterbury Cathedral 英国坎特伯雷大教堂

四、练习

A 请将下列句子翻译成英文。

1. 那天晚上我看到一个广告，至今仍难忘记。

____

2. 那是一个乔丹为耐克鞋拍的广告。

____

3. 那个广告印在了我的脑海里，当然不是因为我以为买了耐克鞋就能像乔丹那样成功，而是因为乔丹那种坚定的决心和毅力。

____

4. 年轻人看广告是不是吸引人，是不是够酷够时尚；而年纪大的人想的更实用一点。

____

5. 看看今天的孩子，我觉得电视对他们的生活和性格的影响大部分都是负面的。它们会让孩子不满足自身所有，并刺激他们要更多的东西，去跟其他小朋友一样。

____

（☞ P274）

B 听 MP3 实战演练。

Topic 25 A Childhood Present 童年礼物

一、考试说明

童年始终是雅思考官钟爱的话题，童年的回忆，童年的游戏，童年的住处……童年话题屡见不鲜。童年的礼物也是“童年”系列话题之一。考生向考官描述完自己小时候收到的礼物后，在第三部分会围绕送礼的习俗展开讨论。“真题演练”部分描述的是童年的生日礼物。在“话题相关材料”部分，考生可以看到国外网友回忆收到过的最好和最差的礼物。

二、真题演练

CUE CARD

Describe a present you received when you were a child

You should say:

what the present was

who gave it to you

how the present was used

and explain how you felt when you got this present.

点题	The most **memorable** gift I received was when I was seven years old, on my birthday, my parents bought me a bike.
事件	They painted it pink for me to match the pink **tassels** that were hanging off the **handlebars**. I learned to ride my bike in the park near our house, and after I learned how to ride I would often ride around in the park while my brother and sister were playing. When my younger brother got his own bike we would ride along the street together.
感受	When I first saw the bicycle I was very excited, and I thought it was very pretty. I was so happy to get it that my father took me out to learn to ride it the same day. After I learned to ride it, I enjoyed it so much that I would ride it whenever I could. I didn't mind having to play by myself if I could ride my bike. I loved the feeling of the wind on my face and through my hair, and seeing the ground speed under my wheels. It was so refreshing when I was hot and **sweaty** to have the cool **breeze** blowing all the time.

重点词句

memorable 难忘的

tassel 穗

handlebars 车把

sweaty 出汗的

breeze 微风

Part 3
Giving gifts in China

1. Do Chinese people often give gifts?

   Yes, we do. Not as much as western cultures, but we receive gifts on our birthday and at Chinese New Year. Sometimes if we visit someone that we don't see very often, they might get a small gift. Of course, when someone gets married, people will give them gifts.

2. What kinds of presents do Chinese people give?

   I think the most popular gift is the Chinese 'hong bao' or 'red envelope'. Money is put in these red envelopes and given at birthdays, weddings, and Chinese New Year. People will sometimes buy other gifts for these occasions. If it is for a child, they might give a toy or **stuffed animal**. Sometimes food is given as a gift, either having been cooked by the giver, or store-bought.

   stuffed animal 动物玩具

3. On what occasions do Chinese people send gifts?

   People send gifts mostly on birthdays or Chinese New Year. These are the traditional times for gift-giving, but as many Western holidays and traditions are slowly becoming more popular in China, it is quite acceptable to give your friends a gift at Christmas, or your sweetheart a gift on Valentine's Day. Even though some people may not know why different festivals are celebrated, they still enjoy the chance to show the people they care about how they feel.

4. If you were going to give a present to a child, what would you give them?

   Well, if it were a boy, I would get him a **Lego set**. The reason why I would choose a Lego set is that it is very fun, and at the same time, it encourages creativity. If it were a girl, I would give her a glass doll. I would give this to her because most little girls like dolls, and if it were glass she would take better care of it and treasure it more because it could break easily.

   Lego set "乐高"牌拼装玩具

5. Do people give the same kinds of gifts to both boys and girls?

   I think some people give both boys and girls the same kinds of gifts because they don't know what to give, so they just get them the same thing. Other people may do this if two children are friends or siblings and the person doesn't want them to fight over different toys, and if they have the same thing, they will be happy. Or people may not know that girls and boys like different things, so they don't think about whether the gift they are getting is suitable for that child.

Importance of gifts

6. Are expensive gifts always better than cheap gifts?

   No, definitely not. A gift doesn't have to be expensive in order to show care for the person receiving it. Often a very expensive gift can show that they were just buying something but not really thinking about what would mean the most to the receiver. This isn't always the case, but I think that a cheap gift can mean just as much or even more than an expensive gift can.

7. Do you think it is necessary for friends to give presents to each other?

   No, it's not necessary. It's nice when friends give each other gifts, but there are other things you can do to show your friend your care. If someone is your friend, you shouldn't expect that they will always get you gifts. True friendship is caring about the other, not looking for how much he can give you.

三、话题相关材料

A 下面是五位网友在讲述他们小时候收到的最好的礼物。

What is the best gift you ever received when you were a child?

1 A mechanical pencil on my 10th birthday. Back then we couldn't afford such pencils, but my brothers saved up to buy it for me. Although it's nothing much now, it was really meaningful for me as I always envied others who had one. My father also got me a pencil box, so everything fit fine. I was so happy then. A week later, someone stole it in school, and it was never found. I never knew who did it.

2 A friend of mine made me a CD and burned 15 songs to it. She wrote in the cover each song's name and why the songs reminded her of me. She had several different kinds of songs, including "Hero" by Mariah Carey. It was by far the greatest present I have ever received and something I will never forget.

3 I remember getting a fluffy, floppy, stuffed dog (I named him Rolf) that had a radio built into him. I think my parents got him at Radio Shack. I could cuddle with him at night while listening to Barry Manilow (it was the 1970s!). I was 7 years old, and thought I was so cool. The batteries corroded in the radio a year later, and the radio had to be pulled out. But the dog had a zipper where the radio used to be. My mom was a health nut back then, always handing me vitamins. Little did she know that Rolf was a very healthy dog with literally oodles of vitamins stuck up in him!

4 My favorite gifts are:

- My father reading aloud to us in the evening, because it gave us a love of books and inquiring minds.

- A book—Black Beauty that my Grandma gave me when I was five; she had received it for Christmas in 1904. She wrote my name in it, too, underneath the original inscription.
- Art supplies, because it gave me a chance to experiment with drawing and painting, and begin a passion for creativity.

5 My favorite gift was a book made by my father titled All About Heather. My dad insists he expresses himself best through writing, so he gave me a book containing several short stories about my life. It starts with my birth. He explains how nervous he was, how he got to take my first picture, and what my mother said when she saw me for the first time. My father gave this book to me on my 16th birthday, and I still have a difficult time sitting down to read it because of the tears that come. It gives me such roots and such a feeling of love and completeness. Now the book is in my new husband's hands. Although not much of a reader, he picks it up every now and then to learn the story of me.

B 最差的礼物。

Holiday gifts can be tricky for both gift givers and gift receivers. Good gifts are often the result of careful planning and consideration, but it takes only a slight oversight or miscalculation for the best intentions to end up as an awkward, unwanted gift.

1 My paternal grandmother is known in our family for giving goofy gifts, and it's become a joke in our family. The worst gift I ever received from her was a pair of bell-bottom overalls with a huge orange button on the front pocket. Later in the year when my aunt and cousins were talking and laughing about the gifts we'd received, I learned that the company that made the overalls had gone out of business before I was even born, and not only that but they had belonged to one of my aunts as a teenager. She purchased them with her babysitting money! Last year our youngest cousin (she was 8) received an angel Christmas ornament with a missing arm. Our grandmother thoughtfully included a note explaining that the ornament was so pretty that she decided to buy it anyway. The One-Armed Angel has become a new tradition in our family. The angel is now being passed around the women in the family with a book/journal that has the original note pasted inside to track her travels. This year I passed her on to another cousin. I even built her a prosthetic arm!

2 Worst Christmas gift: A pair of white plastic hands reaching up from a wooden base. Purpose: to "hold" all your remote controls. The word ugly is not strong enough to describe the gift which would not fit in anyone's decor except perhaps the Monster's.

四、练习

A 请将下列句子翻译成英文。

1. 最让我难忘的礼物是我在7岁的时候收到的。

____

2. 第一次看到那辆自行车的时候我特别兴奋，觉得它太漂亮了。

____

3. 我之所以选择乐高拼装玩具是因为它很有意思，与此同时，它还能激发创造力。

____

4. 礼物的重要与否取决于是谁送的。

____

5. 礼物不一定非要很贵才能显示送礼者对对方的心意。

____

（☞ P274）

B 听MP3实战演练。

Topic 26 News Reports 新闻报道

一、考试说明

用英语讲故事难度很大，一方面要把故事讲出来，一方面还要注意语法，尤其是时态。在回答此话题时，考生如果感觉故事不好讲，也可以寥寥数语将故事梗概讲清楚，然后用较大的篇幅去谈自己的感受，毕竟自己的主观感受相对来说比较好“白活”。“真题演练”讲的是中国反腐败的新闻。无独有偶，在“话题相关材料”列出的《北京周刊》评选出的“2010国内十大新闻”中，反腐败也位列其中。考生可以参照榜单，看看是否关注过这些事件。

二、真题演练

CUE CARD

Describe a news report that you have recently heard or read about.

You should say:

what the story was

how you heard about this story

when you heard the news

and explain your reaction when you heard the news.

点题	Just today I read a story online about a vice mayor getting fired for taking bribes.
渠道	I found the story on the International Herald Tribune website. I found the story because it is one of the websites I **check out** every day, trying to **stay informed of** world events.
感受	I was happy when I heard the news. From what I've seen, China has a **massive problem** with **corruption**, and I think it's about time they started doing something about it. It seems like there is an enormous amount of money wasted every year because officials are either taking bribes or **skimming off the top**, and it does a major amount of damage to the Chinese people. If the government halts this trend, I think it will be a great thing for us. Money will be spent in places where it can do some good rather than **lining the pockets** of people who don't need it. There have been quite a few stories of this nature lately, and it shows an extremely **positive development**. I'm not sure if the government is **going after** all the corrupted officials or just some of them, but either way, it is **a step in the right direction**.

重点词句

lead-up 筹备

take bribes 受贿

check out 看

stay informed of 不断获得消息

massive problem 巨大的问题

corruption 腐败

skim off the top 揩油

line the pockets 中饱私囊

positive development 积极的势头

go after 追捕

a step in the right direction 向正确方向迈出的一步

Part 3
Mass Media

1. How do most people in China get their news?

   Most Chinese people get their news from various newspapers. Everyday, I see people reading newspapers on the bus, on the subway, or on the street. Also many people get their news from the Internet and TV.

2. Are most people in China more interested in local news or international news?

   I think most Chinese people are more concerned with **local news** and **domestic news**, which I'd imagine is the same across the world. Unless there are huge stories going on elsewhere, local news has more of an impact on the average citizen. Also, it is easier to understand news that is about areas that you know **as opposed to** some town in a country you might not even have heard of.

   local news 本地新闻

   domestic news 国内新闻

   as opposed to 相对于

3. Compare newspapers and TV as sources of news.

   I think if you are looking to get a general idea about the day's news, TV is a perfect way. You can get the basics from TV. If you want to get in-depth information, however, newspapers are the way to go. They can dedicate more time to each individual story, so you can learn more about different subjects.

4. How do you think the news media will change in the future?

   News in the future, I think, will come from many more directions. With the creation of **blogs**, more people are able to **report on** many different things, so you will see a lot more news and a lot more analysis. I don't think there is any way that newspapers will be able to compete with this. If people have to choose between getting more news for free online and to pay, they are going to choose to go online.

   blog (weblog) 博客

   report on 报道

5. Are young and old people interested in the same news content?

   I think this question partially depends on how old young people are. If they are in their twenties, I think for the most part, the news they are interested in is the same. Younger people do seem to be more interested in things like celebrities and pop culture than older people, but I think they stay pretty educated about the more important news. Older people are less concerned with the pop culture news, and are more concerned with the news that matters more to the world and their country.

Children and Reading

6. Do you think it's a good idea to teach children to read before they start school?

   Yes, I think it's important to try to teach children how to read at as early an age as possible. The earlier they know how to read, the sooner they can start learning other things. Also, if you teach them early, it may instill a desire in them to keep learning throughout their lives, which would be extremely valuable. I know my parents started me reading very young, and today I think I am **better off** because of it.

   better off 过的好的

7. What kinds of things do children like to read?

   I think kids all over the world like to read books that are either based in the same world they are in (school) or in a world that isn't like this one at all (fantasy/Harry Potter). Everything else, I think, fails to hold their attention. Unless it has a good, entertaining story, kids will not be interested, and I think these kinds of books kids can either **identify with** or can **get wrapped up in**.

   identify with 认同　　　　get wrapped up in 酷爱、着迷

三、话题相关材料

A 补充语汇

conventional media 常规媒体	broadsheet 大报
daily 日报	circulation 发行量
quarterly 季刊	headline 标题
quality newspaper 严肃报纸	editorial 社论
tabloid 小报	column 栏目
classified ads 分类广告	sensational 耸人听闻的
correspondent 通讯员	highlight 重要部分
periodical 期刊	exclusive 独家的
in-depth coverage 深度报道	objectivity 客观性
international news 国际新闻	watchdog 监督者
comic strip 连环漫画	bias 偏见
feature article 专题文章	hearsay 谣言

scandal 丑闻	publicity 宣传
human interest story 富有人情味的故事	news agency 通讯社
timeliness 及时性	reliable 可靠的

B 2010年国内十大新闻

各大媒体在每年年末都会推出自己总结的"Top 10 Stories of the Year"，下面是《北京周刊》(Beijing Review)概括出的2010国内十大新闻榜，受篇幅限制，榜单后只列出了两个新闻的详细内容供大家参考。

TOP 10 DOMESTIC STORIES

1. Efforts to Achieve Social Harmony
2. New Five-year Guidelines
3. Bashing Corruption
4. Rural Development Key to Modernization
5. Green GDP
6. Innovation Nation
7. Food Safety Concern
8. The Earthquake in Yushu
9. Closer Cross-strait Ties
10. Shanghai World Exposition

3. Bashing Corruption

A series of Chinese officals have been arrested because of corruption in this year.

In the wake of a series of sensational corruption scandals involving some high-ranking officials, the Communist Party of China embarked on a reshuffle of the chiefs of the Party's anti-graft bodies at the provincial level, which displays its resolve to halt corruption through strengthened supervision. New graft busters were appointed from outside the municipalities with some having a background in the Party's top anti-corruption body. Earlier this year, disciplinary heads were "parachuted" into their new posts.

10. Shanghai World Exposition

More than 223,000 visitors entered Expo Garden on Sept 2. It was the third day that the number of visitors hovered around 200,000. The high on Aug 21 reached more than 560,000 visitors. It may take visitors less than one hour to get into some famous European pavilions such as the Italy Pavilion. At peak times, it had taken three hours to get in. The number of visitors may surge again after the middle of september during China's National Day holiday and Mid-Autumn Festival.

四、练习

A 请将下列句子翻译成英文。

1. 最近类似的新闻有很多，这显示出一个非常积极的态势。

____

2. 我觉得大部分中国人更关注当地新闻和国内新闻，这一点我想在其他地方也一样。

____

3. 除非其他地方发生了大事，否则总的来说当地新闻对老百姓日常生活的影响更大一些。

____

4. 随着博客的诞生，越来越多的人可以报道新闻，因此你会看到更多的新闻和更多的分析。

____

5. 老年人对流行文化方面的新闻不太关心，他们更关心关系到全世界和自己国家的新闻。

____

（☞ P275）

B 听 MP3 实战演练。

经历类核心级（Topics 27~28）

Topic 27　Public Events 公众活动

一、考试说明

“公共活动”大都涉及当代的民风民俗，材料不难找，但困难之处在于如何用英语去表达。“真题演练”部分 native speaker 讲述的是自己在昆明时参加的一个房地产开发商举办的楼盘促销活动，比较 weird。其实关于该话题网上有很多英文材料，考生只要想好自己要说什么活动，而且这个活动还有点知名度，那么相关材料网上大都可以找到，比如“话题相关材料”就列出了网上搜到的有关北京庙会的介绍，以及吴大维 blog 上对青岛啤酒节的描写。

二、真题演练

CUE CARD
Describe a local event you have attended.
You should say:
what this event was
when and where it was
what happened in the event
and explain what you liked about this event.

点题	Sometime during 2001, when I was living in Kunming, some friends of mine in the Bei Chen area invited me to **a street party** to promote a new **housing compound** that some company had just finished building.
感受	It was a very **bizarre** event. It was held outside in a little park near the new compound. It was a very cute little park with benches and a small playground for little children. I think the event was **funded** by the owners of the compound, because they were giving away food. There was ice cream, soft drinks, beef, lamb, and pork meat sticks, and some other snacks of which I can't remember the names. The only problem, though, was that you had to stand in a line the length of the Great Wall. Sometimes the line would move fast, like when a bunch of the meat was cooked, but other times it just seemed to take forever. I can't remember so well, but I think that you had to be living in the Bei Chen area to attend the party. Oh yes, that's what it was; our friend was living in that area, so we were able to go in for free. The party was so much fun, because it was at night and we were allowed to stay out later than usual. My cousin who lives abroad was visiting and went with us to the party. I don't think I'll ever forget that time.

重点词句

street party 街头活动 | bizarre 古怪的

housing compound 楼盘 | fund 资助

Part 3

Cultural heritage

1. Should businesses support local events?

   I think that businesses should support local events. It not only helps to **create a good image** for the business, but shows customers that the business is interested in their welfare. It can also provide good advertising opportunities for the business. Everyone likes to do business with a community-minded business.

   create a good image 创造一个良好的形象

2. Should the government preserve traditional events like temple fairs?

   I think the government should preserve this kind of event. And furthermore, I think that the best way they can support them is to help financially. Although if you only let the government help to support and sponsor these kinds of events, then companies like Coca Cola, Budweiser, and Mc Donald's will have nothing to do. Therefore, I think it's important to let everyone help to organize and fund the events, but the government should definitely preserve and support these kinds of events.

Community Life

3. Do you think it's important to take part in local activities?

   I personally don't enjoy participating in local events, but for some reason many people actually do. I'd much rather watch the event from a distance. Maybe this is just because I'm lazy, but I just don't really feel the need to go out there and be another nameless person in a crowd that won't miss me at all.

4. Do you think it's important to have a sense of local community spirit?

   If a community wants to prosper, everyone must **make a concerted effort** to put as much into their community as possible. If you don't take care of your community then your community can't take care of you. What I'm trying to say is that if you're in the habit of helping others in your community, then others will be more inclined to help you. It's also important that you don't litter, because if you do then the place will look like a mess. Another thing that would help is that if parents and pet owners would clean up after their kids and pets relieve themselves then there won't be any **excrement** on the grass, sidewalks, and benches.

   make a concerted effort 齐心协力 | excrement 粪便

5. What are the advantages of being part of a close-knit community?

Well, one of the advantages is that your community will look out for you. If you're in trouble you'll get support from your neighbors, and they'll be more likely to accept whatever you decide to do. Also, if you are in a close-knit community, more people will be your friend and invite you and your family over to their house for dinner. Like the saying goes, **a man is only as rich as how many friends he has**.

A man is only as rich as how many friends he has 一个人有多少朋友就有多富有

6. In what ways do neighbors cooperate and help each other in China?

This is a tough question, because I personally don't think that they do. Most of my neighbors are just nosey old **busybodies** who are always trying to find out some new piece of gossip. All the rest are out working all day and when they come home they just want to watch TV or sleep.

busybody 爱管闲事的人

7. How has the sense of community changed in recent years in China?

Before the community was very strong in China. You always did things with your neighbors and helped them in whatever way that you could. Also, whenever anyone did something that wasn't quite right, everyone knew about it, and the person was very embarrassed. But now everyone is out working, and aside from a few old busybodies, no one has time to help or get involved with the affairs of their neighbours.

三、话题相关材料

A 补充词汇

temple fair 庙会	community building 社区建设
book fair 书市	key priority of the government
carnival 狂欢节	政府工作的重心之一
beer festival 啤酒节	improve social, economic and environmental well-
kite festival 风筝节	being
music festival 音乐节	改善社会、经济和环境状况
sponsor 赞助	

B 网上材料

(1)吴大维(David)笔下的青岛啤酒节——

There are many places in China that are very nice, but to my surprise, I went to Qingdao for the first time a while ago, and I liked it a lot!!

It's hard to find sunshine and good beaches in China, but Qingdao has them! I have heard so much about the place and I finally had the pleasure of going there. After I arrived, what I found was bright sunshiny blue skies, nice ocean breeze, and lots of very nice sandy beaches. What's nice about Qingdao is that on certain streets, you can't even find any motorcycles or bicycles because of certain regulations. The streets are clean, and the roads and structures are all very neat and tidy.

What we also ran into was the annual beer festival, tons of people having a good time sipping brew and enjoying the festivities! Qingdao is known for its beer, and there is nothing better than downing a gulp of ice cold brew after a hot afternoon of pure sweating! I love to have a few beers here and there, but I had the time of my life going to the Qingdao Brewery for a little tour. One of the ex-plant managers was showing me around, and let me tell you, the process was amazing! So many people around the world enjoy a nice cold one here and there, but how many people can say they have tasted the freshest beer right off the bottling line? Well, I had the pleasure of doing that while there. The ex-manager let me grab a bottle right after it was capped off the bottling line! Now is there a fresher beer out here? If there is, please let me know! The beer itself is probably no big deal, but to grab something right after it is completed and before it ends up somewhere in Shanghai, or any where else in the world for that matter, is a whole different feeling. We all like to eat freshly cooked food, but freshly brewed beer right after it is done? I don't think that many people can say they have. So if you all have time, next time you down a bottle of brew, think about going to the source and learn a bit more about how it is done. It's a difficult process that'll make you appreciate every sip you take in the future.

摘自吴大维的 blog——http://blog.hjenglish.com/david

(2)有关庙会的描述——

Attending temple fairs （Miao Hui） is high on any Beijing resident's agenda during the Spring Festival. The temple fair began as groups of vendors did business near temples when many pilgrims came to pay tribute to the gods during traditional festivals. The practice grew, gradually turning into a regular event. Now temple fairs are an important and joyful destination for Chinese people during festivals, most especially the Spring Festival or Chinese New Year. In addition to a great variety of Beijing snacks and funny gadgets, temple fairs offer Chinese traditional folk art performances, including stilts, lion and dragon dances, drum beating, diabolo（kongzhu）playing and other activities.

What do you expect from a temple fair:

1）Folk performances: stilt-walking and drum performances are regular activities at any temple fair;

2）Snacks: snacks are displayed in lines of booths. It's one way to taste the many flavours of different ethnic groups across China;

3）Shops: Most of the temple fairs are full of booths providing small, cheap products from tea, pot flowers, paintings, ceramics, books, to birds and toys;

4）Snapshot Opportunities: take your camera when you are on a temple fair trip in Beijing. It's a great insight into the lives of Beijing people of the past and present.

四、练习

A 请将下列句子翻译成英文。

1. 活动是在新楼盘旁边的小公园外举行的。

____

2. 活动很有意思，因为是晚上举行，我们能比平时晚睡觉。

____

3. 这不光为企业创造了良好的形象，还向企业的顾客们表明这个企业很在乎他们的福利。

____

4. 我宁可旁观这个活动。

____

5. 我想说的是只有你在社区里习惯去帮助别人，别人才会愿意来帮助你。

____

（☞ P275）

B 听 MP3 实战演练。

Topic 28 Life-changing Moments 改变人生的事件

一、考试说明

"描述生活中一个重要变化"是雅思口试中的老话题，总体来说难度不大。考生向考官描述完自己的故事后，在第三部分里会围绕生活中各种各样的变化以及社会的变化与其展开讨论。生活中其实有太多的事情可以对我们的一生产生影响，在"话题相关材料"部分，很多国外网友讲述了他们的改变人生的故事。在"真题演练"部分，native speaker 标新立异，讲述了自己与女朋友分手的故事，虽然不开心，但也给自己带来了积极的变化。

二、真题演练

CUE CARD

Describe a positive change in your life.

You should say:

when it happened

where it happened

what the change was

and explain how you have benefited from this change

点题	I think the most positive change that I had in my life, believe it or not, was when I decided to **break up** with my girlfriend.
事件	You see, going out with her started to take up most of my time and I started neglecting my studies and my other friends. My girlfriend became almost like an **obsession** to me. I thought about her all the time, and when I wasn't thinking about her I was out with her. Now don't get me wrong, she was a great girl, my girlfriend. It's just that things got way out of balance in my life. We had been going out for about three years. I knew her from my high school. We had gone out for a walk one evening, and I was really scared to say anything to her because I was afraid that I was going to hurt her feelings. Well, after walking for a while, I finally **got up the nerve to** say something to her, and once it was **out in the open** it really wasn't so bad. She was thinking the same thing, and said that it would be good to just slow things down for a while and see what would happen. **Boy was I relieved**, we had a good laugh over things and parted as friends.
收获	Now although I love her and really do believe that some day we might be together on a more permanent basis, it feels good to just **chill out** with my friends for a while.

重点词句

break up 分手

obsession 着魔

get up the nerve to 鼓足勇气做某事

out in the open 说开

Boy was I relieved 感叹词(表惊讶)

chill out 彻底放松

Part 3
Life Changes

1. What kind of events may be life-changing events?

   Like I said, breaking up or ending a relationship would be one. Having an accident or hurting yourself when playing sports sure is life changing. **Winning the lottery** is another life changing event. Getting married will change your life, too.

   win the lottery 中彩票

2. Do Chinese people change jobs very often? Do you think that's good?

   Yes I think that Chinese do change their jobs pretty often, and I think that it is a good thing. Until you really find a job that you feel comfortable with, then I think it is okay to change jobs. Some Chinese and people around the world have to change jobs because they **get laid off** or their company **gets gobbled up** by some big corporation, and they are forced to leave.

   get laid off 被裁员

   get gobbled up 被吞并

3. How do you think employers could encourage employees not to change jobs?

   Of course they could give a lot of money, but I know that this is not always practical. I think that one thing that would really help people stay in a job is that they are shown some appreciation for what they do. I read that a lack of appreciation is one reason that people go from job to job and just can't seem to find a home. I think if employers would just listen to their employees about their need, that would be a big help, too.

4. Why do so many people in China move to a different city or even go overseas to study or work?

   Well, I think that people are just looking for their **groove** and where they belong. Now that the opportunity is there to travel, people want to take advantage of it, and see where their fortunes lie. There is a big world out there and some people want to find out if it is their "**cup of tea**" as they say. I hate to use so many idioms and I hope that I am using them right, but some people just have the proverbial "**grass is greener on the other side of the fence**" syndrome. They think that once they get there, all their problems will be over.

   groove (俚语)最佳状态

   cup of tea 喜欢或想要的东西

   grass is greener on the other side of the fence 这山望着那山高

5. What do you think are the major challenges of working or studying in another country?

   Well, I guess that one of the biggest ones is that you are going to a different culture, and you are not sure how you are going to fit in. In most countries one of the hardest things to deal with is **prejudice**. People always seem to have a little suspicion of foreigners in their country. I think that loneliness would be another thing that would be hard for someone working or studying overseas. A person would be away from family and friends, and that would be difficult.

prejudice 偏见

Young People and Change

6. Are young people in China today more mature than in the past?

   I don't think so. **If anything**, they are more immature than in the past. In the past, life was harder here in China, and young people had to grow up fast and had to take on responsibility. Now with the country getting richer and only one child per household, they are actually pretty spoiled, and their parents do a lot of things for them.

   if anything 而且、甚至(表强调和递进)

7. What can young people learn from older people?

   They can learn a lot if they want to. They can learn from the vast amount of experience that older people have. They can learn what old people did under circumstances similar to what young people go through. They can learn how to raise a family and how to have a lasting relationship. Also, they can learn how to deal with difficult situations.

8. Do you think young people can adapt to changes easier than old people?

   Not necessarily. I have seen some young people that didn't know how to deal with changes at all, and then I have seen some older people who **take changes without breaking a sweat**. Of course I do know, like the old saying goes about teaching an old dog new tricks, that it is sometimes harder for an older person to change, but they can do it. I think that a lot of young people here in China have a hard time with changes because they have seen such few changes and like the way things are now.

   take changes without breaking a sweat 处乱不惊

Recent Changes in China

9. Do you think China has gone through a lot of changes in recent years?

   I think China has gone through some incredible changes in recent years. China is growing so quickly and at an alarming rate. Even the government is trying to slow it down so that it doesn't overheat. Economically, socially, China is really changing. Since the implementation of the open door policy, one can hardly recognize China, as the joke goes that the "**crane**" is the national bird of China.

   crane 鹤(在此指起重机)

10. What are the most positive changes?

    Well, of course, the economy is one of the most positive changes. Because of this change, China has a lot more money, so the Chinese people have a lot more money too. Joining the WTO has brought about some positive changes. People being able to go abroad easier is also a very nice change. Also more foreigners here in China has been a good change for all.

11. Do you think there will be more changes in the future?

Oh yes, I think that China is going to keep changing. As China takes more of a role on the world stage, this is going to have a big effect on the country. Foreign influence will continue to come into the country and cause changes like more mixed marriages and a mixture of cultures. But **at the drop of a hat**, we could also go back to a more closed society and that would be a big change, but one that is possible.

at the drop of a hat 突然间

三、话题相关材料

A Many things have changed our lives or made an impact. 不管大事小事，好事坏事，都有可能对我们的一生产生影响。下面是国外网友对这样一些事件的回忆。

What has been your most life changing moment or event so far?

1 Meeting my partner. He has helped me open up and become a better person. Since meeting him, my attitude towards life and other people has changed dramatically. Sounds corny, but it is true. If we hadn't gotten together, I'd be a completely different person now. And not a better one!

2 A life-changing event for me was traveling outside of the US for the first time. I realized that I really knew nothing about the other side of the world except for what I'd read or what I saw on TV. I've traveled to over 20 countries now, and it has been really eye-opening about how filtered our news is, how unaware of what's really going on in the world, and how accepting we are of the pictures of other cultures and people in the world that are painted for us on the nightly news.

3 The moment that changed my entire life was the moment when my parents got divorced. At that time and soon after, I got this feeling that now I'm grown up, all of a sudden, and my only aim in life is to keep my mom happy and to face this world and its people, which was very challenging. Although it's all fine now, that moment changed my entire life.

4 When I told the Navy recruiter that I did not want to enlist. Up to that point in my life I had been following everyone's advice. That was my first major decision, albeit a bad one upon reflection, but it was my decision none the less. After that, I started being more independent and making my own choices for good or bad. In other words, I started living my life instead of letting others live it for me.

5 Reading the book "Healing with Angels" by Doreen Virtue (I think Doreen is the first name). It isn't all about angels by the way. Anyway, in reading that, I found out that it is very

likely that I am a star child （Read the book if you wanna know what that is）. For quite some time prior to reading that book, I really felt like although I enjoy my job, it wasn't really contributing to society, and that really bothered me. I wanted a job where I could make the world a better place, but so far I don't really have one. Anyway, the book says that Star Children often don't have a meaningful job, but a job in which they come in contact with many people. Their contribution to society is how they are role models and affect the people who surround them. Reading that made me feel so much better about myself and my life, knowing that it's the people in my life that matter, not what I'm doing for a job. Since then I've been even more positive and caring and try to set a good example every day.

四、练习

A 请将下列句子翻译成英文。

1. 外面的世界很精彩，有些人想去看看那儿有没有自己最想要的东西。

____

2. 有些人就是有"这山望着那山高"的心态，他们以为一旦到了"另一座山"，就什么问题都解决了。

____

3. 我见过一些根本不知道如何去应对变化的年轻人，同时也见过一些对待变化处乱不惊的老人。

____

4. 我觉得中国近年来经历了让人难以置信的变化。

____

5. 越来越多的外国东西会继续涌入中国，从而带来像跨国婚姻、文化融合这样的一些变化。

____

（☞ P275）

B 听MP3实战演练。

经历类进阶级(Topics 29~36)

Topic 29 English Class Activities 英语课堂活动

一、考试说明

英语学习是雅思口语中一个永恒的话题，通常在考试的第一部分出现。“英语课堂活动”可以说是第一个出现在第二部分的有关语言学习的话题。考生要向考官描述自己喜欢的一个英语课堂活动，在第三部分里会围绕英语学习和文化与其展开讨论。课堂活动种类很多，如 presentation, role-play, group discussion 或者 debate 都可以作为素材进行阐述。在“真题演练”部分 native speaker 描述了自己学中文时的情况，虽然有些“跑题”，但答案的参考意义不受任何影响。“话题相关材料”部分为考生推荐了一个网上英语课堂活动库，供考生参考外国人是怎么学英语的。

二、真题演练

CUE CARD

Describe an unforgettable class activity that you have taken part in as part of your English study.

You should say:

what this activity was

when and where you did this activity

how you did it

and explain how you benefited from this activity.

点题	The best foreign language-learning activity I ever had took place in my sophomore year of college in my Chinese class with Mr. Wang.
活动	Every Monday, we would take about twenty minutes of class, and everyone had to stand up and say what they did over the weekend. The mini-speeches didn't have to be long or that **involved**; rather, it was just an opportunity to get everyone up and speaking Chinese. What made the activity fun, though, was not really the assignment. Instead, it was the class that made it interesting. The first couple Mondays, the speeches weren't anything special. Most were pretty boring, and the class had more of a "let's just get this done" attitude instead of an "I like this activity" attitude. The third Monday, however, this all changed. One of the students stood up and told an extremely **creative** story, using a lot of interesting phrases and some truly funny vocabulary. After this, the class all sort of accepted this as the new norm, and every week became a contest to see who could tell the funniest, most creative story. **As a result**, going to class on Monday became something to really look forward to.

收获	In addition, the activity also really helped out our language ability. No longer were we just taking words and phrases out of the book, we were looking for other places, trying to be the most creative. Not only was it really fun, it also encouraged working harder!

重点词句

involved 过分复杂的　　as a result 因此

creative 有创造性的

Part 3

Learning English

1. Why do people learn English in China?

   I believe people learn English in order to **adapt** to the **shrinking** of the world. **In this day and age**, contact and business from country to country is EXTREMELY easy, and as a result, language has become a **barrier** that you must **overcome** if you want to participate. Therefore, learning English for most people is a great way to be able to do business or make friends with foreigners. I think it's really positive.

   adapt to 适应　　barrier 障碍

   shrinking 缩小　　overcome 克服

   in this day and age 在这样一个年代

2. Some people say that if you are going to work in a Chinese company in China, then learning English is a waste of time. Do you agree?

   I do not agree at all with this statement for several reasons. First, how do you know you are always going to be working for a Chinese company? If you can speak English well, you might be able to get a better job in an international company. Secondly, why does language-learning only have to be about business? If you can speak English, you have expanded the number of friends you can possibly make. I have made friends with Chinese people only because they spoke English. I think the above statement is just an excuse given by people who don't want to try to learn new things.

3. What do you think is the best age for children to begin learning English?

   I believe that children should start learning foreign languages as early as possible. If they can, they should try and learn other languages as they are learning their native language. It has been proven that kids can pick up languages easier than adults. They are less **set in their ways** and more open to new things. I have a cousin who has a Mexican mother, an American father, and is living in Cairo, Egypt. He is only one year old now, but is already picking up Spanish, English, and Arabic.

Learning as a child saves a lot of **hassle** as an adult.

set in their ways 固定的、一成不变的 hassle 麻烦

4. Would you say it's better to study English overseas than in China?

I believe that for most people, this is not possible. Either it's too expensive or they can't find the time or a way to live in a foreign country, so it's **out of the question**. However, if they can arrange it, it is definitely easier to learn a foreign language in that country. Being surrounded by people speaking the language you are trying to learn is extremely helpful. The best way to do it, I think, is to take classes of a language to build a base, then go. That way, when you get to the country, you aren't totally **overwhelmed**.

out of the question 不可能的 overwhelmed 不知所措的

5. Do adults have more difficulties than children in learning a foreign language?

Yes, I believe this **wholeheartedly**. Adults who have been speaking one language for a long period of time may find many difficulties in learning a new language. They will also easily fall into the patterns of their native language, making learning hard. Kids, however, are still learning their native language, so they don't have **established** patterns to **fall back on**. As a result, new material is a lot easier for them to learn.

wholeheartedly 全心全意地 fall back on 依靠、求助

established 固定的、成型的

Language and Cultural Diversity

6. Why do people prefer to study English over other languages?

I believe that the reason is mostly economic. English-speaking countries, **for the most part**, make up most of the richest countries in the world. As a result, many people want to learn English so that they can do business with companies in those rich countries. In addition, English has kind of been accepted as one of very few, if not the only, worldwide languages. People all over the world speak English. Therefore, people who want to participate in relationships that **span** the globe find that English is the most common language to do this.

for the most part 总体来说 span 跨越

7. English is now used as an international language. What other languages do you think might develop into international languages?

English is indeed used as an international language. The only other language I can see achieving this status is Chinese. The number of people who speak it is great, and the country is growing economically so quickly that I think more and more people worldwide are going to choose to learn it. The biggest barrier to this, however, is that Chinese is written in characters. It may be a **pipe dream**, but if Chinese changed to *pinyin* as the way to write and read, I think it would explode all over the world. I, speaking as someone trying to learn it, can **testify** as to how much easier that would make learning the language.

pipe dream 白日梦 testify 证明

8. Besides English, what other foreign languages do people study in China?

In China, learning English **reigns supreme**. I imagine that it is by far the most popular language to learn in the country. No other language **comes close**, I think. If I had to choose some other languages for people to learn, I would guess that Japanese and Spanish would be the next two. Japanese is important because of the size of the Japanese economy. Spanish, because it is so similar to English, is fairly easy to learn, and because many people worldwide speak it.

reigns supreme 占统治地位 come close 媲美

9. Compare the future popularity of Chinese and English as foreign languages to study.

English became as popular as it is now because of the extreme wealth and worldwide influence of English-speaking countries (especially the US). People realized that one of the best ways to make money was to do business with Americans, and in order to do this, they had to learn English. I think that China is **approaching** this position now. Its economic influence is spreading extremely fast, and people across the world are realizing that learning Chinese is a great way to make money. As a result, in the future, I think Chinese will start approaching the popularity of English, though probably not ever **overtaking** it.

approach 接近 overtake 赶上

10. Do you think studying foreign languages can benefit world peace? (How?)

Yes, I do believe that if countries can speak to each other easily, tensions are much easier to get rid of. Just as important, however, is studying the culture of other countries. Understanding that other countries might act differently or **take offense** at different actions is a great way to create a more easygoing atmosphere. But yes, language is definitely the first step towards creating a more peaceful environment.

take offense 生气、见怪

11. What difficulties do you think international guests might have when they study Chinese?

There are many answers to this question. First, reading feels like an impossible task. Forcing yourself to **memorize** characters rather than being able to read and figure out the meanings of words is a huge barrier. It is extremely **intimidating** to see the thousands of characters and realize you have to memorize most of them. Secondly, the **tones** are particularly difficult. Learning a language where the inflection can indicate what kind of attitude you have, and realizing that it isn't just what you are saying but how you are saying it that affects the meaning is really difficult. There are also many others, like learning **neutral accents** and proper pronunciation.

memorize 记忆 tone 语调

intimidating 吓人的、打击人的 neutral accents 普通话

三、话题相关材料

A 补充语汇

Dave's ESL Café(http://www.eslcafe.com/)是个很受国外英语教师和英语学习者欢迎的网站，里面有很多学习和教学素材。下面就是一个德国英语教师在课堂上尝试过的一个活动，大家可以参考他讲故事的方法。

Celebrity 10 Questions

Before class, I take index cards and write names of celebrities on them with a magic marker.

In class, I explain to the students that they will have a name of a well-known person stuck to their back. They then have to stand up and circulate around the room, asking each person a maximum of 10 yes-or-no questions about who they might be. (i.e. "Am I alive? Am I female? Am I a politician? Am I young?")

Hopefully they will be able to figure out who they are. The only problem I have encountered is when I use movie stars. I try to select people who my German students would know, but many don't frequent the cinema.

I like this game a lot, since it gets them out of their seats and makes them talk to a large number of people, often those who they wouldn't normally approach in the first lesson. It also works well if you're practicing questions.

—Karen Jochimsen, Marburg/Germany (instructor at the adult ed. center)

四、练习

A 请将下列句子翻译成英文。

1. 每个星期一，我们在班上会用20分钟的时间让每个人站起来讲述一下周末做了什么。

____

2. 但从第三周开始，情况完全变了。有个学生站起来讲了个极有创意的故事，用到了很多有意思的表达方式和词汇。

____

3. 我们不再是单单从书本上搬下一些词和表达方式，我们开始把目光投向其他地方，尝试着去成为最有创意的人。

____

4. 这可能有点痴人说梦，但如果中国人把拼音作为读写语言的方式的话，中文肯定能横扫全世界。

____

5. 英语之所以现在如此盛行，是由于英语国家(主要是美国)的巨大财富和国际影响力。

____

(☞ P276)

B 听MP3实战演练。

Topic 30 Advice 建议

一、考试说明

建议是雅思口语考试中的新话题。考生向考官描述自己得到过的建议，其实本质上还是考查考生讲故事的能力。生活中我们无时无刻不在寻求着建议，接受着建议。在“真题演练”部分native speaker讲述快大学毕业时父亲给予的有关人生规划的建议，在第三部分围绕advice giving展开了讨论。“话题相关资料”部分罗列出国外一些网友讲述的对自己最有帮助的建议，很多也都是人生的道理，供考生借鉴。

二、真题演练

CUE CARD

Describe some advice you received (from a friend or family member) which was useful to you.

You should say:

what the situation was

who gave you the advice

what the advice was

and explain how useful you think the advice was.

点题	The best piece of advice I ever got came from my Dad.
问题	It happened in my junior year of college. At that time, I was just starting to think about what I wanted to do with my life. My dad helped me a huge amount.
建议	Rather than just tell me what he thought I should do, though, he told me a story about his own life. Immediately after he got out of college, he took a job in Florida selling **real estate**. He **ended up** doing that for something like seven years. During the entire time he was doing it, he was pretty unhappy. Sure, he had a pretty happy **home life** and a good family, but his job wasn't **rewarding**. He took it in order to make money, not to be happy. Eventually, he found something that interested him. We moved to Ohio, so he could start a **brewery** with one of his friends from college. The job was much more interesting. He didn't come home at the end of the day relieved to be done with work. He actually enjoyed what he did.
感受	This story taught me an extremely valuable lesson. I shouldn't just jump into a job because it paid well. I should take time to find a job that I would actually like. Money shouldn't be the **number one concern**. It was **due to** this advice that I moved here, to China.

重点词句

real estate 房地产

end up 最终

home life 家庭生活

rewarding 有意义的、值得的

brewery 酿酒厂

number one concern 要考虑的首要因素

due to 由于

Part 3
Advice Giving

1. Have your parents given you much advice?

   Yes, my parents have given me **tons of** advice. They always do it in a way, though, where they aren't just telling me what to do. Instead, they give me some of their wisdom, and let me do with it what I want. **This way**, I can make more **informed** decisions about important stuff.

   tons of 很多的

   informed 明智的、有依据的

   this way 这样的话

2. What kind of advice do parents give their children?

   I've found that it really varies what kind of advice parents give. Many of my friends' parents are really **overbearing**. They try to force themselves into every decision their kids make, be it important （like moving）or unimportant （like buying a bike）. Other parents are really **hands-off**. They let their kids make all their own decisions. This way kids can learn from their own mistakes. I think each way has its advantages and disadvantages.

   overbearing 专横的

   hands-off 不干涉的

3. What kind of advice do friends give each other?

   Friends seem to give each other advice about things that they have experienced before on their own. For instance, I've lived in China, so I can help my friends decide whether it'd be a smart move for them. These situations are useful, because friends are often of the same age, so they can offer a viewpoint from someone who is going through the same kinds of situations. Most of the time, though, friends' advice tends to be about small things, like what clothes to wear or what stuff to buy. These situations aren't really advice, but more suggestions or what they think.

4. Do you think young people should follow their parents' advice?

   No, I don't think young people should follow all of their parents' advice. I think they should listen to what their parents have to say, and use that information to **come up with** their own decisions. Parents are there to help kids out when they need it, but not to instruct their kids how to live their lives. If you rely on your parents too much, you might eventually end up in a situation where they are not around to help you, and you have to make a decision about something you've never thought about on your own before.

   come up with 想出、得出

5. In China, do children ever strongly oppose the advice of their parents?

I'm not too sure. But in my limited experience, it seems that Chinese people really rely on their parents. Therefore, I think that it's rare to see a Chinese person **flat out** denying what their parents suggest they do. It seems that they are far more likely to **take** what their parents say **into consideration** than to not listen to it.

flat out 直截了当的　　　　take... into consideration 考虑在内

6. In China, do young people ever give advice to older people, for example, their parents?

I think, yeah, there's absolutely nothing wrong with giving advice. You can make your opinions known, then whoever you are talking to can choose whether or not to listen to it. Giving advice does nothing more than try to give the person who is making a decision a little bit more information than they had before. This is especially so in the case of parents and children, because so many of parents' decisions affect kids' lives, so the kids should have a say in the decision-making process.

7. Which has more influence on young people, advice from their parents or their friends?

This is a tough but good question. I think that when kids are really young, like under twelve, they rely on their parents more than their friends. When they become teenagers, though, I think they listen to a much larger percentage of their friends' advice. Kids at this age are really **concerned with** being cool and being accepted, and their parents aren't that big of a help to them. Their friends know what is cool and what's not. As they get older, though, I think that people rely on their friends and family pretty **equally**. By this time, I think most people realize the value in everyone's opinions, so they consider what everybody says.

be concerned with 关注于　　　　equally 同等的

8. Have you ever received advice from an expert or professional (other than your parents)?

Yeah, I guess I have, if you consider teachers professional people. **Many a time** I have asked teachers for advice. For example, when I was thinking about moving to China, I asked my Asian Humanities professor what he thought about the idea. He thought it would be a great move, and I took what he said into consideration. Other than teachers, though, no, I haven't really had the need to ask experts or professionals for advice. I haven't made any big enough decisions that would require anyone outside of my friends and family.

many a time 多次

9. In China, is there anywhere where members of the public can get advice?

Yeah, there are places to go for advice. One I absolutely know of is the Internet. Any time I have to make a decision, I look online for different websites that have reviews or suggestions about different things. The Internet is a hugely valuable resource for things like this. Other than that, though, I can't really think of anywhere people can go for advice.

三、话题相关材料

A 生活中我们无时无刻不在寻求、接受并提供着建议。什么是你得到的最好的建议呢？下面是一些国外网友的讲述，看看有没有共鸣。

What's the best piece of advice you have ever received about succeeding in life?

I started college when I was 28. I knew it would take me a long time （10 years）to finish going part time at night, and I was discouraged when thinking about being 38 when I graduated. The advice I got: How old will you be in ten years if you DON'T go to college? So, yes, I finished （at 38）. I even went on to get my Master's, and guess what--they did not put my age on either diploma!

Never date anyone you work with. My dad told me that when I was in high school, and now many years down the road I've seen what office relationships can do to you and how badly they can turn out, and I am thankful for that advice.

Best advice I ever got was from my grandfather on my wedding day. He pulled me aside and told me he'd been married for 53 years, and the one thing he learned was that the woman is the man of the family.

The best advice I ever got was actually more like a motto, but it's always stuck with me. Someone once told me that, "The only people that can offend you are those who are better than you". Basically say, don't let stupid people get to you, which helps when dealing with some of the retards in the world.

There are two actually, you can attract more flies with honey than vinegar （be nice to everyone）, and don't shit where you eat （office romances don't work）. I always adhere to both, and they've held me in good stead.

The best advice I ever got was "take my advice but do not do what I say. Do what you think you should do in your life...you have to make your own decisions." which was from my friend.

四、练习

A 请将下列句子翻译成英文。

1. 那个时候我刚开始考虑人生之路该如何走，我老爸在这方面给了我很大帮助。

____

2. 这个故事给我上了很宝贵的一课。

____

3. 爸妈给了我很多建议，但他们给建议的方式并不是仅仅告诉我该怎么做。

____

4. 有些父母真的是从不干涉孩子，他们让孩子决定自己所有的事情，这样的话他们就可以从错误中吸取教训。

____

____

5. 如果太依赖父母，很可能到最后会出现这样一种情况：爸妈不在身边，而你得面对以前从没有想过的问题而做出决策。

____

____

（☞ P276）

B 听 MP3 实战演练。

Topic 31 An Unsatisfactory Purchase 不愉快的购物经历

一、考试说明

买完东西却发现并不是很称心，遇到这种情况你会如何处理呢？2006年开始，在雅思考场上考生有可能要把这样的经历告诉考官了。第三部分的讨论围绕购物和售后服务展开。在“真题演练”部分native speaker讲述了自己买电热水壶的经历，不过她既没有去退（ask for a refund），也没有去换（exchange），只是提醒自己以后要去一个更信得过的地方去购物，真是够大度的。“话题相关材料”部分列出了大超市的是是非非。

二、真题演练

CUE CARD
Describe an item that you bought that you were dissatisfied with.
You should say:
what the item was
when and where you bought it
why you were not happy with this product.
And explain what you did after you found that it was unsatisfactory.

购物过程	Well, I very much enjoy drinking coffee; unfortunately, I do not always have very hot water. Three months ago I decided to do something about it. I went to the Fu Cheng Men market to buy **a water heater**. I chose the most convenient one: a little pad on which you place your cup and it is supposed to heat the liquid inside. It was being sold for a very reasonable price, and I only had to **bargain** for a short time.
故障	I brought it home, but then forgot about it for about one month. One day I wanted to have some hot coffee and remembered the water heater I had bought. So I went and found it and **plugged it in**. However, When I placed the cup on the pad, it heated the coffee very poorly. In fact, it didn't even make the coffee warm.
处理办法	I was very angry, so I threw it away. Now I have to use a stove to boil the water first. I'm sure next time I decide to buy such a product as a water heater, I will look in a more **reliable place** and probably try to get **a trusted brand**. I will also have to write a note to remind myself of my purchase so that I can discover problems earlier, and thus have time to exchange it.

重点词句

water heater 电热水壶

bargain 讨价还价

plug in 插上电源

reliable place 值得信赖的地方

a trusted brand 值得信赖的品牌

Part 3
Shopping in China

1. Are the services in big stores and small ones the same?

   Of course not. In big stores there are often plenty of attendants to help you with your choice; whereas in small stores, you are left to yourself. Also, if you do not go to a reliable store, you sometimes cannot exchange your purchase if you find fault with it.

2. What services should shops provide?

   They should have people there who are familiar with the store and its product to help you find what you need. Some shops should provide **snack bars** in case you get hungry or thirsty while shopping. I also think it would be helpful if stores had **a delivery service**, so if you were busy, you would not have to do the shopping yourself. Maybe some shops could provide discounts to frequent customers.

   snack bar 快餐厅

   delivery service 送货服务

3. Which do you think is more important in a shop, service or the quality of the goods?

   The quality of goods. I think the quality is most important because if there are no services, people can take care of themselves. Services are simply a luxury, an extra, and pretty much unnecessary. But if the products are not of good quality, then they will not meet the needs of the customer. This, in the end, may make the customer search for another shop.

4. What are the advantages and disadvantages of supermarkets?

   One advantage is that you can find everything you need in the same store. Another is that you can find several brands of the same product, and then make a better selection. I do think, however, that the disadvantages slightly outweigh the advantages. For one, a supermarket can be noisy and large, confusing the new shoppers. Also, prices tend to be higher in big supermarkets.

5. How can supermarkets attract more customers, or retain customers?

   Well, I would say by making sure there are plenty of different options for each product, different varieties and prices, maybe also advertising sales. Of course if they did that they would need to have more sales, so that people feel this supermarket is better than the others. The supermarket should be clean and well kept, and employees should be reliable. Those at the **check-out counters** should know the product, and also know how to use the machines well so that they do not **hold up** the customers.

   check-out counters 收银处

   hold up 耽误

Products

6. What are the advantages and disadvantages of machine-made and hand-made goods?

   I have recently discovered the **superiority** of hand-made products, especially in clothes. When something is personally made, it has **a special feel**, and the quality is much finer. Machines do not have eyes to catch the **defects**. However, when it comes to hand-made products, the production process may not be **sanitary** or those making the product may not be fully reliable in making it correctly.

   superiority 优越性　　defect 缺陷

   a special feel 特别的感觉　　sanitary 卫生的、干净的

7. Do people prefer machine-made or hand-made products?

   I would say nowadays people prefer the machine-made products. I think I may be one of **the odd ones out** when it comes to wanting hand-tailored clothing. But it really depends on the products. Maybe those people who have a little more money can afford to choose things made by hand which have been made correctly and in a clean and satisfactory environment.

   the odd one out 特立独行之人

8. What handmade products do you think will still be popular in the future?

   In my opinion, it would be clothes and some decorations. There are some things that require the classic feeling of quality and uniqueness. Machines often take the creativity out of an object. When something is hand-carved, or hand-sewn, it makes you feel as though this product is special, and is worth more.

9. How do you feel about food additives that are in the food you buy?

   The only good point I know of to food additives is that they make the food look or taste better. Other than that, I have to say they make me afraid to eat certain foods. I won't buy foods that I know have a lot of **preservatives** or MSG. I think these harmful chemicals used in food production should be made illegal. I mean, thousands of years ago, man survived, and even enjoyed his food without these damaging additives.

   preservatives 防腐剂　　MSG 味精

10. What rights do you think consumers have?

    Hmm, slightly difficult question. The **right of choice** maybe. If I go into a supermarket, do I have a choice between food loaded with preservatives and that naturally grown with **organic fertilizers** and nothing added? No, I do not, and I think the right of choice should be provided to consumers. If I were to be able to choose between products with too high a sugar content and those with natural healthy sugar, I would feel much more satisfied.

    right of choice 选择权　　organic fertilizers 有机肥

三、话题相关材料

A 大超市与小商店之争

对很多人而言，超市和购物中心是现代生活不可或缺的一部分。但大超市的扩张的确挤垮了众多的小商店，其中的利弊如何，下面这篇文章供考生参考。

Supermarkets vs. local shops

To many, supermarkets are an integral part of modern life, but should their expansion be at the cost of local stores? TheSite.org looks at the pros and cons of supermarket shopping.

For	Against
Time savers: Let's be honest, life without supermarkets would be total hell. Gone are the days of trawling the high street all day long, and now we can fit shopping into our busy schedules. We're not even restricted by opening hours, with many supermarkets now open 24 hours. **Choice:** Supermarkets now offer the choice of up to 40,000 products—everything from economy to niche products at competitive prices; they provide free car-parking, home deliveries and internet shopping. And you can get supposed seasonal vegetables all year round. **Transport links:** There are bus schemes: a number of outlets offer taxi services; and some are investigating outlets on estates, although the high rate of crimes is putting them off. **Affordable:** Supermarkets have reduced the cost of some grocery shopping and made one-time luxuries into basics, which means many of us whose outgoings often exceed incomings on payday do not starve.	**Overkill:** Supermarket competitiveness can harm local food economies that sustain our market towns and villages, the food producers who supply them, and the people who depend on them. Their monopoly on the market allows them to dictate how much they pay farmers, while at the same time seeking out cheaper food from abroad. **Exclusive:** Not all consumers are in easy reach of a supermarket. Hard as it may be to believe, there are those who have no car, no internet, and whose shopping budgets are too small to qualify for home deliveries. **Unsociable:** The glazed expression of a supermarket check-out girl does not offer the social contact and conversation that can be found in a local shop. **Local shops:** When superstores open, small shops close. Not always, but it does happen, especially when ridiculously over-sized stores open on the local shop's doorstep. **Freshness:** Local markets and shops tend to stock fresher local produce rather than the standardised, symmetrical and blander vegetables you will find in supermarkets.

四、练习

A 请将下列句子翻译成英文。

1. 东西卖的很便宜，所以我没怎么还价。

____

2. 我会去个更信得过的地方，挑个更让人信赖的牌子。

____

3. 商店应该提供快餐厅，以免顾客购物时感到饥饿或口渴。还有，如果商店要是有送货服务就好了。

____

4. 优点之一就是你可以在同一家商店找到所有你需要的。优点之二是同一样商品，你可以找到多个品牌，从而做出更好的选择。

____

5. 如果一个东西是手刻的，或是手工缝制的，你可能会觉得这东西就有了特别之处，因此更值钱了。

____

（☞ P276）

B 听 MP3 实战演练。

Topic 32　Exhibitions 展览

一、考试说明

展览话题难度较大，一是由于大多数考生很少参加展览，二是由于描述展览所需的词汇比较独特。考生向考官描述完自己参观过的展览后，在第三部分里会围绕展览的方方面面与其展开讨论。在选材过程中考生应尽可能选择有文化、历史或考古意义的展览，这样会更切题，而尽量不要描述车展或教育展，因为严格地讲，他们属于 trade fair。在“真题演练”部分 native speaker 描述的是蜡像展，语言自然生动。“话题相关材料”部分提供了对 2006 年国内两个备受关注的展览的介绍，语言更为专业和漂亮。

二、真题演练

CUE CARD
Describe an art exhibition that you visited.
You should say:
when you saw this exhibition
where the exhibition was held
what was on display
and explain your impression of the exhibition.

点题	When I was a little girl, I went to a museum near my home that was exhibiting **life-size wax sculptures.**
内容	It was in a large room of the museum. The wax figures showed people from different occupations and different **poses**. Each looked so real that it almost seemed as if a real person was actually standing there and staying perfectly still. For the first half hour when I was in the room, I was sure that one of the figures would begin to move, and that I would finally prove that they were really just people. The skill of the sculptor was amazing in how each one was perfectly made to exhibit the human body's **texture**, **posture** and size.
特写	I was especially amazed at the wax figure of the cowboy. It seemed that he came right out of an old western movie with his cowboy pants, gun and **spurred boots**. There was also the figure of a woman at a beach, with a swimsuit, towel, sunglasses and surfboard. There was a policeman, his hand held out to stop traffic with a whistle in his mouth. There was a mechanic, with his hand resting on the **hood** of a car that he had just fixed and the illusion of **grease smudges** all over his hands, face and clothes.
感受	As a young girl, I was amazed at how someone could make a statue look so real.

重点词句

life-size 真人大小
wax sculptures 蜡像
pose 姿势
texture 肌理
posture 姿势
spurred boots 带马刺的靴子
hood 前车盖
grease 油
smudge 弄脏

Part 3
Museums

1. Does China have many museums? What kind?

   Yes, there are many. In the places that I've been most of the museums are about **dinosaurs** or stars. There are also some **marine**, bird and insect museums. Often there's a little bit of all of them mixed into one museum.

   dinosaur 恐龙
   marine 海洋的

2. Are museums popular in China?

   Not so popular. They are mostly for children or students. Sometimes you will see a whole family go to a museum or perhaps a young couple, but it is quite rare. Sometimes grandparents would take their grandchildren there.

3. How could museums attract more visitors?

   I think if the museums had more **interactive exhibits**, then they would be more interesting for most people. It would also help people to learn more from actually being able to see first-hand what is happening and how different things work. Having exhibits that change each week or so would make people who have already been there want to go again to see something new. Also people who have not gone yet would want to go as soon as they can so they don't miss something, whereas if it's always the same then they would **put it off**, thinking they catch it later.

   interactive exhibits 互动展品
   put off 推迟

4. Do you think people should have to pay to visit museums?

   I think it's not a good idea for people to have to pay all the time. I think it's a good idea for part or most of the museum to be free, but if people want to see certain parts or participate in special things, then they have to pay. If people have to pay each time they go, and especially if it's expensive, then many won't go or won't go very often. The reason why I think this is bad is that I think it's very educational to be able to look at and learn from all the things in museums.

5. How will museums change in the future?

   I think that museums will become more modernized and more accurate. I think that they will have better and more interesting exhibits. The way they are set up and advertised I think will also improve so that they are more appealing to the general public. I think they will also have more interesting themes displayed and exhibited.

Art Education

6. Do schools in China have art classes?

No, not really. Sometimes they do, but most of the time if the students or their parents want children to study art, they must go to special art classes. Or the schools do have art classes, but they aren't part of the curriculum, and parents must pay extra to have their children attend these classes. More often than not, children in China don't take art classes, and few children ever develop an interest in it.

7. Should arts education be part of the school curriculum?

Yes, it should. I think art is a very important subject, because it not only encourages **self-expression**, but also is a creative art and helps to develop **artistic creativity** in many areas of life, not just art. Also, children who feel they are accomplished and are able to do something more than study do better in other classes and subjects, because they have a higher **self-esteem**. Children who don't know how to do anything other than their basic subjects will **feel inferior to** their **peers,** and will not perform as well in class as they could.

self-expression 自我表达
artistic creativity 艺术创造力
self-esteem 自我满意度
feel inferior to 感觉不如…
peers 同龄人

8. How do you think art classes affect child development?

They help to develop a child's creativity and curiosity. They help a child to express himself through the things he draws, notice the things around him and learn from them. Art also encourages an admiration for nature and living things, so children who have been taught to appreciate art are less likely to do things that are harmful to the environment, to others, or to themselves.

9. What kind of paintings do Chinese people like?

Hmmm, that's a little hard to answer. I think that Chinese paintings are very popular in China. Most people here in China like paintings in the Chinese style or paintings of familiar scenes here. There are also quite a few abstract and realistic paintings and styles that are popular with certain groups of people.

10. Some paintings are very expensive, but people still want to buy them. Why do you think they do so?

I think that most of the time they want to have a very expensive painting so that they can show it off to their friends. Or maybe they feel it makes them look more in style or more fashionable to have expensive paintings by famous people. Some people collect paintings or works of art, so they will get anything they think will look nice with their collections.

11. What benefits can you get from painting as a hobby?

I think there are many benefits. For one, it can be very relaxing to paint, especially if you are outside in nature. Also it can help to take your mind off of any problem or stress that you might have from your work. It will also improve your creativity and help you to think better.

三、话题相关材料

A 下面是国外媒体对中国国内2006年两场备受瞩目的展览的介绍，看看有没有你需要的语言资源。

UK to lend world treasures to China

The British Museum will try to avoid a diplomatic minefield later this month when it lends 272 of its most precious artefacts to the Capital Museum of Beijing in one of the highest level cultural exchanges between the two countries.

None of the items in the Treasures of the World's Culture collection will be Chinese because many people in Beijing refuse to recognise British claims to porcelain, statues and books they say were acquired by imperial force.

According to the United Nations, 1.64 million Chinese artefacts are scattered in 47 museums around the world. Chinese authorities estimate that 10 times that number are in the hands of private collectors. For many Chinese, foreign ownership is a continued humiliation.

The exhibition, which will run from March 18 to June 5, has been hailed by both sides as a breakthrough in relations between the world's oldest national museum and one of the newest of a host of giant cultural institutions built in the Chinese capital.

Ancient Egyptian tablets, Greek busts and the world's oldest tool will be among the items on display in the first major overseas exhibition staged at the new museum—a gleaming structure of glass, steel and stone that opened in December.

Curators on both sides say they hope for an improved climate for further cultural exchanges. In the next few years Beijing will lend the British Museum a number of items. The UK institution will also lend some Chinese treasures to the palace museum in the Forbidden City.

"The Land gives me Rice, Rice gives me Life"

An exhibition of photos taken by rice farmers kick-off this Sunday
to promote sustainable agriculture

Rice is the world's staple food. China's Yunnan province is one of the homelands of rice where thousands of varieties of rice have been farmed using traditional methods spanning thousands of years. The world's rice crop, our environment, farmer's livelihoods and consumer health are all threatened by the imminent introduction of genetically engineered (GE) rice and the use of other unsustainable industrialised farming practices, such as chemical pesticides.

In October 2004, Greenpeace China organised an 8-day "The Road of Rice — The Ecological Agriculture Tour" in Yunnan to celebrate "Biodiversity for Food Security," the theme of 2004's World Food Day. Yunnan province is one of the homelands of rice and still claims one of the richest diversities of rice in the world. Rice farming is intrinsically linked to people's everyday life and culture. The tour showcased the diverse and sustainable rice farming in the region.

During the tour rice farmers were given Polaroid cameras. This was the first time most of the farmers ever held a camera, yet pictures taken were of high standard. It was here that the Yunnan Rice Farmer's Photo project was born. Rice Farmers from different parts of Yunnan province and different cultures, with traditional farming methods learned over generations, were given cameras and invited to document one year in the life of their villages.

Famous Yunnan photographer, Mr.Geng Yunsheng, was hired to oversee the photography and work closely with the photographer-farmers for the duration of the project. Five traditional rice farmers were selected to document one year in the life of each of their 5 villages, and 56 images were selected.

四、练习

A 请将下列句子翻译成英文。

1. 每个蜡像看着都那么逼真，就好像一个真人站在那里一动不动。

____

2. 我对那个牛仔的蜡像尤其感到惊奇。

____

3. 我想如果博物馆有更多的互动展品的话会更有意思。

____

4. 如果人们每次去都要交钱，而且门票还挺贵的话，人们就不会去或者不会经常去了。

____

5. 博物馆布展和宣传的方式也要有所改进，这样才会更加吸引老百姓。

____

(☞ P277)

B 听MP3实战演练。

Topic 33　Being Late 迟到的经历

一、考试说明

“一次迟到的经历”是口语部分的新题。考生描述完自己的故事后，考官在第三部分里会围绕准时的重要性与时间管理等话题与其展开讨论。在“真题演练”部分讲的是自己在朋友的聚会上迟到的经历。在“话题相关材料”部分，提供的是国外网友对如何让自己变得准时提出的一些建议。

二、真题演练

CUE CARD

Describe an (important) occasion you were late for.

You should say:

when this happened

what occasion you were late for

why you were late

and explain what happened as a result of your lateness.

点题事件	One occasion that I was late for was not that long ago. What happened was that I had some important work to do, and there was a deadline on this work. At the time, in our house we need **finances**. Some unexpected things came up, and we were a little short. Then an opportunity came, almost like **a godsend**, a chance where I could make some extra money. On top of that, by the **graciousness** of my friends, who are more like my family, they agreed to help me with this project that had a deadline to it. So I was very happy about that. Meanwhile I started taking care of some business, but then I looked at my watch and noticed I was five minutes late for getting together with my friends. I thought, “here my friends are willing to help me with this project and deadline, and here I am, five minutes late.”
结果	By the time I got there I was 10 minutes late, and there they all were waiting for me. You talk about embarrassing. Well, all I could do was apologize and **thankfully** they all accepted my apology and we moved on.

重点词句

finances 资金
graciousness 亲切、和蔼
godsend 天赐良机
thankfully 感激地

Part 3
Being Late

1. What are some of the excuses that people make when they are late?
   Well, "the alarm didn't go off, the bus was late or I was caught in traffic." Those are just a few of the most-heard excuses. "My mom is sick, and I have to take care of her." is another. "I have to take my brother to school." will work sometimes. "I got caught in the rain." helps in the spring time.

2. Are people in China usually punctual when they have to be somewhere at a certain time?
   Well, I wouldn't say that they are there on time every time, but they are getting there. They are starting to have the same attitude with people in the West that "time is money". It really is a bit of a hard habit to break, as the style of life and the culture have not been that of arriving right **on the dot**. Of course if people really want to be punctual, and it is really important to them, then they will do everything they can to get there on time.
   on the dot 很准时的

3. What do people in China think of people who are late?
   Actually Chinese people are pretty generous overall with people who are late. They are understanding and don't make a big deal out of it. On the other hand, if they are really bothered by people being late, you wouldn't know about it anyway, as most Chinese people don't **reveal their feelings** very easily. Overall they are pretty easygoing on people who are late.
   make a big deal out of it 小题大做
   reveal their feelings 显示自己的情感

4. Do you think it's important to be on time? (Is punctuality important?)
   Yes, I think it is very important to be on time. If you are not on time, then you are basically robbing the time of others. It really shows a lack of respect for others and that you don't think their time is important.

5. For what situations is being on time important?
   Immediately the first thing that comes to my mind is your own wedding. If any event is important I would say that is, getting to your wedding. There is a funny saying in the West. It goes something like this, "He would be late to his own funeral!" I suppose that is a little extreme but funny, though no one has ever been late for that. A job interview would be an important time not to be late. If you want to make a good impression, and they say "first impressions are the greatest ones," then you should try to be there early.

6. For what situations is being on time not very important?

If you were going to go and meet your friends for a game of basketball, and you knew they were going to be there for the afternoon, then you would not have to get there on the dot but would have a little **leeway** on arriving. If you were supposed to be home for dinner, but you came in a little late, that would be understandable. If you were going to your parents for the day, and you came a little late, they would understand. Most situations in which being late isn't too important would involve friends and family.

leeway 自由、余地

Time

7. Do you think modern technology gives us more time, or less?

Definitely less! If anything, modern technology has sped time up with things moving faster everyday. Because of email, now letters are able to be sent and received and answers are expected right away sometimes. With transportation, you can get to places faster and do a lot more. Things are actually moving incredibly fast, and that means less time for all.

8. Did people in the past lead a faster-paced life or a slower-paced life than today?

Well, I think that there is no comparison with the life of the past and today; in the past things definitely went a lot slower. You know that two hundred and some years ago the fastest means of transportation was on the back of a horse, and now you can circle the globe in hours. There was no email or Internet, so information went **creeping** along at a leisurely pace. I think that maybe things were moving so slowly that some people felt bored with it, but now it seems that people are bored with this fast paced modern life that we live.

creep 缓慢移动

9. Do you think the current working hours of most people are reasonable?

I know that in the US people are working more and more hours, and even here in China people have to work overtime. It seems that your work should get accomplished in the time that you have during a nine to five day, but sometimes that doesn't happen. It seems to me that however long it takes to get your work done would be a reasonable amount of hours to put in. I'm sure that people would like to work fewer hours, and that would be nice, but again it depends on what their job and goals are.

10. Is it reasonable for an employer to ask employees to work overtime?

Of course an employer should ask his employees to work overtime if it is really needed. Some people probably think that it is not needed, but if it is going to help the company, then they should be willing to do it. Now if some employees are doing their work and others aren't, and all have to work overtime, then I would say that no—this is not really needed and the problem should be fixed first. Actually I think that if the employee is **conscientious**, then he would volunteer to work overtime if needed.

conscientious 尽职尽责的

三、话题相关材料

A 下面这位女士无论做什么都会迟到，为此她懊恼不已，还贴出求助帖子。网友们倒是很热情，答案五花八门，其中也不乏幽默搞笑者。

Can you tell me how can I become punctual?

HELP!! I am ALWAYS late. Late to work, late to dates, late to church, late to everything! It's really bad because I'm responsible for a lot of things (for example, I'm the church pianist and am STILL late!). The strange thing is that I'm not a lazy or irresponsible person, just not punctual. Is there anyone out there who has conquered the same problem and can tell me how?

1 You are probably focused on yourself a lot. Try to think how it feels to be kept waiting all of the time. Set your clock early, and don't procrastinate with things that need to be done. You just have to change your focus, and you will get the hang of being punctual.

2 Often being late originates from underestimating the amount of time it will take you to get somewhere, so just leave an extra ten minutes early. Forget about "just quickly finishing something up" before you leave, and think about how the other people who got to your destination on time feel about having to wait for you.

3 Get a watch. Get a calendar and use it. Check your calendar daily to verify your schedule for the day. Set your clock forward 15 minutes. Consider riding with a friend that's always punctual. Get married. You being wife will nag you enough to get you where you need to be on time. Otherwise, move back in with Mom...She got you this far, didn't she?

4 Confide in a friend or significant other that you have this problem and are serious about overcoming it. If they agree to help you, keep track of the times you are late and by how many minutes. Once a week meet with your helper, go over how many times you were late and the total number of minutes you were late. Then you must strip and take a spanking from your helper. One swat for every minute late. After the first session, your punctuality will increase each week until your bad habit is broken.

四、练习

A 请将下列句子翻译成英文。

1. 等我赶到的时候，我迟到了 10 分钟，他们都在那儿等我。

____

2. 我能做的就是道歉，让人感激的是他们接受了我的歉意，我们又继续做下面的事情了。

____

3. “闹钟没响、汽车晚点或者堵车了”是我们最常听到的借口。

____

4. 这个习惯真不好改，因为这里的生活方式和文化并不要求无论做什么都要特别准时。

____

5. 这表示你对别人缺乏尊重，因为你觉得别人的时间不重要。

____

（☞ P277）

B 听 MP3 实战演练。

Topic 34 A Time When You Help Someone 帮助别人的经历

一、考试说明

帮助别人的经历大家都有，不管大事小事，因此这个面对这个话题考生不难想出素材来。然而跟其他事件题一样，这个话题难就难在讲故事上。在“真题演练”部分，作者讲述了自己帮助乞丐的经历，在第三部分考官围绕各种各样的帮助题材与其展开了讨论。考生在生活中可能也会发现如果面对别人生活中的问题，我们很容易给出建议和帮助，可一旦这些问题发生在自己身上，我们往往会束手无策，这是为什么呢？在“话题相关材料”部分，考生可以看到很多国外网友对这个现象的解释。

二、真题演练

CUE CARD

Describe a time when you helped someone.

You should say:

who you helped

how you helped them

how you felt when you helped them

and explain how this person benefited from your help.

铺垫	Well, I try to help people whenever I can, even if it is in a small way. I try to help my parents with work in the house, and I usually **help with** the cooking whenever I'm around at the time the meal is being made. If I pass beggars on the street, I often give them something, though not always. Sometimes I'm not sure they are real poor people because I've heard there are a lot of **fakes** who just pretend to be poor or sick.
事件	One time in particular, I passed an old man who was begging. It was early in the morning, and I was on my way to a class. Something inside me caused me to **take special note of** this man. I started to get some money out of my bag for him when it seemed, as if a little voice inside told me to get some food for him instead. I surprised myself at this idea so I hesitated for a moment, but I couldn't **shake the thought**. So I went to the nearby market and bought him some **fresh stuffed buns**, about five of them and a cup of warm **soy milk**. Then I went back to the man and handed it to him, and said some kind words to him. I think he was very happy to have some warm food on **a chilly morning**.
感受	Honestly though, I think doing this might have made me happier than it did him. I really felt good after helping him.

重点词句

help sb. with sth. 帮某人做某事

fake 骗子

take special note of 特别注意到

shake the thought 某想法挥之不去

fresh stuffed buns 刚出锅的包子

soy milk 豆奶

a chilly morning 清冷的早上

Part 3
Helping others

1. In general, why do people help others?

   I think it's the kindness that exists in most human hearts, at least a little. Many of us have needed some help ourselves from time to time, and we know **what it feels like to need something**. We know it feels good to have help from others when we need it, so we want to help others in the same way. Also, as I mentioned before, often it simply makes us happy to help others in some way.

   what it feels like to need something 有所需时是一种什么样的感受

2. Do you think it's important to help people who need help?

   Of course it's important. We have a responsibility to **do our part** whether it's in our family, our workplace, or amongst friends. None of us are like little islands with nothing or no one around us. We influence each other, and contribute to the atmosphere and environment around us, at least we should. And just as we want others to help us, we should naturally be willing to help others.

   do one's part 尽自己的职责

3. How do you feel after you have helped someone?

   Usually I feel very good when I've helped someone. Even if the help I gave was difficult for me or at an inconvenient time. Even if it was a **sacrifice** for me, afterwards it seems that I am happier than when I began, and sometimes I even seem to have more energy or time left for myself. It may sound funny, but sometimes it seems a little like magic how I **end up** with more time or more energy or more money or whatever, after I have **given some away** to another person.

   sacrifice 牺牲

   give away 送给

   end up 结果是

4. Many people only look out for themselves and never think about helping others. What do you think of this attitude?

   I think it's sad. I know it is common, but it's a sad statement of modern life, at least in big cities. I know not everybody is that way, but nowadays a lot of people have become very selfish. It seems that so many people are in such a rush to get rich or get better jobs or into the best schools that they hardly even notice people who need help. Maybe if people were not so **absorbed in their own worlds**, they would see the needs more and would do something about it. At least I hope so.

   be absorbed in their own worlds 沉溺于自己的世界

Helping visitors

5. What is the most important way for a country to help visitors?

   Probably the most common form of help needed by foreigners is help with the language. I've also seen foreigners on the streets who seem to be a little lost. Sometimes they're looking at their maps trying to find a famous tourist spot, so giving directions is another common way to help foreigners. I've done this a few times, and it was an interesting chance to talk to someone from another country.

6. Do you think that countries should help other countries in need?

   Yes, by all means. Our country has helped other countries many times, such as after the **tsunami** caused so much damage in Thailand, Indonesia and India. We also sent aid to the United States after the severe **hurricanes** a few years ago. I think we should look at the world as a very large neighborhood, and if we can try and do as much as possible for our neighbors, everyone is a lot happier and friendlier towards each other.

   tsunami 海啸　　hurricane 飓风

Helping people in society

7. What kinds of people need help in China?

   I think one of the biggest groups in our society needing help is the farmers. It would be better if the wealth and economic progress in our country was more evenly distributed. I live in a fairly prosperous family. We're not rich but we do have plenty, and though I'm happy for this, I feel a little guilty that others have so much less than I do.

8. How does the government try to help these people?

   I think one of the main ways is by investing in business in a certain part of the country so that more jobs are created for the local people. Another way is by providing training, for example in farming, in ways that can increase **productivity**. Also the government should make sure that officials of the provinces are doing their jobs correctly. The government is trying to eliminate corruption at the local level.

9. Are there any non-government organizations in China that help people?

   Yes, there are. At first many of these were foreign, but that is changing now. Although there are still foreign organizations that help people, there are also more and more Chinese **charitable organizations** being set up. I just read some articles about this.

   charitable organizations 慈善机构

10. Where do these organizations get their money from?

    The foreign organizations get their money from overseas. Some of the funding is governmental, but a lot of it comes from **private donations**. Here in China, more individuals are getting involved in charities. It's relatively new, but with the increased income of people, there is more of an awareness of a need to help others who are less fortunate.

private donations 个人捐款

三、话题相关材料

A 我们发现在生活中如果面对别人的问题，很容易给出一些建议和帮助，可一旦这些问题发生在自己身上，我们往往又束手无策，这是为什么呢？

Why do people help others better than they help themselves?

- Because it is easier said than done. You are projecting what you want to do yourself. Lots of people help others when 90% of them have the same problems going on. That's why we look to our friends. Also we know what we want to do, but we need that extra push from our friends.
- Because we are too close to our own situations to see things clearly most of the time. That is why it is so often helpful to seek outside input.
- It's easy to give advice, but it takes discipline to actually do what you advise people to do. Sometimes it's easier to be on the outside looking in.
- It is easier to do this because when we deal with our own problems, we find it hard to be really honest with ourselves. So helping a friend is easier since we have the ability to stand back from the problem he/she has and view it more objectively.

四、练习

A 请将下列句子翻译成英文。

1. 我们也经常会需要别人的帮助，因此我们知道有所需时是一种什么样的感受。

____

2. 不管是在家里，单位还是朋友之间，我们有责任尽我们的职责。

____

3. 听上去可能有点好笑，但当我把自己的时间、精力、金钱等用于帮助别人，我反而得到了更多的这些东西，这真是不可思议。

____

4. 人们都急着挣钱，找好工作，进好学校，以至于很少去关注那些需要帮助的人。

____

5. 在中国，越来越多的人开始投身于慈善事业。

____

（☞ P277）

B 听 MP3 实战演练。

Topic 35　Busy Days 忙碌的日子

一、考试说明

随着生活节奏的加快，中国人越来越忙，管理时间的技能也显得日益重要。本题中考生要向考官描述一段忙碌的日子，在第三部分里会围绕时间管理和如何放松与其展开讨论。面对该话题，考生应该不难想出要说的东西，如果实在困难，还可以讲讲雅思考试或学校里的期末考试，就像“真题演练”部分 native speaker 讲述的就是自己考试前突击准备的情况。在“话题相关材料”部分，提供的是一个国外中学生发出的有关时间管理方面的求助贴和热心人的回帖。

二、真题演练

CUE CARD

Describe a time when you are very busy.

You should say:

when this time is

what you do at this time

how you arrange your time

and explain how you feel after this busy time is over.

点题	Usually at the end of the term, my teachers start giving me **a bunch of** homework to help me prepare for the exam.
事件	I have 6 classes: Chinese, math, science, history, geography and English, and each teacher gives me so much homework that by the end of the week I have **a stack of** papers that look the size of a small book. I must complete all this homework before the next week begins or I will face a **penalty**. So what else can I do but get busy and start **burning the candle at both ends** and **burning the midnight oil** until the work is done. It means forget about basketball and watching TV and even just **fooling around** with my friends. It means **stinging eyes** and large **yawns** during the day. It means brain **overload** for a while.
事后感受	Now how do I feel when it is over? Well, how does a tree feel after a storm? How does a branch feel when the weight is gone? How does a bird sing after the rain? I know that I am getting a bit **poetic**, but actually it feels quite good to be relieved of this pressure. I like to go out in the sunshine and fresh air and just walk around to enjoy life for a while.

重点词句

a bunch of 一束、一捆

a stack of 一摞

penalty 处罚

burn the candle at both ends 操劳过度

burn the midnight oil 熬夜

fool around 消磨时光、寻开心

stinging eyes 眼睛酸疼

yawn 打呵欠

overload 超载、超负荷

poetic 富有诗意的

Part 3
Time Management

1. Do you manage your time effectively?

   It really depends on what I'm doing. If I'm in a lazy mood, I tend to do whatever first comes to mind, but when I am more active, I usually organize what I'm supposed to do by importance. Sadly **more often than not** I forget to organize my thoughts and end up wasting a lot of precious time. But I'm working on changing all that.

   more often than not 通常(口语)

2. Do you like making detailed plans?

   I don't usually make detailed plans for the work I'm doing, but I really like the outline method, where you just list the main points and sub-points of your project. Then you can clearly see what you need to **accomplish** and how realistic your **time frame** needs to be. But for the most part I don't **particularly** like drawing detailed plans.

   accomplish 实现

   time frame 期限

   particularly 特别地

3. What are the advantages of making plans?

   One advantage, like I said before, is that you can clearly see what it is you need to accomplish and better plan about how much time you need to accomplish it. Another advantage is that important details are less likely to be left out. Quite a few times I've had to go back and redo something that I was working on just because I **overlooked** a small but important detail, which in the end cost me a lot of extra time, and sometimes money. Thankfully I've been getting better at **time management** and have fewer problems than before.

   overlook 忽视

   time management 时间的管理

4. Do you use any special tools, such as a computer, to help you draw up plans?

   Like I said, I'm an extremely lazy person, so I usually try to be as simple as I can when drawing up plans. I'll usually use a sheet of paper and a pencil to write up whatever it is I'm planning. The only problem is that I often lose the paper and have to go back and rewrite it. This is, in my opinion, a huge waste of time, so I've been thinking about using my computer to make my plans, and hopefully save time... and paper.

5. Do you keep a diary?

I've tried on several occasions to start a diary, but I usually forget about it after a week or so. I think I've started about seven diaries in my life time, and the longest one lasted for about 2 months. Diaries just don't seem to work for me, so I think I'll spend my time doing more profitable things, like playing my guitar. Maybe some day I'll start a diary and actually keep it but for now I think I'll just stay away from them.

Leisure Time

6. Compare the way old people and young people spend their leisure time.

Many old people spend their leisure time indoors, sitting down, reading a book or resting; or they might go outside for a **brisk** walk in the evening. Many of them enjoy watching TV or knitting. Young people, on the other hand, enjoy a variety of things. Many do the same things I mentioned that old people do, but in my opinion there are many more options available if you are young. You can play sports, go clubbing all night, participate in **extreme sports**—like **bungee jumping** or **sky diving**—that might give an older person a heart attack.

brisk 轻快的 | bungee jumping 蹦极
extreme sports 极限运动 | sky diving 跳伞

7. Do people today have more leisure time than before?

I think that since modern **appliances** have cut down the amount of unnecessary physical work we need do, there is more time for leisure. You don't have to gather wood to make a fire, and you don't have to spend 1 or 2 hours lighting your fire. Cell phones and instant messaging make it possible to communicate immediately with your friends and associates, cutting back on time needed to wait for telegraphs or snail mail replies. The only problem is that even though everything is so much easier, there are other **complications** that people in the past didn't have, such as traffic jams and long lines at the supermarket. Also it really depends on the person, because I know some people who never rest or take time off. They're always working and never stop. But I also know some guys who are the total opposite: they make every excuse why they can't do what's being asked of them, and I imagine that in the past it was the same.

appliance 器具、设备 | complication 复杂情况

8. Do you think leisure time is important? (Why?)

Yes, I think that leisure time is very important. Like the saying goes, "all work and no play makes jack a dull boy." If you're working nonstop and never take the time to **let your hair down**, you'll most likely get **stressed out** and even get sick. If I don't take some time to just relax a bit every week, I end up getting sick, and have to stay in bed for a few days. So in my opinion leisure time is **vital** to maintaining health and **sanity**.

let your hair down 放松（口语）　　stressed out 因压力而累垮的

vital 非常重要的　　sanity 理智

9. How have leisure activities changed in China in the past few years?

Well, for one thing, many more Chinese, mostly young people, have been spending a lot more time on their computers, either playing games, studying, doing research and business, or any number of things. Before, if you wanted to relax, you just went for a walk, read a book, or **played mahjong** with friends. Now the possibilities are endless. Many people still relax in the traditional ways, but many more are finding new and different ways to spend their leisure time.

play mahjong 打麻将

10. How do you think leisure-time activities will change in the future?

You know what? I have absolutely no idea! I mean, 10 years ago, did you think that modern technology would be as advanced as it is now? Music players **for that matter** are also getting smaller, slimmer and more **compact**. A few years from now you might be able to get an mp3 player in a little chip under your skin that's controlled by your brain.

for that matter 同样的　　compact 紧凑的、不占空间的

三、话题相关材料

A 管理时间对很多人而言是个很大的挑战。面对日益快节奏和忙碌的生活方式，我们更需要培养管理时间的技巧。下面是一个外国中学生发出的求助信息和别人给她的建议，你有没有更好的建议？

How do you teens keep organized in school and still manage your time well? I have a really hard time with that and really want to get better. Please help me. Teens and adults are welcome to answer.

1 Try to prioritize. Take it easy initially, plan a day at a time, and mark your little achievements. Once you have done that, increase the duration to 2 days...

2 Well, it's one thing to have ways to manage your time. It's another to have the discipline to stick with it. I've found that an extremely helpful way to manage time after school is to get right into doing and finishing your homework. That should always be the first thing you do—it's about making priorities and sticking with them... but again, that also has a lot to do with your ability to stay disciplined to do it.

3 I think the first thing you should do is to monitor where your time is going now. For a couple of weeks, don't change anything that you are doing but take note of where your time is going. Update frequently so you don't forget where your time was spent.

At the end of two weeks you will now have a good idea about where most of your time is being spent. Now, make a list of your priorities in terms of what must be done.

How much of your time are you actually spending on those priorities? You will probably notice that much more time than necessary is being spent on things that have nothing to do with school activities. It is your goal to cut out the time wasters and devote the saved time to more productive activity. Until you are really aware of where your time is being spent, you can't really do a lot about it.

Good luck with your schooling.

三个人的建议中都提到了"priority（轻重缓急）"，可见它在制订时间计划时的重要性，毕竟Everyone starts the day with 24 hours, no more and no less. How much we achieve within these 24 hours depends on how well we manage what is important to us, i.e. our priorities.

四、练习

A 请将下列句子翻译成英文。

1. 所以除了晚睡早起、点灯熬油赶活之外我还能做什么呢？

____

2. 如果碰到我懒散的时候，我会想到什么做什么；如果碰到我"奋发向上"的时候，我会根据重要性来安排我要做的事情。

____

3. 这样的话你就可以清楚地看到自己要实现什么以及时间该怎么安排才现实。但通常我不是特别喜欢制定很详细的计划。

____

4. 正如我刚才说过的，优点之一就是你可以清楚地看到自己要实现什么以及如何更好的安排时间。优点之二是你就不太可能丢失一些重要的细节。

____

5. 所以在我看来，休闲时间对保持身心健康至关重要。

____

（☞ P278）

B 听MP3实战演练。

Topic 36 Practical Skills 实用技能

一、考试说明

实用技能，作为学术能力的重要补充，是生活中必不可少的能力。在这个话题卡中，考生要讲述自己的一技之长。很多人马上会想到做饭、开车之类的技能，这些固然可以讲，但“实用技能”包括的远不止这些，比如在“真题演练”部分，native speaker 讲述的就是自己弹吉他的技能。第三部分会围绕实用技能的重要性以及它在教育中位置等话题展开讨论。“话题相关材料”部分补充了一些实用技能的名称和英国《泰晤士报》网站上关于“学校要不要开设生活技能课”的辩论片段。

二、真题演练

CUE CARD

Describe a practical skill that you have.

You should say:

what this skill is

how you learned it

when you use this skill

and explain how this skill is useful to you.

点题	Well one skill that I have is **playing the guitar**.
学习过程	I learned it when I was young. I learned how to play because I had many friends that played the guitar and when they played and sang, I knew I just had to learn. At first it was a little difficult because to be quite frank, I really didn't see myself as someone who was **musically inclined**. I had to tell myself that I could do it and little by little, a **note** here and a **chord** there, I managed to **pick** it **up**. Even now I have a long way to go with playing but I have found it enjoyable not just for myself, for others have said they enjoy it as well. I have had a few guitars and although there are different styles and qualities, to me it seems that as long as they have **strings** on them and you can **tune** them they are fine.
有用之处	I use the guitar to **cheer myself up** when I am **feeling a little down** and also use it to teach songs to others. I have never made money teaching guitar but I have made a little money playing and singing. I don't know if I would want to pursue this skill as a career but as long as I still enjoy it, I am going to do it.

重点词句

play the guitar 弹吉他

musically inclined 有音乐天赋的

note 音符

chord 和弦

pick up 学会

string 弦

tune 调音

cheer oneself up 让某人开心

feel a little down 感觉心情有点差

Part 3
Practical Skills

1. Compare the importance of practical skills and academic skills.

   Well actually both are much needed in society. It seems to me that practical skills such as knowing how to cook a meal or clean a house or take care of children are **slipping**, whereas academic skills such as teaching a class or doing research seem to be **on the rise**. This is not bad in itself because there need to be people who are thinking about how things work and how to improve them, but the skills needed for everyday life shouldn't be looked on as any less important than others.

   slip 下跌

   on the rise 上升

2. How can people learn practical skills?

   A lot of these skills can be learned at home with their mother and father and family. Skills such as **sewing**, **budgeting** or **maintenance** can be learned from an aunt or uncle, grandfather or grandmother. If more difficult trades want to be learned, such as **plumber** or **electrician** or **mason**, there are **vocational schools** that could teach those. **The main thing** to learning a skill is the **motivation** that is involved.

   sewing 缝纫

   budgeting 理财

   maintenance 日常维护

   plumber 水管工

   electrician 电工

   mason 砖瓦工

   vocational schools 职业学校

   the main thing 最重要的事情

   motivation 动机

Children and practical skills

3. What practical skills do children learn at school in China?

   I'm afraid that there are not many. Academics are stressed so highly in schools that they seem to **overshadow** practical skills. I suppose students probably learn to listen to their teacher and how to behave and sit for long periods at a time and apply themselves. They also have to learn how to **interact amongst themselves** in a satisfactory way. They have to learn how to get up on time and be at their school, which teaches them responsibility. I guess it would help to define what practical skills we are talking about.

overshadow 使显得不重要　　interact amongst themselves 相处

4. Do you think children should learn some practical skills at school?

I think that children should learn practical skills at school. This would help to **prepare them for life outside of school.** A lot of times not much thought is put into how to manage money or take care of an apartment but I think these skills would be helpful. Life in the working world can be a lot different than the **sheltered life of schooling**, so having some practical skills such as those learned from a part-time job would be beneficial to a student.

prepare them for life outside of school 为离开学校的生活做准备

sheltered life of schooling 学校里养尊处优的生活

5. How useful will these skills be to the children after they leave school?

Well as I was saying in the previous question, these skills would be very helpful to children after they leave school. When a teenager goes from high school to college he has to start managing things on his own without the security of mom and dad. **Even more so** when a young adult graduates from college or university, he would also be very **grateful** to have some practical knowledge on how to **survive in the working world**.

even more so 更是如此　　survive in the working world 在工作的世界中生存下去

grateful 感激的

Adult education

6. Do you think it's useful for adults to attend classes to further their education?

Sure, why not, if it is something that they find useful in their lives and something that they enjoy. Learning is lifelong and I don't know if it has to stop in old age. Now I know that a lot of times these adults are looked upon as teachers, but if they feel so inclined why not attend a class to further their education. If they are not able to keep up with the young students then this would be a **detriment**, but if there are no **disruptions** why not?

detriment 损害　　disruptions 分裂，混乱

7. What kinds of courses exist in China for adults?

There are wonderful exercise classes that are available for adults in China. I don't know if you have seen large groups of older women out on the streets performing with various **percussion instruments**, but these are classes that help them to work together and perform for audiences. There are dancing classes available. There are even English classes available for senior citizens in China. There are Tai Chi classes also available to seniors here. As time goes on and the country develops there will be more classes that will be available for seniors.

percussion instruments 打击乐器

8. What are some reasons why adults might attend classes?

Well I guess one of the main ones is that they are working and they need to keep up with the latest technology that will help them to **stay abreast of** the latest in their fields. Sometimes they might even be thinking of **switching careers** so they take classes to get the training to do so. Other times they might just want to learn some things in their spare time that will **enhance their life** on a recreational level. Other times their bosses might want them to learn some special skill for the good of the company.

stay abreast of 跟得上　　enhance their life 充实生活
switch careers 转行

9. Who do you think should pay for adult education—the government, the student or the company (if it is a work-related course)?

Again it depends on the course and why they are taking it. If it is for personal gain or gratification then of course students should be responsible to pay for it. If the government is offering a course and adults are interested in it then it is already paid for. If it is going to move the company ahead and bring financial results then of course the company should pay for it. Now if the company can't pay for it and it interests the individual then it is up to him to get the money together to attend the class.

三、话题相关材料

A "practical skills"包括各种各样的技能，除了样题中提到的弹吉他之外，下面这些技能同样是生活中常见的实用技能。

cooking 烹饪
gardening 园艺
sewing 缝纫
making tofu 豆腐制作
woodwork 木工
driving 驾驶
soap-making 肥皂制作
outdoor survival 野外求生
first aid skills 急救
parenting 育子
money skills 理财
home economics 家政
housekeeping 做家务
massage 按摩
clay modeling 泥塑

B 英国《泰晤士报》网站上曾刊登过一场"学校要不要教学生生活技能"的辩论，部分内容刊登如下，供大家参考。

Should schools teach children "life skills"?

Tony Blair wants schools to send pupils out into the world able to cook, communicate, enjoy the theatre and handle home finances. The three Cs (cooking, communicating and culture), with emphasis on non-academic learning, may upset traditionalists, but some will see it a vital move towards turning pupils into well-rounded members of the community. What do you think?

- Most of what is being proposed was taught to me by my parents. Strangely enough, I always believed that is the parents' role to impart knowledge of life to their children. Since apparently one in six children can barely read or write, it might be more useful if they could learn that first from the school.
- The idea of introducing practical life skills to our children before they get into the rat race is a wholly justified one. If our children are aware of the pit falls regarding loans, credit cards, mortgages and self-employment, then maybe our financial debt as a nation could be lowered. Too many corporations prey on naivety.
- I wished that my son could have had a different kind of education when he was younger. I think learning life skills is vital, at home and in the classroom. Some people have high IQs but completely lack common sense, and have no people skills at all. I think it is important for young people to learn about their environment, how to handle bank accounts for when they leave school, and to go back to basic cooking lessons instead of studying food technology. Schools are obsessed with league tables and GCSE results, putting a lot of pressure on young people.

四、练习

A 请将下列句子翻译成英文。

1. 一开始有点难，因为说实在的，我并不觉得自己属于那种有音乐天赋的人。

____

2. 当我情绪低落时我会弹吉他让自己开心起来，我也可以弹着吉他教别人唱歌。

____

3. 文化知识的学习在学校里被过分地强调，以至于实用技能方面的学习都被忽略了。

____

4. 我认为孩子应该在校内学习实用技能，这会帮他们为校外的生活做准备。

____

5. 工作后的生活跟学校里那种养尊处优的生活大不一样，因此学点实用技能（比如说找份兼职工作）对学生来说是很有益处的。

____

（☞ P278）

B 听 MP3 实战演练。

假想类进阶级（Topics 37~40）

Topic 37　To Start A Small Business 创业

一、考试说明

自主创业是很多人的梦想，现在也成了时尚。雅思口语反映生活中新现象、新趋势，自主创业的话题也开始出现在了口语话题中。考生向考官描述完自己的创业计划后，在第三部分双方会围绕创业的方方面面展开讨论。在“真题演练”部分 native speaker 讲述了自己想开个手工首饰店的想法；“话题相关材料”部分则为考生提供了美国小企业管理局对自主创业者的一些指导和建议。

二、真题演练

CUE CARD
Describe a small business that you would like to own.
You should say:
what this business would be
how you would start/open this business
how you would run this business
and explain why you would like to run this kind of business.

点题	I've always been interested in different kinds of **handcrafted jewelry**, such as **macramé**, **beading**, **Chinese Knot** tying, and other kinds of knotting and stitching with cord or wire. So I'm thinking I'd like to go into business selling and making that kind of jewelry.
运作	It wouldn't even have to be a big production, just a few people making and selling **bracelets**, necklaces, and other **accessories**. Maybe if we become popular and more people start buying our products we could even open a small shop and take special orders. We could also have classes, where we teach people how to make their own jewelry. I was thinking that my cousin could help me since she is quite good with her hands; I think she has some friends who are good at macramé so they could help also. We could put an ad in the newspaper or on the Internet and sell our wares that way. During holidays we'd travel around China and sell our jewelry at famous parks and places that tourists frequent. We'd each just make the things that we're best at so that we get a bunch of quality products in as short an amount of time as possible.
原因	The main reason I'd start a business like this is because it's something that I enjoy doing, and I don't think I could work at a job that I don't like.

重点词句

handcrafted jewelry 手工首饰
macramé 装饰用流苏花边
beading 珠饰
Chinese Knot 中国节
cord or wire 绳子和铁丝
bracelet 手镯
accessories 配饰

Part 3
Small business

1. What challenges and difficulties do people face when they try to open a small business?

   One of the main challenges for small businesses is just staying open. Most small businesses close within a year after they're open, so if they get past that **hurdle** the next most important thing that they'll have to **tackle** is getting long-term customers. Depending on what kind of business they're starting they'll also have to advertise their products and services. Good advertisement is really what makes the difference between the success and failure of their business.

   hurdle 障碍　　tackle 应付，解决

2. What are some of the advantages and disadvantages of small businesses compared to large companies?

   One advantage of having a small business is that you don't have to **be tied down** by company rules, regulations, and **protocols**. You are free to operate as you please and don't have to worry about getting the approval of the CEO or some other person higher up on the ladder than you. There are some disadvantages, though, to having a small business. The main one is that if you're not careful, the big businesses will put you out of business by slashing their prices or advertising heavily. You see, they can afford to make their prices lower than yours simply because they have more money.

   be tied down 被束缚　　protocols 礼仪，行为方式

3. How can small businesses benefit the people in their community?

   Small businesses are able to cater to the **whims** and wishes of the people that they are near. They get to know their customers and can specialize in taking care of them. Small businesses can even watch out for community members: if they are used to seeing them and they notice a change in their routine, the business could report this to someone who would be concerned about them. Having a small business, like a restaurant for instance, creates a family-like feeling in the neighborhood, as opposed to going to McDonald's for instance, where they **don't know you from Adam**.

   whim 心血来潮，冲动　　not know you from Adam 根本不认识你

4. Compare small shops with big (international) department stores and supermarkets.

   I really don't think there is any comparison. Small shops **retain a personal touch** and give you the feeling that the owners are more than people who just want to make money. Small businesses make you feel that you are contributing to keep the community going by shopping there. Of course the big

stores have a lot more variety and are able to have sales and cut their prices when they need to.
retain a personal touch 保留着人情味

Other possible questions

5. What kinds of small business are most popular in China?

Well you see them everywhere and new ones pop up almost daily, what are they? Well, you guessed it, beauty salons and hairdressers and haircutters. If you walk down any given street you will see one or two on each corner. People are much more interested in style and being in fashion, so that is why these businesses are so popular. If you look around you will see so many new hairdos.

6. Why do some people open their own business?

People want to be able to say, "this is mine." They want to be able to do something on their own. They want to see something grow that they had a direct part in. People also want to make money, of course, and this might even be the main reason.

7. What qualities does a small business owner need to have?

A small business owner would have to be diligent with his business, wanting to make sure that things are done right. He would need to have patience, the ability to wait until the business starts succeeding. He would have to have plenty of capital to **get** his business **off the ground**. A small business owner would also have to have a sense of humor, to laugh when he feels like crying.
get off the ground 开始成功

8. How have small businesses changed in recent years in China?

There is a lot more freedom here in China to start your own business and make it succeed. There are a lot more small businesses than in the past. Because of China's entry into the WTO, there are a lot more products and therefore more businesses. As I mentioned before, style is becoming more popular so more businesses open to keep up with it.

9. How do you think small busineses will change in the future in China?

I think that people are working together more and want to get their small businesses going and progressing so that they can branch out and grow. You will see small businesses **flexing their muscle** in the rural areas and expanding their support base. You will see small businesses affecting life much more than they do now. Small businesses are the future of China and will continue being so as time goes on.
flex their muscle 一展拳脚

10. Compare owning and running a small business to being an employee in a large company.

I think that I am passionate about this. I feel that owning and operating a small business is everything good and working as **a cog in a wheel** for a large company is everything bad. Maybe it's just me, but I like to experiment and try new things and when you have your own business you can do this. I've got to feel like I am making a difference; owning a small business would do this for me.

a cog in a wheel 无足轻重的位置

三、话题相关材料

A 自主创业是很多年轻人的梦想，但从梦想跨越到现实的路上充满挑战和陷阱。美国有个专门的政府机构 Small Business Administration 帮助那些有志于创业的人们。下面是他们设计的整个创业流程以及创业计划中最重要的 7 个要素和成功创业人士的共同素质，看对你有没有启发。

创业流程

1 Plan Your Business
- > Get Ready
- > Write a Business Plan

2 Start Your Business
- > Find a Mentor
- > Finance Start-Up
- > Buy a Business
- > Buy a Franchise
- > Name Your Business
- > Choose a Structure
- > Protect Your Ideas
- > Get Licenses and Permits
- > Pick a Location
- > Lease Equipment

3 Manage Your Business
- > Lead
- > Make Decisions
- > Manage Employees
- > Market and Price
- > Market and Sell
- > Understand Fair Practice
- > Pay Taxes
- > Get Insurance
- > Handle Legal Concerns
- > Forecast
- > Advocate and Stay Informed
- > Use Technology
- > Finance Growth

4 Getting Out
- > Plan Your Exit
- > Sell Your Business
- > Transfer Ownership
- > Liquidate Assets
- > File Bankruptcy
- > Close Officially

CHECKLIST FOR STARTING A BUSINESS

Owning a business is the dream of many Americans. Starting that business converts your dreams into reality. However, there is a gap between dreams and reality. Your dreams can only be achieved with careful planning. As an entrepreneur, you will need a plan to avoid pitfalls, to achieve your goals and to build a profitable business.

This checklist is designed to help you get started. It has seven key components:

- Identifying Your Reasons
- Self Analysis
- Personal Skills and Experience
- Finding a Niche
- Market Analysis
- Planning Your Startup
- Finances

Do You Have What It Takes?

Many successful entrepreneurs have similar traits and characteristics. Learn what these are and what you can do to improve on your own.

- Persistence
- Desire for immediate feedback
- Inquisitiveness
- Strong drive to achieve
- High energy level
- Goal-oriented behavior
- Independent
- Demanding
- Self-confident
- Calculated risk-taker
- Creative
- Innovative
- Vision
- Commitment
- Problem solving skills
- Tolerance for ambiguity
- Strong integrity
- Highly reliable
- Personal initiative
- Ability to consolidate resources
- Strong management and organizational skills
- Competitive
- Change agent
- Tolerance for failure
- Desire to work hard
- Luck

Many entrepreneurs also had a role model to influence them early on, or parents who were entrepreneurs. Two traits necessary for successful entrepreneurs are creativity and innovation.

四、练习

A 请将下列句子翻译成英文。

1. 我们可以在报纸上或网上做广告，在网上卖我们的产品。

____

2. 我想开一家这样的公司的主要原因是我的确喜欢这东西。

____

3. 我们各自做自己最擅长的，这样就可以在最短的时间内生产出一批高质量的产品来。

____

4. 好的广告是生意成败的决定因素。

____

5. 他们想看到一个事物的成长并且能在其中发挥直接作用。

____

（☞ P278）

B 听 MP3 实战演练。

Topic 38 A Large Sum of Money 大笔钱财

一、考试说明

该话题是口语考试中典型的“虚幻类”话题，总体难度不大，因为很容易借题发挥；惟一的难点就是第二部分长发言时的时态问题，因为是虚拟，所以尽量使用情态动词“would”。考生向考官描述完自己的花钱计划后，在第三部分双方会围绕与金钱相关的话题展开讨论。在“真题演练”部分native speaker讲了很多计划，比如开发新能源、帮助战争国家恢复以及举办音乐会等，纵横捭阖，跨度较大，不建议考生参考。“话题相关材料”部分的资料倒是可以参考，内容都是网友对“赚钱后干什么”问题的回应。

二、真题演练

CUE CARD

Describe what you would do if you received a very large amount of money.

You should say:

who you would share it with

what you would buy

what else you would do

and explain how you would feel about getting so much money.

点题	It really depends on how much money a “large amount” is. If it’s in the trillions I’d probably buy up most of Europe or maybe North America.
想像	I would be my own little king and have everyone **pay homage to** me. There would be no more wars because I wouldn’t let them happen. I would be fair to all people. We would **commission** all of the nuclear scientists to try to discover an economical, plentiful, and **non-toxic substitute** for **gasoline and diesel**. There would be less pollution, because if you want to drive a gas powered vehicle you’d have to pay a fine. As far as noise pollution, there would be less, because there would be fewer things to complain about. I would **sponsor** rock festivals so that everyone could **partake of** the beauties of music. All my subjects would love me, because they’d know I am trying my best not to be like all of the leaders in the past who gave into their own desires and lusts; instead I would give the people what they want. I would use all the money that would normally be spent on wars to help poorer nations, improve the lives of **war-torn countries**, and build a big **rollercoaster theme park**. When all this is done and with whatever money I have left I would get the best, most expensive guitar on the market and hire a super-skilled guitar player to teach me all he knows. I’d really enjoy that.

重点词句

pay homage to 向某人表示敬意
commission 委任，委托
non-toxic 无毒的
substitute 替代品
gasoline and diesel 汽油和柴油
sponsor 主办
partake of 共享
war-torn countries 被战争蹂躏的国家
rollercoaster 过山车
theme park 主题公园

Part 3
Money

1. Is money important to you?

   Money isn't really that important to me, but you need money to live and if you don't have money, then you can't do anything. But I'm really against the idea of just spending your whole life trying to make a bunch of money so that you can die a rich man. Most of the people who do that don't even get to enjoy the money they have, and they're never content with what they have because they always want more.

2. Do you think children are given too much pocket money in China?

   It really depends on how much they're getting. Some kids definitely get **way** more than they need, and others don't get enough. There are some families where the parents hardly have enough money to pay their bills and get food; I don't think these families should **feel obliged to** give their children money that they don't have. But if they do have money, then it would be nice to give at least some spending money to their children.

   way 大大的，远远的
   feel obliged to 感到必须要做某事

3. How do you think parents could teach the value of money to their children?

   If you give your children only a small amount of money each week then they'll have to learn to make it last. It might take a while for them to learn, and they might be broke for the first few months, but after a while they'll realize that **money doesn't grow on trees** and will respect its value. Of course there are children who always want everything they see, and if the parents give it to them then the kids won't value money at all.

   money doesn't grow on trees（谚语）钱不是树上掉下来的

4. Do you think it is important to let children learn **money skills**?

   I think that's a wonderful idea. If all kids knew how to do banking, open a savings account and cash checks, their parents would have a lot more leisure time. And even if the parents still do the banking, at least when their kids grow up they won't be totally helpless. In fact, they'll **have a big jump on** the other kids their age.

   money skills 理财能力
   have a jump on sb. 比别人有优势

5. Do you think people should be paid extra when they work overtime?

If you pay someone extra to work overtime then you're, in a sense, giving them an **incentive** to work harder. When the work day is over, most people just want to go home and relax. Some people are **workaholics** and don't think anything of working until 3 or 4 in the morning and getting up at 6 a few hours later to go back to work. But these people are rare. So if you want more people to work later an overtime **bonus** is a very good idea.

incentive 激励　　workaholic 工作狂

bonus 奖金

Money and Society

6. What kinds of jobs have higher pay? Why?

Jobs like designing and repairing computer software, lawyers, doctors and surgeons, building designers, scientists, and Hollywood actors are some better paying jobs. All these jobs require years of study, research, and lots of experience in that field.

7. What occupations do you think will get high salary in the future?

People who are multilingual will be highly sought after in the future. As the world is becoming more international, people who speak more than 2 languages fluently will be greatly needed. English is the main international language right now, but there are billions of extremely intellectual individuals who can't speak or understand English. These people don't want to get left out of all the fun and games that are happening in the rest of the world, so they need translators who will be able to make them understood by people of different races.

8. Is pay the most important factor in a job?

The most important factor is, as most fun loving people know, how much vacation time you get; not only time off, but **paid time off**. Another important thing to keep in mind is what kind of work it is. Some work is just boring and nobody likes doing it—except for boring people. But if you really want to excel in your work, pick something that you feel comfortable doing, something that you're good at. The **workplace environment** is also very important. Some offices are **stuffy** and **drab**, whereas others make you feel fresh and alive.

paid time off 带薪假期　　stuffy 空气污浊的

workplace environment 办公环境　　drab 无聊的

9. What is the primary source of income for the Chinese government?

The primary source of government income is taxes. Taxes are the way that governments support all their projects around the country. Whether they're building skyscrapers, roads, or schools in **impoverished** counties, all this funding comes from taxes. Another way to put it is that you're supporting the government, because you're the one paying the taxes. Whenever you see government officials on the news doing something or another, you can know that you are actually responsible, since it is you who made it possible for them to do it.

impoverished 贫困的

10. Do you think the government should let people know how it spends money?

You know, that would be very nice. I've always wondered what exactly is going on behind those closed doors. Naturally some things just can't be talked about because they're state secrets, and some things you probably don't want to know about, such as how much money was spent on this banquet, or that convention, or how many liters of gasoline their vehicles consume each month. But I would like to know exactly what they're spending my money on.

三、话题相关材料

A 如果你像比尔·盖茨那样富有，你会做什么？

If you had as much money as Bill Gates, what would you do with it?

- Put some in the bank, have a long family holiday abroad, pay off loans, buy my own apartment and car.
- I would first pay off all my bills, then give some money to charity, then my husband and I would take a nice, long vacation.
- I'd spend it on buying myself a little house and making it lovely then with what's left I would by a few malamutes. I wouldn't quit work because I would die of boredom and being stuck at home, but it would be nice to go part-time, that way I wouldn't have to take on all the stress at work.
- I'd buy a new car, a house, give some money to the Make-a-Wish foundation, and put the rest in stocks so I can make more money to give away. Plus I'd stash some in a bank on the Cayman Islands.
- I would go shopping and then donate the rest to a good cause.
- I'd help as many friends and family as I could. I don't need much.
- I'd go shopping, hire personal instructor to shape up my body, travel around the world, buy a mammoth house for my parents, donate to the poor and needy, and last but not least I would invest in my corporation.

四、练习

A 请将下列句子翻译成英文。

1. 这真的取决于“很多”到底是多少。

____

2. 我会主办摇滚音乐节，这样所有的人都可以分享音乐之美。

____

3. 钱对我没那么重要，但我们要生存确实需要钱。如果没钱什么事都做不了。

____

4. 如果你每星期只给你孩子一点点钱，那他就不得不学着如何去省着花。

____

5. 办公环境同样重要：有些办公室空气污浊，毫无生气；而有些办公室却让你感觉清新而有活力。

____

（☞ P279）

B 听 MP3 实战演练。

Topic 39　A Goal You Want to Achieve 想做成的一件事

一、考试说明

"想做成的一件事"是雅思中的新话题，总体来说难度不大，讲述将来总比讲述过去和现在容易。考生向考官描述完自己的想法后，第三部分双方会围绕"成功"展开讨论。在"真题演练"部分考生讲自己想结婚却困难重重，讲的在情在理。"话题相关材料"部分为考生提供了国外网友的"New Year Resolution"，里面有很多点子可以拿来当自己的"想做成的一件事"。

二、真题演练

CUE CARD

Describe something that you would like to succeed in doing in the near future.

You should say:

what it is

how difficult you think it will be

what you should do to prepare for this

and explain why you want to succeed in doing this.

点题	Well, when it comes to my business life, my work and career, I am still **contemplating** my options, but right now, the real problem for me is getting married.
困难	It is very hard to find a suitable match simply because I cannot please everybody. I must think about what my family wants, what the world around me would be pleased with, and the last person on the list to worry about is me. It will take a lot of searching, a lot of concentration. In my life, my schedule seldom permits free time, much less time to date, and I am often too shy to begin **from scratch**. I do not have many close friends, and those that I do have are either married or do not make a very good match for me. An extra difficulty is that I am not too good at the whole parents-in-law situation; I would find myself quite unhappy with this traditional way of living. Many Chinese must "**put up**" with their husband or wife, and also their parents and relatives, and must receive **critiquing** or judgment from all sides. I do not want to live this way, and I don't want a partner that I must "put up with", I want to have love in my life.

解决方法	But traditions are traditions and I must follow some kind of pattern. Thus, my first step might be to ask my parents and my aunt and uncle to look for a suitable partner for me, and then we can begin by writing each other, and when we feel we have enough common ground, we can arrange a meeting.

重点词句

contemplate 思忖，仔细考虑　　put up 忍受
from scratch 从无到有，从零开始　　critique 批评

Part 3
Success

1. How would you define "success"?
Hmm, there are so many ways to define it. I believe success is feeling my life is worth living, and being a good person to those around me. If I have a partner, or children, or relatives dependant on me, I would consider it a success if I were able to provide them with a good life style and everything they need. Success would mean my reputation as a good person travels ahead of me. It would mean I would have a goal and hope for life, and would stand out amongst others.

2. Do you think most people want to succeed in life?
I would imagine they do. But as I said, there are many ways to define success. It is the inborn desire of a human to want to be the best they could be, to want more. Everybody wants life to be worthwhile, they want their husband or wife to be proud of them, they want their children to admire them, and they want **a sense of fulfillment**. It's natural.
a sense of fulfillment 满足感

3. When do people most want to be successful?
Well I would say it's after they realize that life is a struggle and that they must **make it** on their own. When we are young we can depend on others and do not feel the need to make something of ourselves. It's when the pressure **kicks in** and the understanding comes to us that we find we must choose for ourselves whether we will be happy or sad, a success or a failure. When we grow up and are more mature, we begin to have others depend on us, **looking to** us, and we feel the responsibility to do our part in the world.
make it 成功做某事　　look to 依靠，指望
kick in 开始出现

4. What kind of success is most important to Chinese people?
Well, originally it was about being a good provider for one's family, finding one's children a good husband or wife, having enough land to **live off**. But now that China is much more open, people

begin to feel success is about making enough money to never have to worry about anything. It's also about giving that feeling of relaxed and easy living to their children. Get them into the best school, buy them a house so they don't have to work, hand life to them **on a silver platter**. This is beginning to be the image of success, and the people of this country are **bombarded** with advertisements, movies and pictures of the easy life, the rich and famous, and they feel this is the only way to succeed. I myself feel it has its downsides, and must really consider what I want for my life.

live off 维持生计　　bombard 轰炸

on a silver platter (得到得)不费力气

5. Do you think that successful people are always happier than unsuccessful people?
   Again, this depends on your idea of success. But whatever it means to a person, if they are dissatisfied with **the cards they are dealt** and do not realize they can determine their success, then yes, I imagine they are not happy at all. But sometimes, those that we think are successful on the outside, or what we see of them, are not happy, they do not consider their life worth the trouble. So no, I do not think "successful" people are always happier than "unsuccessful" people.
   the cards they are dealt 他们发到的牌(喻指生活现状)

Success and reward

6. How should parents reward their children for success, for example, for doing very well in exams at school?
   I believe parents should give their child the sense that success is their reward. They should help the children to feel a sense of pride in their accomplishments and not always expect to receive a candy bar or a trip to the amusement park for every good deed. It is true that children need encouragement, but they should realize that the reason they worked for the good score on the exams was because learning is important and will help their lives to be better. They should not be thinking, "I am studying hard and getting a good score because my mother promised me new toys or extra money." They will never become truly successful if they are dependent on that candy bar, or those new toys.

7. How do teachers in China reward students for doing well?
   They may give the best student the title of "class monitor". In school we always had class monitors and being the monitor meant that we were responsible and trusted people. Often the students need good grades and good reputations or connections to assist them later when they get out of school or wish to get into a good university or college. If a student is exceptional, then at the end of the year or semester the teacher can write a letter or paper describing the student's good qualities. Such documents may help to prove students' worth or abilities later in life when they are in search of a job.

8. How do bosses in China reward employees for a job well done?
   It depends, sometimes, it means extra money, and sometimes it means promotion. But then

sometimes, the bosses do not reward their employees, and simply demand that each worker be giving their best for whatever pay is offered. Chinese are naturally hard workers, it's in their blood. So because of this, the mentality is, "they are working for me, they give their best day in and day out because it's their job and duty as humans." On top of that, there are so many people who can work and need work, so there is not too much value placed on the employees.

Competition versus cooperation

9. Which do you think is a better attitude for children to have: a strong spirit of competition or a strong spirit of cooperation with others?

Both. One can be competent but if they cannot cooperate with others, they will meet with failure in their life. No matter where you go, what position you hold in a company, you will have to work with others, communicate and cooperate with them. If all you are capable of is competition, how can anyone else benefit you? Whatever those children choose to do, they will desperately need both skills.

10. Do you think that too much competition could damage the spirit of cooperation in society?

Of course. By that I mean that competition can eventually lead to war, as has happened on a number of occasions in Central America. If you promote competition so much in comparison to **fair play** and good sportsmanship then the wrong values are being **espoused**. Cooperation is based on working together to help the whole. When you foster this spirit then you are contributing to society.

fair play 公平竞争　　　　espouse 拥护、信奉

11. Some people say that success means being number one and that being number two is valueless. What do you think?

This is really an immature way to look at life. I really believe that you just have to get up and keep trying no matter who is in first or even second place. Just finishing the race has its rewards. Forget about what others are doing and just get on with life, this is my philosophy, which I try to live by.

三、话题相关材料

A 每年年初是制定新年计划的时候，考生或许能从国外网友的 New Year's Resolution 里找到自己想说的话题。

What's your New Year's Resolution this year?

Smile more, try to be less bitter, go on a diet, lose some weight and get my life back into perspective and spend more time living instead of sleeping.	**One** of my resolutions is probably the same as most people: to loose 15 pounds. I am going to accomplish it by training for a 50 mile organized bike ride in April that I have done before and am really looking forward to!

Try to improve in certain things like relationships with friends, relatives, and boyfriend. Make 2007 a better year than the previous years! And sleep earlier since I stay up too late and try not to be on the computer 12 hours a day. And maybe even cut out the junk food!

I am really going to try to be a better person. All I do is to try to have fun and I see myself saying mean things to people. I haven't really talked about anyone in a while. But, when I do I'm telling the truth about them. Like if someone asked me to tell them the truth about the way they look I have no choice but to tell them. I try to be nice about it. I haven't hurt anyone's feelings with the way I say it. Well, I hope I didn't because I'm a real straight-up person who will tell it like it is. So I'm trying to be nicer to people than I was in 2006. It's going to be kind of hard to keep my comments to myself, but I will try.

四、练习

A 请将下列句子翻译成英文。

1. 我必须要考虑我的家庭想要什么，我周围的人在乎什么，最后要考虑的才是我自己。

____

2. 我认为成功是感觉自己的生命很有意义，对周围的人友善。

____

3. 当我们长大了，更成熟了一点后，就开始有人依靠我们，指望着我们，我们感觉要在这个世界上承担起自己应尽的责任。

____

4. 我觉得父母应该让孩子感觉到成功本身就是一种回报。

____

5. 这是一种很不成熟的生活态度。

____

（☞ P279）

B 听MP3实战演练。

Topic 40 A Meal 一顿饭

一、考试说明

Food是雅思中的常见话题，各部分都曾经考过。本单元话题卡是食物系列中比较新的一个话题卡，考生需向考官描述自己要请别人吃的一顿饭。第三部分会围绕饮食及其变化展开。在“真题演练”部分native speaker选择了火锅，讲的头头是道。在“话题相关材料”部分，大家可以看到英文版的中国饮食文化基本介绍，相信介绍中基本涵盖了描述中国饮食传统的必备词汇。

二、真题演练

CUE CARD

Describe a meal you would like to invite your friends to.

You should say:

who you would invite

where you would eat this meal

what you would eat

and explain why you would choose to eat this food.

点题	I would like to invite my friends to a **hot pot** meal.
人物	I would invite my closest friends, the ones that I hang out with and have the most in common with. I would of course invite my girlfriend so that she could meet my friends. That is important to me. I think my girlfriend should know what I am like when I am with my friends.
地点	I would find a nice restaurant with a good atmosphere where the waiters are friendly and the owners are working to give you the best experience you can have. I would not choose a big, **monstrous** place where everything would seem so impersonal, but instead a restaurant that has **a family ambiance**.
食物	I would order hot pot with lots of meat, lamb, pork, beef, fish, tofu...mmm...I am getting hungry just thinking about it. I would also order some nice vegetables and noodles, and to top it off, some ice cold beer to wash it down.
解释	I really like hot pot because of the atmosphere it creates of everyone eating together and pulling things from the pot and **dipping** it in their favorite sauce, just relaxing and enjoying the food and the friendship.

重点词句

hot pot 火锅

monstrous 巨大的

a family ambiance 一种家的氛围

dip 蘸

Part 3

Diet

1. What kinds of food do Chinese people like to eat?

   Many Chinese like to eat their vegetables cooked. They enjoy eating food that is fried, steamed, and sometimes boiled, but rarely eat baked food. The only time they will eat baked goods is when they have cakes from the store. Most Chinese food is cut in bite-sized pieces before being cooked and served.

2. How important is eating a healthy diet?

   I think eating healthy is a very important part of life. If you don't give your body what it needs then it won't be able to function well. This is why what you eat is so important to how well you are able to do things. Eating well even improves study.

3. Are there many vegetarians in China?

   I believe there are a fair amount of **vegetarians**. Most Chinese already eat very little meat, so without even trying they are almost vegetarians. However, I think if they had the chance, many Chinese would eat more meat than they do now. Though as health awareness increases I believe there will be a rise in the number of vegetarians in China.

   vegetarian 素食主义者

4. Is the food that people eat today in China different to the food that people used to eat in the past?

   I think that in many ways it is quite the same. I do know that in recent years there has been a rise in the number of fast-food restaurants. Many people, especially of the younger generation, enjoy going to these restaurants. The actual Chinese food, though, has not seen much change over the years.

5. How do you think the way we eat will change in the future?

   Our eating habits will of course affect the way we will live in the future because of the effect it has on our health. If we eat well then we will have better health as we get older. I believe, though, that as time goes by fast food will become more popular. We will be entering a time in history where going fast will mean the difference between success and failure, so the food industry will change to accommodate the population's demand.

6. Is fast food popular in China?

   Yes, fast food is very popular here in China. I believe the main reason is because the taste is very different from that of Chinese food. This appeals to the youth of China. Also the advertisements of most fast food restaurants portray their food as cool or western food.

Eating Habits

7. Who do most Chinese people usually eat with?

   Chinese will usually eat with their family, classmates, or colleagues. Most couples eat together as often as they can. When eating out you will often see groups of friends out together. You can also see families sharing some time together over a nice meal.

8. Do you think it's important for people to eat with their family?

   I think that when you eat with your family it strengthens the **family bonds**. It helps you get to know each other better and learn more about what each are doing in their lives. It's very sad when families don't see each other often. Often in China mealtimes are the only time a family spends together.

   family bonds 家庭凝聚力

9. Do Chinese people often eat out?

   I think most families rarely eat out. Usually either the mother or the grandmother of the family will cook and prepare the food. It is more common for young singles and professionals to eat out, either alone or with classmates or colleagues. Often married or dating couples will spend a dinner together for special occasions or to get to know each other more.

10. What kind of restaurants do young people in China prefer?

    I think they prefer fast-food or western restaurants. Often it's because it's considered cool to eat or take people out to these kinds of restaurants. Or, they enjoy the food because it tastes different from Chinese food. They also may want to accustom themselves to western food and culture, because they want to be comfortable around foreigners or they would like to travel abroad.

11. How do you think restaurants have changed, over the past few years?

    Before, the restaurants did not cater to foreigners at all. The menus were all in Chinese and had no pictures. Now more restaurants, especially in areas with many foreigners, will have menus in English and pictures for those who are not familiar with Chinese dishes.

12. How do you think restaurants will change in the future?

    I think that in the future all or nearly all restaurants will have food to cater to different nationalities and food preferences. I think that the standard of both food and service will also improve. They will also probably be more sanitary.

三、话题相关材料

A 中国饮食入门

The Art of Chinese Food and Drink

Cooking has occupied a lofty position in Chinese culture throughout history. The great Chinese philosopher Lao Zi once said of the art: "Governing a great nation is much like cooking a small fish."

Chinese food can be roughly divided into the Northern and Southern styles of cooking. In general, Northern dishes are relatively oily, and the use of vinegar and garlic tends to be quite popular. Wheat, processed into pasta, also plays an important role in Northern cooking; noodles, ravioli-like dumplings, steamed stuffed buns, fried meat dumplings, and steamed bread are just a few of the many flour-based treats enjoyed in the North of China. The best known regional variations of Northern Chinese cuisine include those of Beijing, Tianjin, and Shandong.

Representative of the Southern cooking styles are Sichuan and Hunan cuisine, famous for their liberal use of chili peppers. Within the whole of Southern cooking, the Jiangsu and Zhejiang regions emphasize freshness and tenderness, while Guangdong cuisine tends to be somewhat sweet and always full of variety. Rice and its bi-products, including noodles, cakes, and congee, form the typical foundation for Southern dishes.

In Chinese cooking, color, aroma, and flavor share equal importance in the preparation of every dish. Normally, any one entree will combine three to five colors, selected from ingredients that are light green, dark green, red, yellow, white, black, or caramel-colored. Usually, a meat and vegetable dish is prepared from one main ingredient and two to three secondary ingredients of contrasting colors. They are then cooked appropriately, incorporating the proper seasonings and sauce to create an aesthetically attractive dish.

Color, aroma, and flavor are not the only principles to be followed in Chinese cooking; nutrition is also an important concern. The principle of the harmonization of foods can be traced back to the Shang dynasty scholar Yi Yin. He relates the five flavors of sweet, sour, bitter, piquant, and salty to the nutritional needs of the five major organ systems of the body (the heart, liver, spleen/pancreas, lungs, and kidneys), and stresses their role in maintaining good physical health. In fact, many of the plants used in Chinese cooking, such as scallions, fresh ginger root, garlic, dried lily buds, tree fungus, and so forth, have properties of preventing and alleviating various illnesses. The Chinese have a traditional belief in the medicinal value of food, and that food and medicine share the same origin. This view could be considered a forerunner of nutritional science in China. Notable in this theory is the concept that correct proportion of meat to vegetable ingredients should be maintained; one-third of meat-based dishes should be vegetable ingredients, and one-third of vegetable dishes should be meat. In short, the correct ingredient proportions must be adhered to in the preparation of each dish or soup in order to ensure full nutritional value.

The Chinese have a number of rules and customs associated with eating. For example, meals must be taken while seated; there is a set order of who may be seated first among men, women, old and young; and the main courses must be eaten with chopsticks, and soup with a spoon. Chinese banquets are arranged on a per table basis, with each table usually seating ten to twelve persons. A typical banquet consists of four appetizer dishes, such as cold cut platters or hot hors d'oeuvres; six to eight main courses; then one savory snack-type dish and a dessert.

The methods of preparation include stir-frying, stewing, steaming, deep-frying, flash-frying, and pan-frying. A dish may be savory, sweet, tart, or piquant. The main colors of a dish may be red, yellow, green, white or caramel. Food garnishes, such as cut or sculptured tomatoes, Chinese white radishes and cucumbers, may be used to add to the visual appeal of a dish. All of these elements contribute to making Chinese food a true feast for the eyes and nostrils as well as the taste buds.

四、练习

A 请将下列句子翻译成英文。

1. 我想找一家环境不错、服务质量好的餐馆。

____

2. 一想起来这道菜我就觉得饿了。

____

3. 我不会找那种特别大的餐馆，那种餐馆会给人很疏远的感觉；我会找那种有家的感觉的那种。

____

4. 我之所以特别喜欢吃火锅是因为喜欢它所营造的那种气氛。

____

5. 我觉得跟家人吃饭会增强家庭凝聚力。

____

（☞ P279）

B 听MP3实战演练。

练习题答案

人物类

Topic 1 老人

A

1. He has taught me a lot about just being happy with the things that I have to do and also to take time to enjoy life.
2. Things were a lot more difficult than they are now, but through it all he always maintained a happy outlook on life.
3. I would like to grow up and be like him in some ways, I wouldn't say that he is perfect in any way, but then who is?
4. The elderly have a lot of influence in their family's lives.
5. Another role that they play is cheerleader for the family.

Topic 2 孩子

A

1. I love this child very much because she is always so happy and I can't help but feel happy too.
2. Spending time with MaoMao has helped me to see that I can have a positive attitude towards my life and be happy even though I am no longer a child and have many responsibilities.
3. That way he will have good health and also learn how to communicate and interact with his peers.
4. Home schooling is more personalized and focused on the individual student's needs, whereas that personal attention is not available in public schools due to there being many other students.
5. The fathers now are busier with their careers and are often not at home, so the mother is left with the job of disciplining their child.

Topic 3 名人

A

1. He's well over two meters tall, but unlike most tall players, he has a lot of skill, not just a height advantage.
2. Despite all his fame, he doesn't have a big head, and stays cool.
3. I think the disadvantages outweigh the advantages.
4. Whatever personal things happen in your life will often become common knowledge to everyone.
5. And being famous isolates you from the real world, so that you can't see what's really going on in people's lives.

Topic 4 有探险精神的人

A

1. During the time she was studying at university, she was always active in sports and often organized excursions with fellow students.
2. She even backpacked in Tibet for two weeks with only 400 RMB in her pocket.
3. The Chinese youth wish to challenge themselves, which often leads them to extreme sports like snowboarding, rollerblading, rock climbing and trick BMX.
4. Going on an adventure or doing an activity requires risks, tests our strength and capabilities, and gives us a thrill and feeling of triumph.
5. The challenges children face and experience today are very different from the past.

Topic 5 领袖人物

A

1. Once he saw what he wanted to do, he didn't wait around until graduation, but instead grabbed the opportunity while he could and took off with it.
2. Being a leader will help to bring out the best in someone.
3. Be a good example. Try your best to understand and not order children around.
4. A leader with integrity can be trusted and will be admired for sticking to strong values.
5. Creativity means thinking differently, being able to get outside the box and take a new and different viewpoint on things.

Topic 6 邻居

A

1. She had made a special dish from her hometown and she brought me a little bowlful.
2. I think she is a very motherly type of person.
3. It makes me feel good that even though I live away from my family, I have a caring person like her as a neighbour.
4. I think neighbours are very important because they are some of the people that you are around every day.
5. One thing that is important for children to learn in life is how to relate to others. It is actually a good opportunity for them to learn this in their interactions with the people they live close to.

地点类

Topic 7 家乡建筑物

A

1. The church is about 30 or 40 meters high, not very big. It is made of red brick, and the architecture,

as I said before, is in the Old Russian style.

2. Now it is a very famous tourist attraction, and visitors from around China and the world go to see it and take pictures.
3. I think it's important because it is a historical relic, and a little peaceful place in the busiest part of the city.
4. No matter how many skyscrapers and tall apartment buildings are built, it still has an old and friendly flavor.
5. It will probably be many years before this trend is reversed.

Topic 8 童年房间

A

1. The room was not so big, about 5 square meters.
2. Because of the window and door there was plenty of light and fresh air, which made it a very nice place to work.
3. They learn how to get along with the people they share a room with, and they learn to share their toys, which is very important later in life.
4. The layout of houses and rooms are pretty standard and stay almost the same. One thing that does change is the material that the furniture is made out of.
5. In the old days there were not many parks or public facilities, and the ones that were around were often small and unkempt. The plants were not taken care of and the ground was often dirty and littered.

Topic 9 休闲健身中心

A

1. I love to go to the Karaoke bar that they had there and sing to my heart's content.
2. If I felt tired after studying or working all week, I would go to the massage center and after just an hour there I felt on top of the world.
3. One of the most common ways that Chinese people like to relax is to go out to a restaurant with their friends or family and enjoy a good meal together.
4. Sometimes the Chinese men in particular drink a little too much and end up with health problems.
5. Being active gives us more energy, reduces stress and makes us feel good.

Topic 10 旅馆

A

1. I personally liked this hotel and enjoyed staying there. All of the maids and cleaning staff were very cheerful and the hotel carried an air of joy and happiness.
2. Tourism not only helps to bring in money, but also helps to influence and modernize China.

3. It should also have a few places for recreation and exercise, such as a gym, swimming pool, and sports equipment room.
4. The most important thing is for the hotel employees to be able to understand the tourists and guests.
5. The rooms were stunning too—very well decorated and very clean and modern. The staff are, without exception, polite and helpful, without being pushy.

Topic 11 图书馆

A

1. It is in a very new building that has some beautiful urban sculptures standing on the grounds around it.
2. Besides having a good stock of books, it also provides office equipment such as a good copy machine.
3. I think that the atmosphere in the library is conducive to reading because number one, it is one of the quietest places you can go.
4. It may sound like fantasy, but with all the progress in technology I think it is very possible.
5. Also I am in favor of having works of art in libraries. Not necessarily originals but good quality copies of famous works are both attractive as well as educational.

喜好类

Topic 12 电影

A

1. I really enjoyed the movie from start to finish.
2. Just by watching a movie and seeing what a character does in certain circumstances can help you to know what to either do or not do.
3. Film is a powerful medium and brings many parts of life to the public for observation.
4. I think that the rating system is too simplistic and many more guidelines and ways to classify movies are long overdue.
5. This movie caused quite an uproar when it was released as some people really loved it and others hated it.

B

1. 《满城尽带黄金甲》
2. 《伤城》
3. 《疯狂的石头》
4. 《大红灯笼高高挂》
5. 《十面埋伏》
6. 《天下无贼》

7. 《霸王别姬》
8. 《重庆森林》

Topic 13 户外活动

A

1. I really enjoy running. Not the fast sprinting kind of run, but rather the more drawn-out jogging kind of run.
2. I usually like to run when the weather is warm but not too hot.
3. I also like the rush that you get when you push yourself farther than you've ever gone before.
4. Most middle-class working people do not get sufficient amounts of exercise, and as a result are weak and more prone to sickness.
5. If you're always indoors then you'll get weak and sick easier; whereas if you work outside then you're getting fresh air and sunshine, which are two things that everyone needs to stay healthy.

Topic 14 最喜欢的季节或月份

A

1. The sky is blue and the weather is nice and warm.
2. Another thing I like to do during spring time is get up early and climb mountains.
3. The air always seems fresher in the spring, the sky is bluer, the grass greener, and the people friendlier.
4. During the winter the weather may go below zero, and in the summer it might get as hot as 40° Celsius.
5. More responsibility should fall on the shoulders of the government because they have the means to do more than the average citizen.

Topic 15 经常走的一段路

A

1. Every time, I would wear my iPod and listen to music that fit the mood of the walk and weather.
2. Also, walking in parks gives people a taste of nature in a concrete world.
3. Walking does a lot of good for your mental health. It provides a great escape from the working world, and gives the mind a good opportunity to just wander.
4. But people that value life more than money probably walk more often because they want to enjoy themselves every once in a while.
5. In my opinion, the best way to get people to walk more would be to build more places where people would enjoy walking. Parks and/or nice tree-lined streets would be a good way to start.

Topic 16 体育赛事

A

1. The atmosphere in the stadium was so exciting. Everyone was shouting, whistling, cheering, and just making noise.
2. Exercise keeps you healthy. It's been proven that people who exercise get sick less.
3. If kids don't win their natural reaction is to cry or get mad. This doesn't really help them in life. When they grow up they'll find that you don't always win the first time round, you just have to keep trying and keep going on with your life.
4. The game is so much more alive and real than if you were just watching it. You feel like if you yell louder then your team might actually have a greater chance of winning.
5. Also if someone decides to streak at halftime then you won't have to worry about the sports channel switching to the anchors who talk about the game.

Topic 17 外国文化

A

1. Prior to visiting, I knew almost nothing about the culture, but staying there, even for such a short time, really opened my eyes.
2. It's an extremely laid back, relaxed culture. Their main goal in life is to be happy.
3. It's important to be educated about the world and not just shut yourself into your own country.
4. Reading about people's experiences in foreign lands is the next best thing to being there.
5. Some people have different opinions because they are really concerned with the loss of culture, but for me, the benefits outweigh the drawbacks.

物品类

Topic 18 服饰和时尚

A

1. This pair caught my eye because they were simple and matched my clothes and accessories.
2. I chose them because they can be worn on many different occasions and still be appropriate.
3. Loose types of clothing are most comfortable. I like to have nice, neat, stylish clothing, too.
4. Fashions of today change drastically in a very short period of time. Often certain clothes will only be in style for one year or so before another, very different style is in.
5. I like everything comfortable and stylish, but not too vulgar of course. I carefully pick my clothes and outfits, but at the same I don't want to look like I spent hours putting it all together.

B

A-5　B-1　C-2　D-3　E-4

Topic 19 野生动物

A

1. They usually hunt and live alone, and only meet other tigers during the mating season.
2. Tigers have had a place in Chinese culture for thousands of years. They are found in Chinese literature new and old, and are the subject of many famous paintings.
3. I hope more efforts will be made in the future to protect the tiger's living environment.
4. Many Chinese are only now beginning to learn about the importance of protecting wild animals, as well as the environment they live in.
5. Wild animals don't always directly affect people, but often, they fill a special role in the balance that we are also part of, and affect other species or plants that we are directly dependent on.

Topic 20 电器

A

1. Computers have changed so much since they first came out.
2. I think we will have electrical appliances that will do many of the jobs and duties that require less thinking.
3. One of the main effects of using electronic communication is that the communications become less personal.
4. People will more often turn to their machines for entertainment rather than spending time with others or getting exercise.
5. There are some advantages to using modern home and office equipment. One of the main ones is that more things get done and often we can complete projects and assignments very quickly.

Topic 21 重要的信件

A

1. If this doctor hadn't taken the time to write me, I just don't know what would have happened to me.
2. You have to word things carefully and make sure they get the point, but be subtle.
3. A hand written letter has a more personal touch.
4. Emailing is more than just writing; it really is a way of life, and this way of life wasn't really available here in China before.
5. Computerization is moving in and taking over, so for the sake of speed we will see the slower methods of communicating—such as handwritten characters—become a lost art and a casualty of modern times.

Topic 22 读物

A

1. It is a collection of the writer's works including three novels and forty short stories.

2. I was given the book as a present, and I was immediately fascinated by the raw, beautiful but very real world the writer experienced and wrote about.
3. Like most countries it depends on individual preference, but I would say it is not so popular an activity as in countries where the pace of life is slower.
4. These stories are sometimes the first education a child receives.
5. People need to have heroes they can look up to and learn from.

Topic 23 家具

A

1. It's convenient for me because my room is small and I don't have space for a lot of furniture.
2. It's not a very beautiful piece of furniture, but it has definitely been one of the most practical things I've bought in a long time.
3. A very popular furniture store right now in China is IKEA, this is a store from Sweden and its style of furniture is a big change from the recent and distant past.
4. I'd say he needs to be artistic and imaginative. At the same time a designer also has to have quite a bit of practical sense.
5. Nowadays people live in flats and often these are in tall buildings if in big cities. In the past most lived in houses even if they were small.

Topic 24 广告

A

1. That night I saw an advertisement that has forever stuck in my mind.
2. It was a commercial for Nike shoes with Michael Jordan.
3. I couldn't get that commercial out of my mind, not because I thought buying Nike shoes would make me as successful as Michael Jordan, but because of his unflinching determination and perseverance.
4. Young people look at how appealing the advertisement is, if it's cool, hip, or fashionable; whereas older people tend to be more practical-minded.
5. Looking at today's children, I would have to say advertisements have predominately had a negative influence on their lives and on their character. Ads create a discontentment with what children have and a desire to own more and to be like everyone else.

Topic 25 童年礼物

A

1. The most memorable gift I received was when I was seven years old.
2. When I first saw the bicycle I was very excited and I thought it was very pretty.
3. The reason I would choose a Lego set is because it is very fun, and at the same time, it encourages

creativity.

4. The importance of the gift depends on the person who is giving it.
5. A gift doesn't have to be expensive in order to show care for the person receiving it.

Topic 26 新闻报道

A

1. There have been quite a few stories of this nature lately, and it shows an extremely positive development.
2. I think most Chinese people are more concerned with local news and domestic news, which I'd imagine is the same across the world.
3. Unless there are huge stories going on elsewhere, local news has more of an impact on the average citizen.
4. With the creation of blogs, more people are able to report on many different things, so you will see a lot more news and a lot more analyses.
5. Older people are less concerned with the pop culture news and are more concerned with the news that matters more to the world and their country.

经历类

Topic 27 公众活动

A

1. It was held outside in a little park near the new compound.
2. The party was so much fun, because it was at night and we were allowed to stay out later than usual.
3. It not only helps to create a good image for the business, but it shows customers that they are interested in their welfare.
4. I'd much rather watch the event from a distance.
5. What I'm trying to say is that if you're in the habit of helping others in your community, then others will be more inclined to help you.

Topic 28 改变人生的事件

A

1. There is a big world out there and some people want to find out if it is their "cup of tea" as they say.
2. Some people just have the proverbial "grass is greener on the other side of the fence" syndrome. They think that once they get there all their problems will be over.
3. I have seen some young people that didn't know how to deal with changes, at all, and then I have seen some older people who take changes without breaking a sweat.
4. I think China has gone through some incredible changes in recent years.

5. Foreign influence will continue to come into the country and cause changes like more mixed marriages and a mixture of cultures.

Topic 29 英语课堂活动

A

1. Every Monday, we would take about twenty minutes of class, and everyone had to stand up and say what they did over the weekend.
2. The third Monday, however, this all changed. One of the students stood up and told an extremely creative story, using a lot of interesting phrases and some truly funny vocabulary.
3. No longer were we just taking words and phrases out of the book, we were looking for other places, trying to be the most creative.
4. It may be a pipe dream, but if Chinese changed to pinyin as the way to write and read the language, I think it would explode all over the world.
5. English became as popular as it is now because of the extreme wealth and worldwide influence of English-speaking countries (especially the US).

Topic 30 建议

A

1. At that time, I was just starting to think about what I wanted to do with my life. My dad helped me a huge amount.
2. This story taught me an extremely valuable lesson.
3. Yes, my parents have given me tons of advice. They always do it in a way, though, where they aren't just telling me what to do.
4. Other parents are really hands-off. They let their kids make all their own decisions. This way kids can learn from their own mistakes.
5. If you rely on your parents too much, you might eventually end up in a situation where they are not around to help you, and you have to make a decision about something you've never thought about on your own before.

Topic 31 不愉快的购物经历

A

1. It was being sold for a very reasonable price and I only had to bargain for a short time.
2. I will look in a more reliable place and probably try to get a trusted brand.
3. Some shops should provide snack bars in case you get hungry or thirsty while shopping. I also think it would be helpful if stores had a delivery service.
4. One advantage is that you can find everything you need in the same store. Another is that you can find several brands of the same product, and can make a better selection.

5. When something is hand-carved, or hand-sewn, it makes you feel as though this product is special, and is worth more.

Topic 32 展览

A

1. Each one looked so real that it almost seemed as if a real person was actually standing there and staying perfectly still.
2. I was especially amazed at the wax figure of the cowboy.
3. I think if the museums had more interactive exhibits then they would be more interesting for most people.
4. If people have to pay each time they go, and especially if it's expensive, then many won't go or they won't go as often.
5. The way they are set up and advertised I think will also improve, so that they are more appealing to the general public.

Topic 33 迟到的经历

A

1. By the time I got there I was 10 minutes late and there they all were waiting for me.
2. All I could do was apologize and thankfully they all accepted my apology and we moved on.
3. "The alarm didn't go off, the bus was late or caught in traffic." Those are just a few of the most-heard excuses.
4. It really is a bit of a hard habit to break, as the style of life and the culture have not been that of arriving right on the dot.
5. It really shows quite a lack of respect for others that you don't think their time is important.

Topic 34 帮助别人的经历

A

1. Many of us have needed some help ourselves from time to time and we know what it feels like to need something.
2. We have a responsibility to do our part whether it's in our family, our workplace or amongst friends.
3. It may sound funny, but sometimes it seems a little like magic how I end up with more time or more energy or more money or whatever, after I have given some away to another person.
4. It seems so many people are in such a rush to get rich or get better jobs or into the best schools that they hardly even notice people who need help.
5. Here in China more individuals are getting involved in charities.

Topic 35 忙碌的日子

A

1. So what else can I do but get busy and start burning the candle at both ends and burning the midnight oil until the work is done.
2. If I'm in a lazy mood I tend to do whatever first comes to mind, but when I am more active I usually organize what I'm supposed to do by importance.
3. Then you can clearly see what you need to accomplish and how realistic your time frame needs to be. But for the most part I don't particularly like drawing detailed plans.
4. One advantage, like I said before, is that you can clearly see what at is you need to accomplish and better plan how much time you need to accomplish it. Another advantage is that important details are less likely to be left out.
5. So in my opinion, leisure time is vital to maintaining health and sanity.

Topic 36 实用技能

A

1. At first it was a little difficult because, to be quite frank, I really didn't see myself as someone who was musically inclined.
2. I use the guitar to cheer myself up when I am feeling a little down and also use it to teach songs to others.
3. Academics are stressed so highly in schools that they seem to overshadow practical skills.
4. I think that children should learn practical skills at school. This would help to prepare them for life outside of school.
5. Life in the working world can be a lot different than the sheltered life of schooling, so having some practical skills such as those learned from a part-time job would be beneficial to a student.

假想类

Topic 37 创业

A

1. We could put an ad in the newspaper or on the Internet and sell our wares that way.
2. We'd each just make the things that we're best at so that we get a bunch of quality products in as short an amount of time as possible.
3. The main reason I'd start a business like this is because it's something that I enjoy doing.
4. Good advertisement is really what makes the difference between the success and failure of their business.
5. They want to see something grow that they had a direct part in.

Topic 38 大笔钱财

A

1. It really depends on how much money a "large amount" is.
2. I would sponsor rock festivals so that everyone could partake of the beauties of music.
3. Money isn't really that important to me, but you need money to live and if you don't have money, then you can't do anything.
4. If you give your children only a small amount of money each week then they'll have to learn to make it last.
5. The workplace environment is also very important. Some offices are stuffy and drab, whereas others make you feel fresh and alive.

Topic 39 想做成的一件事

A

1. I must think about what my family wants, what the world around me would be pleased with, and the last person on the list to worry about is me.
2. I believe success is feeling my life is worth living, and being a good person to those around me.
3. When we grow up and are more mature, we begin to have others dependent on us, looking to us, and we feel the responsibility to do our part in the world.
4. I believe parents should give their child the sense that success is their reward.
5. This is really an immature way to look at life.

Topic 40 一顿饭

A

1. I would find a nice restaurant with a good atmosphere where the waiters are friendly.
2. I am getting hungry just thinking about it.
3. I would not choose a big, monstrous place where everything would seem so impersonal, but instead a restaurant that has a family ambiance.
4. I really like hot pot because of the atmosphere it creates.
5. I think that when you eat with your family it strengthens the family bonds.

IELTS™

IELTS Speaking band descriptors (Public version)
雅思考试口语评分标准（公众版）

Band	Fluency and coherence	Lexical resource	Grammatical range and accuracy	Pronunciation
9	• speaks fluently with only rare repetition or self-correction; any hesitation is content-related rather than to find words or grammar • speaks coherently with fully appropriate cohesive features • develops topics fully and appropriately	• uses vocabulary with full flexibility and precision in all topics • uses idiomatic language naturally and accurately	• uses a full range of structures naturally and appropriately • produces consistently accurate structures apart from 'slips' characteristic of native speaker speech	• uses a full range of pronunciation features with precision and subtlety • sustains flexible use of features throughout • is effortless to understand
8	• speaks fluently with only occasional repetition or self-correction; hesitation is usually content-related and only rarely to search for language • develops topics coherently and appropriately	• uses a wide vocabulary resource readily and flexibly to convey precise meaning • uses less common and idiomatic vocabulary skilfully, with occasional inaccuracies • uses paraphrase effectively as required	• uses a wide range of structures flexibly • produces a majority of error-free sentences with only very occasional inappropriacies or basic/non-systematic errors	• uses a wide range of pronunciation features • sustains flexible use of features, with only occasional lapses • is easy to understand throughout; L1 accent has minimal effect on intelligibility
7	• speaks at length without noticeable effort or loss of coherence • may demonstrate language-related hesitation at times, or some repetition and/or self-correction • uses a range of connectives and discourse markers with some flexibility	• uses vocabulary resource flexibly to discuss a variety of topics • uses some less common and idiomatic vocabulary and shows some awareness of style and collocation, with some inappropriate choices • uses paraphrase effectively	• uses a range of complex structures with some flexibility • frequently produces error-free sentences, though some grammatical mistakes persist	• shows all the positive features of band 6 and some, but not all, the positive features of band 8
6	• is willing to speak at length, though may lose coherence at times due to occasional repetition, self-correction or hesitation • uses a range of connectives and discourse markers but not always appropriately	• has a wide enough vocabulary to discuss topics at length and make meaning clear in spite of inappropriacies • generally paraphrases successfully	• uses a mix of simple and complex structures but with limited flexibility • may make frequent mistakes with complex structures, though these rarely cause comprehension problems	• uses a range of pronunciation features with mixed control • shows some effective use of features but this is not sustained • can generally be understood throughout, though mispronunciation of individual words or sounds reduces clarity at times

IELTS™

IELTS Speaking band descriptors (Public version)
雅思考试口语评分标准（公众版）

Band	Fluency and coherence	Lexical resource	Grammatical range and accuracy	Pronunciation
5	• usually maintains flow of speech but uses repetition, self-correction and/or slow speech to keep going • may over-use certain connectives and discourse markers • produces simple speech fluently, but more complex communication causes fluency problems	• manages to talk about familiar and unfamiliar topics but uses vocabulary with limited flexibility • attempts to use paraphrase but with mixed success	• produces basic sentence forms with reasonable accuracy • uses a limited range of more complex structures, but these usually contain errors and may cause some comprehension problems	• shows all the positive features of band 4 and some, but not all, the positive features of band 6
4	• cannot respond without noticeable pauses and may speak slowly, with frequent repetition and self-correction • links basic sentences but with repetitious use of simple connectives and some breakdowns in coherence	• is able to talk about familiar topics but can only convey basic meaning on unfamiliar topics and makes frequent errors in word choice • rarely attempts paraphrase	• produces basic sentence forms and some correct simple sentences but subordinate structures are rare • errors are frequent and may lead to misunderstanding	• uses a limited range of pronunciation features • attempts to control features but lapses are frequent • mispronunciations are frequent and cause some difficulty for the listener
3	• speaks with long pauses • has limited ability to link simple sentences • gives only simple responses and is frequently unable to convey basic message	• uses simple vocabulary to convey personal information • has insufficient vocabulary for less familiar topics	• attempts basic sentence forms but with limited success, or relies on apparently memorised utterances • makes numerous errors except in memorised expressions	• shows some of the features of band 2 and some, but not all, the positive features of band 4
2	• pauses lengthily before most words • little communication possible	• only produces isolated words or memorized utterances	• cannot produce basic sentence forms	• speech is often unintelligible
1	• no communication possible • no rateable language			
0	• does not attend			

分数	流利性与连贯性	词汇多样性	语法多样性及准确性	发音
9	● 表达流利，极少出现重复或自我纠正的情况；出现犹豫是基于思考内容，而非寻找合适的词汇或语法 ● 表达连贯，衔接手段的使用完全恰当 ● 完全且恰当地展开话题	● 准确自如地使用词汇来谈论任何话题 ● 自然且准确地使用习语	● 自如得体地使用语法结构 ● 除了出现英语为母语者也会犯的口误外，始终使用准确的语法结构	● 准确运用丰富多样的发音特点，能表达微妙的差异 ● 表达过程中始终灵活地使用各种发音特点 ● 听者理解毫无障碍
8	● 表达流利，偶尔出现重复或自我纠正的情况；出现犹豫通常是基于思考内容，仅在少数情况下是寻找合适的语言 ● 连贯且恰当地展开话题	● 词汇使用丰富，运用自如及灵活，表达意思准确 ● 熟练地使用非常见的词汇及习语，偶尔欠准确 ● 按需进行有效的改述	● 灵活地使用多种语法结构 ● 除极其偶然情况下出现的不当或简单的 / 非系统性错误外，大部分语句准确无误	● 使用多样的发音特点 ● 表达过程中灵活地使用多种发音特点，但偶尔出现偏差 ● 表达过程中始终易于听者理解；母语的口音对听者理解的影响极小
7	● 表达详尽，并无明显困难，或不失连贯 ● 有时出现与语言相关的犹豫或出现重复及 / 或自我纠正 ● 具有一定灵活性地使用一系列连接词和语篇标记	● 灵活地使用词汇讨论各种话题 ● 使用一些非常见的词汇及习语，对语体及词汇搭配有所认识，但有时词语选择不甚恰当 ● 有效地进行改述	● 较灵活地使用一系列复杂的语法结构 ● 虽然反复出现一些语法错误，但语句通常正确无误	表现出 **6** 分水平中所有积极表现，但也表现出 **8** 分水平中部分积极表现
6	● 表现出充分交流的意愿，但有时由于偶尔的重复、自我纠正或犹豫而缺乏连贯性 ● 能使用一系列连接词及语篇标记，但无法保持一贯恰当	● 有足以详尽讨论各种话题的词汇量，虽然有时使用不当但意思表达清晰 ● 基本上能成功地进行改述	● 结合使用简单与复杂的句型，但灵活性有限 ● 使用复杂结构时经常出现错误，尽管这些错误极少造成理解困难	● 使用多种发音特点，但掌握程度不一 ● 展现出某些有效使用发音特点的能力，但不能持续表现这一能力 ● 表达过程中听者基本能理解，但部分单词或音发音不准确导致有时清晰度下降
5	● 通常能保持语流，但需通过重复、自我纠正及 / 或降低语速来维持表达 ● 过度使用某些连接词及语篇标记 ● 能用简单的语言进行流利的表达，但在进行更为复杂的交流时则表达不畅	● 能谈论熟悉或不熟悉的话题，但使用词汇的灵活性有限 ● 尝试进行改述，但有时成功有时失败	● 能使用基本的句型，且具有合理的准确性 ● 使用有限的复杂句式结构，但通常会出错且会造成某些理解困难	表现出 **4** 分水平中所有积极表现，但也表现出 **6** 分水平中部分积极表现
4	● 作答有明显停顿，且语速有时缓慢，出现频繁重复及自我纠正 ● 能连接简单句子，但重复使用简单的连接词，有时缺乏连贯性	● 能谈论所熟悉的话题，但对不熟悉的话题仅能表达基本意思，且经常用词不当 ● 很少尝试改述	● 能使用基本句型并正确使用一些简单句型，但极少使用从句 ● 常出现错误，且会造成误解	● 使用有限的发音特点 ● 尝试表现多种发音特点，但频繁出现偏差 ● 经常出现发音错误，对听者理解造成一些困难
3	● 表达过程中出现长时间停顿 ● 连接简单句的能力有限 ● 仅能简单作答，且经常无法表达基本意思	● 使用简单词汇表达个人信息 ● 讨论不熟悉的话题时词汇匮乏	● 尝试使用基本句型，但准确度有限，或依赖预先背诵的几句话 ● 除预先背诵的内容外，错误很多	含有 **2** 分水平中部分表现以及 **4** 分水平中部分积极表现
2	● 大部分词汇间出现长时间停顿 ● 几乎无法进行沟通	● 仅能说出零散的单词或预先背诵的几句话	● 不能使用基本的句型	表达通常无法理解
1	● 无法进行沟通 ● 无可供评分的语言			
0	缺考			